Voltaire's Essay on Epic Poetry

A STUDY AND AN EDITION

BY
FLORENCE DONNELL WHITE

Phaeton Press

New York

1970

Originally Published 1915
Reprinted 1970

Library of Congress Catalog Card Number — 74-90363
Published by PHAETON PRESS, INC.
SBN #87753—044—0

FOREWORD

The subject of this dissertation was suggested to me in 1906 by Mr. Lucien Foulet, at that time professor of French in Bryn Mawr College. Under him the work was begun. I wish to express my warm appreciation of his stimulating advice and interest.

I worked upon the subject in Paris and in London in the summers of 1907 and 1911. In 1913, since Mr. Foulet had left America some years before, Professor A. Schinz, now head of the Department of French at Smith College, under whom I had worked in another field at Bryn Mawr, was kind enough to take over the direction of my dissertation at the request of the Graduate Committee of Bryn Mawr. I am the more appreciative of his courtesy in doing so since he is not a specialist in Voltaire. In the direction of this work he has given his attention particularly to form and presentation of the subject-matter. I have to thank him for unfailing kindness and much helpful criticism. I am also indebted to Dr. S. C. Chew Jr. of the Department of English of Bryn Mawr for valuable suggestions.

PREFACE

In the year 1727, while Voltaire was living in England, a small volume was issued by a London book-seller, under the title: *An Essay upon the Civil Wars of France, extracted from curious Manuscripts and also upon the Epick Poetry of the European Nations, from Homer down to Milton, by Mr. de Voltaire.* It passed through several editions in England and Ireland between 1727 and 1761. Despite the use of the singular " Essay," the title makes it clear that there were two distinct pieces of work. Both were translated into French and published, the *Essay on Epic Poetry* in Paris in 1728, that on the civil wars of France at The Hague in 1729.

The French translation of the *Essay on Epic Poetry* was reprinted with Voltaire's *Henriade* in an edition of his works, Amsterdam, 1732. The following year, however, when he published the *Henriade* separately, the author replaced the translated essay by a French version of his own making, which he announced as quite different from the English and adapted to the taste of the French public. This version, together with the original translation of the *Essay upon the Civil Wars*, is to be found in standard editions of Voltaire's works immediately after the *Henriade*.

In their English form the essays are difficult of access and therefore little known. That they were even more inaccessible in the past may be seen from the fact that three scholars writing in London or in Paris in 1778, 1807 and 1828 respectively, discussed in detail a point in the English *Essay on Epic Poetry* which a glance at the text in question would have elucidated.[1] One of them, Beuchot, the accomplished editor of the 1828 edition of Voltaire, felt called upon to adduce evidence that an English version of the two essays had actually appeared.[2] Although these essays have been not infrequently cited, and even quoted by a few modern writers, notably Ballantyne,[3] no study of them has been made.

[1] Cf. p. 96, note 5, *post.*
[2] Cf. *Oeuvres de Voltaire*, Garnier frères, VIII, pp. 264,302, note 4. All references to Voltaire's works other than the letters of the years 1726-1729 and the *Lettres philosophiques* are to this edition, unless otherwise specified.
[3] Ballantyne, *Voltaire's Visit to England*, pp. 123 ff.

Written by a Frenchman who had been in England but a year and a half and at a period when few Frenchmen learned English, their most obvious interest is linguistic. Less evident but in reality more important than the question of the language is that of the content. In this respect the *Essay on the Civil Wars*, a brief historical treatise, although of considerable interest, has naturally less to offer. Furthermore it can be read in the French translation in Voltaire's works, whereas the translation of the *Essay on Epic Poetry* has, like the English original, become very rare. The latter is therefore the more interesting of the two essays and it is to it that our discussion will be confined.

Many critics, aware of the existence of the English *Essay*, have assumed that the French and the English versions were in the main identical. As a matter of fact they differ markedly in places and furnish an unusual opportunity for the comparison of certain of Voltaire's views in 1727, the period when he was becoming acquainted with English ideas, with those he held on the same subjects several years after his return to France, as well as of the forms under which he thought best to present those views to two different nations.

The ideas in the *Essay* are in themselves of real importance. We have here an early example of what Joseph Texte has called literary cosmopolitanism: brief and informal criticisms of Homer, Virgil, Lucan and of certain modern poets, Italian, Spanish, Portuguese and English, at a time when the study of comparative literature was rare in France.

Moreover, the essays, both English and French, are intimately connected with the author's own epic, the *Henriade*, which was his chief interest for many years and was long considered his foremost claim to immortality.

This dissertation concerns itself with the circumstances of the publication of the English essays, chapter I; with Voltaire's use of English, chapter II; with the French translation of the *Essay on Epic Poetry*, chapter III; with Voltaire's French version of the *Essay*, chapter IV; with the content of the English version, chapter V. It also includes the republication of the text of the *Essay on Epic Poetry* according to the edition of 1727, with notes and an appendix.

For any investigation having to do with Voltaire's stay in England the way has been paved by the work of Baldensperger, Ballantyne, Churton Collins, Foulet and Lanson, dealing with that significant part of the French author's life of which little was known in former years. In this field Gustave Desnoiresterres may be called a pioneer.

For the complete titles of all the works to which reference is made in this dissertation see the bibliography following the appendix.

CHAPTER I

THE PUBLICATION OF THE ENGLISH ESSAYS

Immediate cause of Voltaire's journey to England—His intention of publishing the Henriade *there—Voltaire in England, 1726 and 1727—Efforts to gather subscriptions for the* Henriade—*The English essays intended to predispose the British public in favor of the poem—Date of publication of the essays—Editions.*

Before discussing the publication of the English essays, it is well to recall why Voltaire went to England.

"The immediate reason for his leaving France was his quarrel with the Chevalier de Rohan-Chabot and the difficulties in which it involved him." Foulet has shown that the quarrel dates from the latter part of the month of January, 1726.[1] At that time Voltaire was thirty-one years of age. He was extremely prosperous and indeed he had never known more than temporary financial embarassment.[2] Since his school days he had been associated with members of the nobility, many of whom were apparently his warm friends. His daring wit made him a favorite in the pleasure-loving society of the time and he had every reason to consider himself on a firm footing of equality with persons far above him in rank. He had acquired literary renown as the author of a successful tragedy, *Oedipe*, and of an epic poem which was thought to be on a plane with the *Iliad* and the *Aeneid* and to have made good a marked deficiency in French literature. It is true that he had more than once been exiled from Paris but under circumstances that had in no wise injured his social position and had only added to his reputation for audacious wit and to his renown in general. The same may be said of his eleven months' imprisonment in the Bastille, May, 1717—April, 1718, under the charge of writing a satire against the government. At the period in which we are interested Voltaire seems to have been justified in believing his position secure.

---

[1] Foulet, *Corr.*, p. 219. All references to the letters of Voltaire falling between the dates February 4, 1726 and April 18, 1729 will be made to this edition.

[2] Cf. Lanson, *Voltaire*, pp. 20 ff.

For that reason the events of the first months of 1726 were a revelation to him. The beginnings of the quarrel between Voltaire and the Chevalier de Rohan-Chabot were insignificant. Heated words passed between them at the Opera, and again a few days later at the Comédie française. They became so angry as nearly to engage in a hand to hand combat. Very shortly after, when Voltaire was one day dining with the Duc de Sully, he was called to the door and soundly beaten by hirelings of the Chevalier.

When this became known, what was Voltaire's astonishment to find himself deserted by practically all his associates, who were unwilling to side with a bourgeois poet in his quarrel with a nobleman, although that poet had been their intimate friend for many years and, in the latest development of the quarrel, had been distinctly ill-treated. Voltaire was in a position to appreciate thoroughly and for the first time the inequality of classes in France.

It is said that he wished to engage in a duel with Rohan but was given no opportunity. The police were ordered to prevent a meeting between the two and by way of a final precaution the poet was imprisoned in the Bastille, April 17, a proceeding calculated to make him feel still more keenly the lack of personal liberty prevailing in France and the injustice of the French social order. About two weeks later he was released on the condition that he should leave Paris and remain at least fifty leagues distant from the French court.[1] It is now admitted that he chose the place of his exile himself. In letters written from the Bastille to a government official Voltaire asked permission to go to England.[2] This permission was readily granted, for the government was glad to have him leave French soil. It was natural that he should wish to withdraw far enough and for sufficient time to allow the affair with Rohan to blow over. It is not surprising that he chose as a place of refuge a country in which his interest had already been aroused by English friends in Paris, particularly Lord Bolingbroke, and where liberty was said to prevail.

---

[1] Foulet, *Corr.*, p. 18.
[2] *Ibid.*, p. 10: "Je demande avec encor plus d'instance la permission d'aller incessament en Angleterre." Cf. also *ibid.*, p. 14.

Although this incident was the immediate cause of Voltaire's crossing the channel, it appears that it merely hastened the fulfilment of an intention he had had for some time in connection with the publication of his epic.[1] The poet's correspondence previous to 1725 shows that the *Henriade*, begun in 1716 or 1717, had been his foremost interest for a number of years. It was to arrange for having it printed that, in 1722, he visited Holland and spent several weeks at The Hague.

Although it celebrated one of France's great kings, the *Henriade*, because of its bearing upon religious intolerance, was displeasing to the French government as well as to the Catholic church. To his surprise, Voltaire had not been able to obtain the necessary " privilège " for publishing it openly. He therefore had had an edition printed hurriedly and in secret at Rouen and smuggled into Paris in December, 1723. In this, its earliest and incomplete form, the poem had won great praise from the public but no degree of approval from the government. Other clandestine and unsatisfactory editions, issued, in some cases at least, without the author's knowledge, had appeared during 1723 and 1724.[2] The ban laid upon his poem had served moreover to arouse public interest in it, and Voltaire, who was constantly working over the text and arranging for illustrations, was eager to publish a complete and satisfactory edition.

In a letter of August or September, 1725, he expresses his intention of issuing such an edition outside of France, " à Londres, à Amsterdam ou à Genève." [3] Foulet has suggested that Geneva was mentioned in this connection merely out of compliment to the Swiss gentleman to whom the letter was addressed.[4] The poet's choice, then, lay between Amsterdam and London. Now both Lord Bolingbroke, whom Voltaire had known well in Paris, and Pope, to whom a copy of the poem had been sent in 1724, had praised the *Henriade* highly.[5] Moreover, because of the tale of Henry IV's visit to England and the part played by Queen Elizabeth, the subject-matter was such as to interest the English more than any other people outside of France. It was natural

---

[1] Cf. Foulet, *Rev. d'Hist. litt.*, 1906, pp. 9 ff.
[2] Cf. Bengesco, *Voltaire*, I, pp. 99 ff.
[3] *Oeuvres*, XXXIII, pp. 107, 108. This letter was wrongly dated by Moland and redated by Foulet, *Rev. d'Hist, litt.*, 1906, p. 6, note 3.
[4] *Ibid.*, p. 7.
[5] Cf. Pope, *Works*, ed. Elwin and Courthope, VII, pp. 401-402, and *Oeuvres de Voltaire*, XXXIII, p. 84.

then that the author should have preferred England, as a country offering at the same time liberty for publishing his poem, an interested public, and influential patrons.

The following month, October, 1725, Voltaire wrote to King George I of England a letter recently published in the *Athenaeum:* " Sire il y a longtemps que je me regarde comme un des sujets de votre majesté. jose implorer Sa protection pour un de mes ouvrages cest un poeme epique dont le sujet est Henri quatre le meilleur de nos rois . . . jai respecté la relligion reformée; jai Loue l'illustre Elisabeth D'angleterre. jai parlé dans mon ouvrage auec liberté et auec verité. uous etes Sire le protecteur de l'une et de l'autre; et jose me flatter que uous m'accorderez uotre roiale protection pour faire imprimer dans uos états un ouvrage qui doit uous interesser puisqu'il est l'eloge de la vertu cest pour apprendre a la mieux peindre que je cherche auec empressement lhonneur de venir a londres vous presenter les profonds respects et la re-connaissance auec laquelle jai l'honneur detre Sire de votre majesté le tres humble et tres obeissant et tres obligé Seruiteur." [1]

Foulet quotes a letter written by Lord Bolingbroke in December, 1725, which seems to indicate that Voltaire had asked him also to lend his influence to the publication of an English edition of the *Henriade.* [2] In April, 1726, asking permission to go to England, Voltaire spoke of " l'Angleterre, où je devois aller depuis longtemps." [3] At any rate it is certain that when he left France his chief concern was to issue a satisfactory edition of the *Henriade.* Both in Paris and in London this purpose was definitely recognized. [4]

---

[1] *Athenaeum*, January 11, 1913, p. 45.

[2] *Rev. d'Hist. litt.*, 1906, p. 8, quoted from Desnoiresterres, I, pp. 368-369.

[3] Foulet, *Corr.*, p. 14. Cf. p. 2, note 2, *ante.* It is significant that, during the weeks between his quarrel with Rohan-Chabot and his imprisonment, when Voltaire's whereabouts were unknown, he was reported to have gone to England. Foulet, *Corr.*, p. 220.
    Cf. *ibid.*, p. 6 (Début d'avril): "Je n'attends que ma convalescence pour abandonner à jamais ce pays-ci."

[4] Cf. letter of Horatio Walpole to Bubb Dodington, Paris, May 29, 1726: " Mr. Voltaire, a French poet...being gone for England in order to print by subscription an excellent poem, called *Henry IV.*" Foulet, *Corr.*, pp. 37-38. The same statement occurs in a letter from Walpole to the Duke of Newcastle. *Ibid.*, p. 41. Cf. also *British Journal*, May 14, 1726: " Tis said he [Voltaire] will publish at London a large edition of his famous Poem of the *League*, whereof we have only an imperfect copy." Quoted by Ballantyne, p. 19.

The date of Voltaire's arrival in England has been much debated. It is now generally accepted as about the middle of May, 1726. Of his first weeks in the country nothing definite is known. After a hurried and secret trip to Paris, the poet established himself toward the middle of August at Wandsworth, a small town near London, where he was the guest of the merchant Faulkner whose acquaintance he had made in Paris. There he lived in retirement and spent his time chiefly in reading and in study, desiring to familiarize himself with English literature and English institutions. It was probably late in October or in November that he moved to London.[1] Early in 1727 he was presented at the court of George I. His letters seem to indicate that London remained his headquarters until late spring. At the end of May he was evidently in the country. There are no letters to give us direct information as to his whereabouts between June and December, but in December we find him again in London. During this year he led an active life, mingling with people of various classes, parties and professions, and probably paying visits in numerous English homes. Before summer he had made the acquaintance of both Pope and Swift, the two living English writers whom he most admired.

The letters of this early period show that Voltaire had the *Henriade* constantly in mind. In August, 1726, he writes to Thieriot in a melancholy strain: " Si le caractère des héros de mon poème est aussi bien soutenu que celui de ma mauvaise fortune, mon poème assurément réussira mieux que moi." [2] In the letter of October 15 we read: " I had a mind at first to print our poor *Henry* at my own expenses in London, but the loss of my money is a sad stop to my design: I question if I shall try the way of subscriptions by the favour of the court." [3] We have definite evidence of the carrying out of this idea in a letter from M. de Broglie, French ambassador in England, to M. de Morville, March 3, 1727: " Le S. de Voltaire . . . est prest à faire imprimer à Londres, par souscription son poème de la *Ligue*. Il me sollicite de lui procurer des souscrivants, et M. de Walpole s'employe de

---

[1] Foulet, *Corr.*, p. 70, note 1.
[2] *Ibid.*, p. 43.
[3] *Ibid.*, pp. 60-61.

son côté tout de son mieux pour tâcher de luy en faire avoir le plus grand nombre qu'il sera possible."[1] It appears that during the year 1727 Voltaire was active in his own cause and that his efforts were being supplemented by friends and acquaintances. In December, 1727, he writes to Swift: "Can I make bold to intreat you to make some use of yr interest in Ireland about some subscriptions for the *Henriade*, which is almost ready and does not come out yet for want of little help. The subscriptions will be but one guinea in hand."[2]

In the letter just quoted occurs the first allusion to the English essays to be found in Voltaire's correspondence: "You will be surprised in receiving an English essay from a French traveller."[3] The fact that the writer sends Swift this little volume at the same time with an urgent request for subscriptions for his epic, would suggest on the face of it a connection between the essays and the enterprise in question. This connection is definitely expressed in a passage occurring at the end of the *Advertisement to the reader* preceding the essays in the edition of 1727: "As to this present Essay, it is intended as a kind of Preface or Introduction to the *Henriade*, which is almost entirely printed, nothing being wanting but the printing of the Cuts."[4]

Despite the efforts of the poet and his friends, the complete edition of the *Henriade* which he had so long desired to publish was still delayed for lack of sufficient subscriptions. The foremost reason for the publication of the essays is thus very evident and eminently practical. Keen business man that he was, Voltaire meant them to serve as an advertisement. It was not mere chance that the subjects of the two essays particularly fitted them to prepare the way for the *Henriade*, one of them dealing with the civil and religious wars of France, the very wars described in the poem, and the other with epic poetry, the class of literature to which the poem belonged. The second essay called attention

---

[1] Foulet, *Corr.*, pp. 86-87.

[2] *Ibid.*, pp. 110-112. This letter appears in the Garnier edition of Voltaire's correspondence (XXXIII, p. 175) in a rather inaccurate French translation with no indication of the original's having been written in English.

[3] The manuscript copy of this letter, preserved in the British Museum, bears the words, probably in Swift's handwriting, "in receiving an English essay, Monsr. de Voltaire, Dec. 14, 1727," and "Monsieur Voltaire, R[eceived] Decemb. 21st, 1727." Foulet, *Corr.*, p. 109, note (a).

[4] Cf. p. 77, *post*.

in a flattering way to the fact that, while France, almost alone among European nations had no such poem, England on the contrary, boasted a model. At various points the author lays emphasis upon those characteristics of poets and poems which the reader recognizes as having their counterpart in the *Henriade*, a method of influencing the critic in favor of the poem which was about to appear.[1]

The real purpose of the volume was at once recognized and interest in the *Henriade* was aroused. This is shown by the following item which appeared in January, 1728, in an English magazine, *The Present State of the Republick of Letters*: " We also hope every day to see Mr. De Voltaire's *Henriade*. He has greatly raised the expectation of the curious, by a beautiful Essay he has lately published upon the Civil Wars of France (which is the subject of his Poem), and upon the Epic Poets from Homer down to Milton." [2]

The publication of the essays and the appeal to Swift bore good fruit, for in February an advertisement of the *Henriade* was printed in London newspapers and in March the quarto edition of the poem appeared with a dedication to Queen Caroline.[3] There was a list of nearly three hundred and fifty English and Irish subscribers headed by the King and Queen. This edition was a great success financially and otherwise. Other and less expensive editions were published in London later in the year." [4]

But quite apart from the motive just discussed, which must, it is true, have determined the subject-matter in great measure, we may recognize in the *Essay on Epic Poetry* a real desire to make a contribution to what is now called comparative literature and to open men's eyes to its value. As early as 1722 Voltaire had felt the necessity of taking into account the different " geniuses " of different nations before passing judgment on their literature.[5] This idea is expressed in various ways in the text

---

[1] Cf. pp. 56, 60, *post*.

[2] Quoted by Ballantyne, p. 149.

[3] King George II and Queen Caroline came to the throne in June, 1727. Cf. Bengesco, I, p. 103. Bengesco speaks of this dedication as addressed to Queen Elizabeth, a mistake due, perhaps, to the fact that the " great Elizabeth " is mentioned in its opening sentence.

[4] Cf. *ibid.*

[5] Cf. *Oeuvres*, XXXIII, p. 84: " Il [Bolingbroke] possède Virgile comme Milton; il aime le poésie anglaise, la française, et l'italienne; mais il les aime différemment, parcequ'il discerne parfaitement leurs différents génies."

of the essay itself and the mere bringing together of poets of various nations was a step toward its realization.

The date of the publication of the essays may be determined approximately. They had already appeared December 14 (o. s.), 1727, when Voltaire wrote to Swift. Additional evidence is found at the beginning of the *Advertisement to the reader*, in the sentence: " It has the Appearance of too great a Presumption in a Traveller, who hath been but eighteen Months in England, to attempt to write in a Language, which he cannot pronounce at all." [1] Eighteen months from the middle of May, 1726, which has been accepted as the approximate time of Voltaire's arrival in England, would place the writing of the *Advertisement* of the English essays in November, 1727. The *Advertisement* was certainly written some time before the volume appeared in print. In view of Voltaire's anxiety to secure subscribers in Ireland, it is probable that he sent the essays to Swift immediately upon their publication. Since the letter to Swift is dated December 14, it seems probable that the first edition dates from early in December (o. s.), 1727. [2]

That the essays had some vogue in England is to be inferred from the number of editions issued. [3] Four of these still exist. They will be enumerated in the order of their appearance. The first, as just stated, was published in London in 1727; it formed a small octavo volume of 130 pages. The essay on epic poetry begins on the thirty-seventh page. [4] Within a few weeks, January 8, 1728, the London newspapers announced the second edi-

---

[1] Cf. p. 75, *post.*

[2] The Essays were announced in the *New Memoirs of Literature* for the month of December. Foulet, *Corr.*, p. 110, note 1.

[3] Cf. also *Mercure de France*, June, 1728 (an account of the French translation of the *Essay on Epic Poetry*): " L'ouvrage dont il s'agit a autant de succès icy qu'il en a eu à Londres."

[4] The full title of this edition reads: *An Essay upon the Civil Wars of France extracted from Curious Manuscripts, and also upon the Epick Poetry of the European Nations, from Homer down to Milton. By Mr. de Voltaire, London, Printed by Samuel Jallason, in Prujean's Court, Old Baily, and sold by the Booksellers of London and Westminster, MDCCXXVII.* Of this first edition there is preserved in the British Museum (show case XII) a copy bearing the inscription in Voltaire's handwriting: " to Sir hanslone " (Hans Sloan). From the *British Journal*, Dec. 2, 1727, it appears that Sir Hans Sloan had, when Voltaire's essays appeared, just been elected President of the Royal Society (of Science): " The same day [Nov. 30] Sir Hans Sloan was chosen President of the Royal Society for the year ensuing." Voltaire was elected a member of this society, Nov. 3, 1742.

tion.[1]   This appeared under the same title as the first with the further information that Mr. de Voltaire was " the author of the *Henriade*," and that the second edition of his essays had been corrected by himself.[2]   In 1731, some two years after Voltaire's return to France, an edition of the essays announced as the fourth, the third of those still existing, was published in London, together with a translation into English of the author's *Discours sur la Tragédie*, the original of which had appeared in Paris shortly before.[3]   The fourth of the editions now accessible was published in Dublin in 1760 with the same title as the others mentioned, but adding: " By Mr. de Voltaire. To which is prefixed a short account of the author by J. S. D. D. D. S. P. D." [4]   This series of letters has been considered to designate Jonathan Swift, D.D., Dean of Saint Patrick's, Dublin,[5] a supposition which is borne out by the account itself: " The author of the following Discourse, Monsieur de Voltaire, is a young *French* Gentleman, and allowed to be the most celebrated Poet of that Kingdom. He hath been some years composing an *Heroick Poem* upon *Henry the Great*. But being falsely accused for writing a Libel, he was put into the *Bastile*, and confined there in a Dungeon several Months, till the true Author was discovered. He there suffered much in his Health, and having been known to some *English* persons of Quality then at Paris, he was invited over to *England*. His

[1] *Daily Journal* and *Daily Post*. Cited by Ballantyne, p. 114.
[2] This edition was printed for " N. Prevost and Company at the Ship, over against Southampton Street in the Strand, MDCCXXVII." The price is announced on the title page as 1s 6d. Copies of this edition are to be found in the British Museum (2), in the Bibliothèque nationale (2) and the Library of the University of Paris (1).
[3] The title, the same as that of the two editions already discussed, is followed by the words: *By Mr. de Voltaire, Author of the Henriade. The Fourth Edition, Corrected—To which is now prefixed A Discourse on Tragedy—With Reflections on the English and French Drama By the same Author, London, Printed for N. Prevost and Company over against Southampton Street in the Strand, MDCCXXXI.*
There are two copies of this edition in the British Museum. With one of them is bound a criticism of the *Essay on Epic Poetry* which appeared shortly after the publication of Voltaire's essays and to which we shall frequently refer: *Remarks upon M. Voltaire's Essay on the Epick Poetry of the European Nations*, Paul Rolli, London, 1728; and *No. 1 of the Herculean Labour or the Aegean Stable cleared of its Heaps of Historical, Philological and Geographical Trumpery* by M. Ozell, at the end of which is subjoined the first Canto of the *Henriade*— a translation we are told " to be continued if encouraged."
[4] This edition was printed for William Ross, Bookseller in Grafton Street, Dublin. There is one copy of it in the British Museum.
[5] Churton Collins (*V. M. R.*, p. 69) says simply in this connection that the introduction was erroneously attributed to Swift since he was not living in 1760.

Heroick Poem is finished [in 1728, according to a foot-note], and now printing in London by Subscription, being encouraged by the Crown and most of the Nobility. He had not been above eleven Months in *England*, when he wrote the following Treatise, intended as an Assistance to those who shall read his *Poem*, and may not be sufficiently informed in the History of that Great Prince." Clearly this somewhat inaccurate account was written at the beginning of 1728 before the publication of the subscription edition of the *Henriade* in March.[1] It was shortly before this that Voltaire had sent Swift a copy of the first edition of the essays and had asked his help in gathering subscriptions.[2] It is entirely reasonable to suppose that Swift conceived the idea of reprinting the essays in Ireland as an easy way of interesting the Irish public in Voltaire's epic. The tone of the preface shows that the writer wishes to advertise the poet and the poem. The edition of the essays published in 1760, fifteen years after Swift's death, is probably merely a reprint of a 1728 edition now lost.[3]

We have thus far considered five editions. There is reason to believe that there was still another, published between 1728 and 1731, probably earlier than 1730 (or in that year). This conclusion is drawn from passages in prefaces of certain editions of Voltaire's works, taken in connection with the fact that the 1731 edition of the essay was called the fourth when it appeared. In the preface preceding a reprint of the *Essai sur la poésie épique* in an edition of Voltaire's works of 1746 we read: "On imprima en effet à Londres un essai de lui sur la Poésie Epique en Anglais, et il y en a cinq éditions."[4] Granting that there were already five editions in 1746, we must acknowledge the existence at that time of two in addition to the extant London editions of 1727, 1728 and 1731. One of these two may well have been the 1728 Dublin edition. That the other was an edition published in London between 1728 and 1730, or during the latter year, seems very likely from a passage contained in the preface of the 1730

---

[1] Bengesco (II, p. 4, note 2) says that this account must have been written by Swift toward 1731 or 1732. He gives no reasons for this assumption, which is entirely opposed to the evidence.

[2] Cf. p. 6, *ante*.

[3] This supposition is borne out by the fact that the edition of 1760 follows the text of the London edition of 1727, the one from which the 1728 Dublin edition would have been compiled.

[4] *Oeuvres diverses de M. de Voltaire*, A Londres, 1746.

edition of the *Henriade* in which mention is made of " l'essai sur la poésie épique, imprimé plusieurs fois à Londres." [1]

That the English edition of 1731 is called the fourth, although, if we accept the conclusions above, four had already appeared, is not surprising. It is quite conceivable that an English publisher would not take into account the reprinting in Ireland of the first edition of the essays. On the other hand, the Irish edition would naturally be included in a summary of the history of the essays such as that contained in the preface of 1746. [2]

---

[1] *La Henriade*, Nouvelle édition. A Londres, 1730. As a matter of fact this edition was published in France (cf. Bengesco, I, p. 104) toward the month of November. Foulet, *Corr.*, p. 301; *Oeuvres*, XXXIII, p. 201.

[2] The inaccurate statements concerning the original publication of the English essays which recur in editions of Voltaire's works and elsewhere, may be traced back to a period surprisingly near their first appearance. In the preface to the 1730 edition of the *Henriade* we read of the "*Essay sur la Poésie Epique*, composé en anglais par M. de Voltaire en 1726." The same date is given in the Amsterdam edition of 1732, while in that of 1733 the essay is spoken of as " cette esquisse qu'il donna en langue anglaise en 1728."

An example of incorrect assertions made by bibliographers is the statement of Wm. T. Lowndes, (*The Bibliographer's Manual*, London, 1857-64, X, revised 1881-'85, X, p. 2791) that the *Essay on Epic Poetry* was published in London in 1726 and secondly that it was published together with the *Essay on the Civil Wars of France*, in French and in English in 1727.

CHAPTER II

THE LANGUAGE OF THE ESSAY ON EPIC POETRY

Voltaire's interest in England and knowledge of English while still in France—Evidence of his study and use of English during his first year in England—Examination of the language of the Essay on Epic Poetry and of the English letters of Voltaire—Conclusion that the language of the Essay *is largely Voltaire's and that the disparaging comments of certain critics are without weight.*

It is easy to understand Voltaire's reasons for publishing his essays in English rather than in French. Appearing in English, they would advertise the *Henriade* more successfully since they would arouse curiosity as to the work of a foreigner and could be read by a wider public. Moreover they were sure to bring their author some measure of the admiration he always craved. The question at once arises as to how well Voltaire was fitted to undertake formal composition in English and to what extent he worked independently.

Had Voltaire any familiarity with English before he left France? In the Collège Louis le Grand, young Arouet did not study any modern language.[1] Although Frenchmen of the time often acquired some knowledge of Italian and Spanish, English was, in the early years of the eighteenth century, " un idiome jusque-là universellement ignoré et qu'on se faisait gloire de ne pas apprendre." [2]

On the other hand a distinct effort was already being made by means of reviews and translations to spread throughout Europe, and especially in France, English ideas,—the knowledge of English science, philosophy, and literature.[3] This propaganda was

[1] Pierron, *Voltaire et ses Maîtres*, pp. 39 ff.
[2] Texte, *Jean Jacques Rousseau et les Origines du Cosmopolitisme littéraire*, p. 77.
[3] *Ibid.*, pp. 17 ff. and p. 42.

chiefly the work of refugees driven out of France by the Revocation of the Edict of Nantes and residing in England or in Holland. So active were they in Holland that that country is recognized as having served in intellectual matters as an intermediary between England and France. Now Voltaire had twice visited Holland,—as a young man, in 1713, and again in 1722; he had been associated with at least one family of refugees,[1] had had dealings with book-sellers,[2] and had talked with many sorts of people.[3] Keenly curious in the face of new experiences, there, as well as in France, he probably came under the influence of this more or less organized movement for the spreading of English ideas.

His interest thus aroused is sure to have been furthered by his acquaintance in Paris with representative Englishmen, particularly the exiled Lord Bolingbroke. At the end of the year 1722 Voltaire visited Bolingbroke at his country place, La Source, near Orléans. The Englishman spoke French extremely well. What we know of the topics he discussed with his guest is significant for one who studies the *Essay on Epic Poetry*. They talked of history, and of Italian, French and English poets, including Milton. That Voltaire already contrasted English learning with French polish appears from the sentence in which he then characterized Lord Bolingbroke: "J'ai trouvé dans cet illustre Anglais toute l'érudition de son pays et toute la politesse du nôtre." [4]

His interest in England and in English literature would seem to have led the young poet to acquire some familiarity with the English language. This may be inferred from a letter he wrote to his friend, Cideville, in September, 1723, concerning Fenton's English tragedy, *Mariamne*. "Quelque bonne," he says, " que pût être la traduction anglaise, elle m'aurait assurément fait moins de plaisir que votre lettre. . . . Vous devriez bien quelque jour venir à la Rivière-Bourdet, apporter la *Mariamne* anglaise, et voir la française." [5] Further evidence of Voltaire's ability to read English may, perhaps, be seen in a letter of Pope's.

---

[1] In 1713 he had been sent back to Paris from Holland because of a love-affair with the daughter of a refugee.

[2] Cf. p. 3, *ante*.

[3] *Oeuvres*, XXXIII, pp. 73-74: ("A la Haye, 7 octobre, 1722.") " J'ai vu avec respect cette ville, qui est le magasin de l'univers. . . . Je vois des ministres calvinistes, des arminiens, des sociniens, des rabbins, des anabaptistes, qui parlent tous à merveille, et qui, en vérité, ont tous raison."

[4] *Ibid.*, p. 84.

[5] *Ibid.*, p. 90-91.   Foulet (*Rev. d'Hist. litt.*, 1906, p. 12, note 8) has shown that this letter should be dated September rather than June, 1723.

Writing to Caryll in December, 1725, a few months before Voltaire came to England, the English poet spoke of having " formerly had some correspondence about the poem on the League with its author."[1]   If such a correspondence took place it seems likely that Pope's letters at least would be written in English since, at that very period, he speaks of understanding French but imperfectly[2] while Voltaire states in the *Lettres philosophiques* that Pope read French with difficulty, could not speak a word, and was incapable of writing a French letter.[3]

In 1724 Lord Bolingbroke had returned to France and in February Voltaire was again with him at Ablon.[4]   In April, writing to Bolingbroke, Pope spoke of the " friendship and intimacy " with which Bolingbroke honored the young French poet.[5]   This renewed contact with the illustrious Englishman must have served

[1] Cf. Pope, ed. Elwin and Courthope, VI, p. 288. We have no trace of this correspondence. It may well have dated from the year 1724 when Bolingbroke sent Pope a copy of the *Henriade*. A passage in a letter from Bolingbroke to Pope written in February of that year seems to support this assumption. Bolingbroke speaks of Voltaire " who says that he will introduce himself to you, and that the muses shall answer for him." The explanation of this statement is contained in the last sentence of the letter: " But I will say no more of it [Voltaire's *Mariamne*], since he intends to send it to you."   Cf. *ibid.*, VII, p. 398.

The entire sentence in the letter to Caryll reads: " I had read the Mariamne before our friend had sent it, having formerly had some correspondence about the poem on the League with its author." It appears so evident that Pope is referring to two different persons when he speaks of *our friend* and *the author of the League* that Courthope's note: " Caryll, it seems, brought over as a present from Voltaire, a copy of his Mariamne," is on the face of it unsatisfactory. On the other hand the very fact that Pope mentions his correspondence with Voltaire as an explanation of his having read *Mariamne*, makes it seem probable that, according to his intention stated by Bolingbroke, the French poet had early in 1724 " introduced himself " to Pope and sent him a copy of his tragedy.

[2] Cf. *ibid.*, VII, p. 401, Letter to Bolingbroke, April 9, 1724: " It is but this week that I have been well enough in my head to read the poem of the League with the attention it deserves . . . I cannot pretend to judge with any exactness of the beauties of a foreign language which I understand but imperfectly."

[3] Lanson, *Lettres phil.*, II, p. 140, (variant first found in 1756): " Ce que je sais, ainsi que tous les gens de lettres d'Angleterre, c'est que Pope, avec qui j'ai beaucoup vécu, pouvait à peine lire le Français, qu'il ne parlait pas un mot de notre langue, qu'il n'a jamais écrit une lettre en Français, qu'il en était incapable, & que s'il a écrit cette lettre au fils de notre Racine il faut que Dieu sur la fin de sa vie lui ait donné subitement le don des langues pour le récompenser d'avoir fait un aussi admirable ouvrage que son *Essai sur l'homme*." Cf. Rigault, *Histoire de la querelle des anciens et des modernes*, p. 443. " Profondément versé dans la langue française, dont il [Pope] comprenait les finesses les moins accessibles aux étrangers," an interesting contrast to Pope's own testimony!

[4] *Oeuvres*, XXXIII, p. 83, wrongly dated by Moland, "A la Source, 1722." Cf. Foulet, *Corr.*, p. 31, note.

[5] Pope, VII, p. 402.

to stimulate Voltaire's interest in things English. In the autumn of 1725 his thoughts were turned toward England in connection with the publication of the *Henriade*. So far as his last months in France are concerned, it is frequently stated that, during the weeks intervening between his quarrel with the Chevalier de Rohan and his imprisonment, he devoted some of his time to the study of English and from his own pen we know that his friend, Thieriot, brought him English books while he was in the Bastille.[1] All this leads us to conclude that when he left France, Voltaire had at least a reading knowledge of English.

If we put any faith whatever in Voltaire's account of his first impressions of England, it would appear that at the time of his arrival in that country he was able to understand something of what he heard and to converse with people whom he met, not all of whom could have spoken French.[2] Duvernet, whose testimony, though often unreliable, is interesting as that of one of Voltaire's first biographers, explains the poet's withdrawal to Wandsworth by saying: "Il se retira dans un petit village et ne rentra à Londres que lorsqu'il eut acquis une grande facilité à s'exprimer."[3] There is no doubt that during this retirement he spent much time in the study of English literature as well as in conversation with his host. That he was strongly impressed with the necessity of learning thoroughly the language of a country in order to understand its literature, appears from a sentence contained in the *Lettres philosophiques* in which the writer recommends a course much like that which he himself followed: "Si vous voulez connoître le Comédie Anglaise, il n'y a d'autre moyen pour cela que d'aller à Londres, d'y rester trois ans, d'aprendre bien l'anglais, & de voir la Comédie tous les jours."[4]

A brief English note-book of Voltaire's, discovered in Petrograd and recently published,[5] belongs apparently, from the dates

---

[1] *Oeuvres*, XLVIII, p. 6.

[2] Cf. Lanson, *Lettres phil.*, II, pp. 256 ff., Supplément.

[3] *Vie de Voltaire*, p. 65.

[4] Lanson, *Lettres phil.*, II, pp. 109-110. Voltaire expressed at various times his idea of the importance of learning the language of other countries. Cf. p. 70, *post*. Cf. also p. 75, *post*: "I look upon the English Language as a learned one, which deserves to be the Object of our Application in France."

[5] *The English Review*, February, 1914, pp. 313 ff.

which occur at various points, to the summer of 1726.[1]   Although fragmentary in style and containing many peculiarities of construction, it shows that the author used the written language early in his stay and expressed himself in it comprehensibly.   A long English letter of October, 1726, to his intimate friend, Thieriot, shows a much better command of the language and is significant as an early example of Voltaire's custom of using it in his private correspondence.[2]   At the time of writing this letter, he evidently had a considerable knowledge of English but he still made elementary errors in construction, errors which Foulet's critical edition shows were in several cases corrected later, either by Voltaire himself or some other person.[3]   In this letter we have evidence that the writer possessed a discriminating appreciation of certain English works, and felt that familiarity with the language was essential to the full understanding of them.   Speaking of Pope he writes: " I hope you are acquainted enough with the English tongue to be sensible of all the charms of his works.   For my part I look on his poem call'd the *Essay upon criticism* like on a poem superior [corrected to *as superior*] to the *Art of poetry* of Horace; and his *Rape of the lock*, la boucle de cheveux, [that is a comical one],[4] is in my opinion above the *Lutrin* (de) of Despreaux; I never saw so amiable an imagination, so gentle graces, so great varyety, so much wit, and so refined knowledge of the world."   On the other hand, that he could blame as well as praise is seen from the last sentence of the letter: " But 'tis time to put a stop to my English talkativeness.   I fear you will take this

---

[1] Cf. *The English Review* p. 315: " Thirty and one of july one thousand and seven hundred twenty and six, I saw floating islands nyre (near) St. Om . . . " If St. Om refers to St. Omer, which lies on the road from Paris to Calais and is built on reclaimed marshland, this entry is of real importance in connection with Voltaire's secret trip to Paris, the date and circumstances of which have been much discussed.   P. 316: " 1726, in the month of august."   P. 318: " Mr. Blwet told me this day 20 July that he was married to fortune's daughter, who is mis'fortune."

[2] Cf. Foulet, *Corr.*, pp. 142-143, 21 April (o. s.), 1728.   " My dear Tiriot, I write to you in English for the same reason that Abbot Boileau wrote in Latin; I mean, that I should not be understood by many over-curious people." Cf. also *Oeuvres*, XXXIII, p. 181.   " Voici qui vous surprendra, mon cher Thieriot; c'est une lettre en français.   Il me paraît que vous n'aimez pas assez la langue anglaise, pour que je continue mon chiffre avec vous."

[3] Foulet, *Corr.*, pp. 53 ff.   For the history of the manuscript of this important letter and of its publication, cf. *ibid.*, pp. xxxv-xliv.

[4] The brackets are Voltaire's.

long epistle for one of those tedious English books that I have advised you not to translate."[1]

A letter to Pope of November, 1726,[2] when Voltaire was established at Lord Bolingbroke's house in London is, if one may judge by the form in which it has come down to us, a further indication of his proficiency in English. It was no doubt during this winter that the poet formed the habit, as a definite means of improving his English, of going regularly to the theatre where he followed the play, text in hand. This custom is described in the *General History of the Stage* written by Chetwood of the Drury Lane Theatre. " The noted author about twenty years past resided in London. His acquaintance with the Laureat brought him frequently to the theatre where (he confess'd) he improved in the English Orthography more in a week than he should otherwise have done by labour'd study in a month. I furnished him every evening with the play of the night which he took with him into the Orchestra (his accustomed seat). In four or five months he not only conversed in elegant English but wrote it with exact Propriety." [3]

It is likely that during the summer of 1727 Voltaire was boarding at the house of a scarlet-dyer in Wandsworth.[4] Lanson has reprinted a story which has to do with that period and which shows the French poet engaged in a definite study of the spoken language. The story is told by an apprentice to the schoolmaster in the parish of Wandsworth. The passages which interest us most read as follows: " Voltaire desired to be improved in the English tongue: and in discourse [with the master][5] chanced to fall on the subject of water baptism [which was treated between them],[5] till, for want of understanding each other, they were so set, they could proceed no further. . . . During his stay at

---

[1] Voltaire himself tells us that he wrote the first act of *Brutus* in English prose while in retirement at Wandsworth, " chez . . . M. Falkner, ce digne et vertueux citoyen " (*Discours sur la tragédie, Oeuvres*, II, p. 311), a statement which seems to refer to the year 1726. Goldsmith (*Works*, IV, p. 27) quotes what purports to be an extract from this English version, but Goldsmith's statements concerning Voltaire are singularly unreliable.

[2] Foulet, *Corr.*, p. 70.

[3] P. 46, note. Cf. Churton Collins, *V.M.R.*, p. 22; Ballantyne pp. 48-49. Lanson (*Lettres phil.*, II, p. 92) reproduces a list of plays presented in London during Voltaire's stay in England, beginning with Sept., 1726. In a passage in the French version of the *Essay on Epic Poetry* Voltaire refers to plays which he probably saw during the winter of 1726-27. Cf. also Genest, *Some Account of the English Stage*, III, pp. 184-196.

[4] Foulet, *Corr.*, p. 93, note 2.

[5] These phrases are bracketed in the text.

the scarlet dyer [sic] in Wandsworth, I had to wait on him several times, and heard him read, in *the Spectator* chiefly. At other times he would translate the Epistle of Robert Barclay." [1]

Only seven of Voltaire's letters of the year 1727 have been preserved. It is significant that of these seven, four are, with the exception of two or three sentences, written in English.[2] A fifth closes with an English paragraph.[3] In this paragraph and in three of the letters, since the manuscripts exist, we are sure of having the original form of the English. It is clear, forceful and idiomatic with only occasional slips, showing a marked improvement upon that of the letter of October, 1726. A few quotations will serve to show the writer's interest in the language and his ability to use it: "I am mightily glad for your [Thieriot's] improvement in English; I hope you won't take hereafter the *Rape of the lock* pour une serrure; but remember that there is no other way to get the true English pronuntiation than to come over into England." [4] "I advise you to sit still for a month or two, to take care of your health, and to improve your English till the book of Mr. Pemberton comes out." [5] "There you [Swift] will find two or three of my intimate friends who are yr admirers and who have learn'd English since I am in England." [6] "It was indeed a very hard task for me to find the damn'd book which under the title of *Improvement of Humane Reason* is an example of nonsense from one end to the other, and which besides is a tedious nonsense and consequently very distasteful to the French nation who dislikes madness itself when madness is languishing and flat. The book is scarce, because it is bad, it being the fate of all the wretch'd books never to be printed again. So I spent almost fortnight in the search of it, till at last I had the misfortune to find it. . . . Indeed you deserve to read it to do penance for the trouble you gave me to enquire after it, for the tiresome perusal I made of some part of this whimsical stupid performance, and for your credulity in believing those who gave you so great

---

[1] Lanson, *Lettres phil.*, I, pp. 20-21.
[2] Foulet, *Corr.*, pp. 88 ff., 93 ff., 101 ff., 109 ff.
[3] *Ibid.*, p. 85.
[4] *Ibid.* It appears that Voltaire himself had considerable difficulty with the pronunciation of English. Cf. p. 75, *post*, where he speaks of English as a "Language which he cannot pronounce at all, and which he hardly understands in Conversation."
[5] *Ibid.*, p. 96.
[6] *Ibid.*, p. 103.

an idea of so mean a thing." ¹   That Voltaire made opportunities
for practice in writing English is further seen in a sentence at the
end of this letter in which he speaks of having recently sent an
English theme to the Chevalier des Alleurs in Paris.²

From all this evidence it is reasonable to conclude that, at
the end of the year 1727, Voltaire was capable of writing for publication in English.³ There remains the question as to the measure
of assistance he received from the English friend to whom one
may assume he submitted his manuscript.

In his correspondence and elsewhere Voltaire conveys the impression that he was wholly responsible for the language of the
essays published under his name.   His statements take for the
most part the form of apologies.   One such apology appears in
the *Advertisement to the reader* already quoted.⁴ Another occurs
in the letter to Swift written shortly after, in the characteris-
tically flattering words: " Pray forgive an admirer of you who
ows to yr writings the love he bears to yr language, which has

¹ Foulet, *Corr.*, pp. 88-89. It is worth noticing in this connection that the
brief English poem which Voltaire wrote, probably to Lady Hervey, has been
dated 1727. *Oeuvres*, X, p. 607 and note.

² *Ibid.*, pp. 98-99.

³ As *ex post facto* evidence may be cited nine English letters written by Voltaire during the remaining months of his stay in England (Foulet, *Corr.*, pp.
113, 114, 122, 134, 142, 150, 154, 165, 168), the English dedication to Queen
Caroline contained in the 1728 edition of the *Henriade* (*ibid.*, p. 118), and two
special notices of some length contributed to the *London Daily Post* in connection with the publication of this edition (*ibid.*, pp. 126, 131).   Notes for the
history of Charles XII taken in English are preserved in the Bibliothèque
nationale (Bengesco, I, p. 376).   Churton Collins (*V.M.R.*, p. 55) speaks of
having seen in a private collection in England a note-book of Voltaire's containing English as well as French notes.

Shortly after his return to France Voltaire went so far as to declare that
he found difficulty in writing French, so accustomed had he become to the use
of English. This statement occurs in the *Discours sur la Tragédie, Oeuvres*, II,
pp. 311-312: "Je vous avoue, mylord [Bolingbroke], qu'à mon retour d'Angleterre,
où j'avais passé près de deux années dans une étude continuelle de votre langue,
je me trouvai embarrassé lorsque je voulus composer une tragédie française.
Je m'étais presque accoutumé à penser en anglais; je sentais que les termes
de ma langue ne venaient plus se présenter à mon imagination avec la même
abondance qu'auparavant: c'était comme un ruisseau dont la source avait été
détournée; il me fallut du temps et de la peine pour la faire couler dans son
premier lit."

Voltaire continued his interest in the English language, as well as in English things in general, throughout his life. His correspondence of later years
contains English letters, addressed for the most part to Thieriot and Falkner.
At Ferney he received many English visitors and often conversed with them
in their own language.

⁴ P. 8, *ante*.   Cf. pp. 75, 88-89, *post*.

betray'd him into the rash attempt of writing in English."[1] Again at the end of March, 1728, Voltaire writes to an unknown correspondent: " I have been tempted to send you an essay of mine which I have been bold enough to print in English above two months ago." [2] In a letter written some five years later, he returns to the same subject: "Mais si vous aviez été deux ans, comme moi, en Angeleterre, je suis sûr que vous auriez été si touché de l'énergie de cette langue que vous auriez composé quelque chose en anglais." [3]

These personal statements, assuming as they do that Voltaire received little or no assistance, require the support of internal evidence. What can be learned from an examination of the text of the *Essay on Epic Poetry*? Voltaire speaks of this essay as " a slight performance " which is " but the sketch of a very serious work," [4] and indeed its charm lies in the fact that it is entirely unpretentious and everywhere simple, clear and direct. It could easily enough be the work of a foreigner of unusual ability who had a thorough grasp of English construction.

There is naturally much which differs from present-day idiom. It is not to be expected that the language will reveal actual errors of importance since it is almost certain that the manuscript was more or less carefully read by an English friend of the author. There remain, however, many words and phrases, which in themselves, are indicative of French authorship. Most of them are forms allowable in eighteenth century English but less common than parallel forms and nearer to the French. Since they were like the French they would suggest themselves more naturally than others to a Frenchman and since they were permissible they would not meet with objection from the English reader of the manuscript. Furthermore there are a few pronounced Gallicisms which evidently escaped the eyes of this English reader and were later brought to Voltaire's attention. The fact that these were altered either in the *Errata* or in the second edition proves that

---

[1] Foulet, *Corr.*, p. 110.

[2] *Ibid.*, p. 137. It may be that " two months ago " refers to the publication of the second edition of the essays in the month of January.

[3] *Oeuvres*, XXXIII, p. 399. Cf. also a sentence occurring in Voltaire's French version of the *Essay on Epic Poetry*: " Lorsque j'étais à Londres, j'osai composer en anglais un petit *Essai sur la poésie épique.*" *Oeuvres*, VIII, p. 360.

[4] Foulet, *Corr.*, pp. 154, 155.

they were considered incorrect at the time and therefore that the manuscript was not exhaustively revised by an English-speaking person before it was sent to the printer.

As examples of spelling and forms of words which are noticeably like the French may be mentioned, *interesses*,[1] *Metamorphose*,[2] *Teints*,[3] *Richesses*,[4] *Pic*,[5] *Toilette*,[6] and *Mosquee*.[7] In every case authorities at our disposition[8] show that these were permissible English forms but that in the eighteenth century they were either archaic or less usual than others. It is especially significant that in the *Errata* of 1727, *Pic* was changed to *Pike* while in the 1728 edition *Toilette* was replaced by *Toilet* and *Mosquee* by *Mosque* and in 1731 *interesses* was in one case corrected to *interests*.[9]

In several cases where either the omission or the use of the article seems abnormal it may be explained as a confusion due to the difference between English and French usage. In three of these cases corrections have been made: the phrase *to the Christ*[10] was corrected in the *Errata* of 1727 to read *to Christ*, *in the Sight of the Cape*[11] was altered in 1728 to *in Sight of the Cape* and *of Virgin Mary* to *of the Virgin Mary*.[12]

There are many sentences in which the position of the adverb, although possible in English, is significantly like that of the French. For example, *to have much laboured;*[13] *bears secretly an ill Will;*[14] *makes sometimes amends;*[15] *which animated sometimes the Author;*[16] *who wears always a Mask.*[17]

In the use of auxiliaries the sequence of tenses is more char-

---

[1] Pp. 91, 98, *post*
[2] P. 94, *post*. The form metamorphosis also occurs once in the *Essay*, p. 139, *post*.
[3] P. 91, *post*.
[4] P. 96, *post*.
[5] P. 119, *post*.
[6] P. 105, *post*.
[7] P. 116, *post*.
[8] Cf. especially the *Oxford Dictionary*.
[9] Cf. also *Argonautes* (p. 111, *post*), changed to *Argonots* in 1728 and *Michel Cervantes* (p. 129, *post*), corrected in 1728 to *Michael*.
[10] P. 110, *post*.
[11] P. 108, *post*. Cf. Notebook of Voltaire, *English Review*, p. 313: "Jewish relligion is the mother of (the) Christianity."
[12] P. 117, *post*.
[13] P. 81, *post*.
[14] P. 92, *post*.
[15] P. 109, *post*.
[16] P. 125, *post*.
[17] P. 139, *post*.

acteristic of French than of English. A peculiar form of an aux-
iliary, to be explained perhaps by the French, is to be noticed
in the sentence: "One may judge . . . if to say to *Agamemnon*,
that *Achilles* is the most valorous of the present Chiefs, ought to
be [i.e., would be, cf. *devait être*] very acceptable to *Agamemnon*."[1]

Other expressions difficult to classify are worth noting—for
instance: *there are infinite Things*[2] [des choses infinies] corrected
in the *Errata* to *there is an infinite Number of Things; there is what
to laugh at*[3] [de quoi rire]; *in comparison of*[4] [en comparaison
de]; *Thirst of Glory*[5] [la soif de la gloire]; *whatever it be*[6] [quoiqu'il
en soit], where one would expect *however it may be*.

One sentence which appears in the 1727 edition is particularly significant: " But in my Opinion, the best reason for the
Languour which creeps upon the Mind of so many Readers, in
Spight of the Flashes which rouse her now and then, is, that *Homer*
interesses us for none of his Heroes." [7] In the *Errata* and in
the edition of 1728, *her*, the French grammatical gender, has been
changed to *it*, the English natural gender. A second but less
striking instance of the same sort is the phrase, " which the Fleet
finds in her Way home." [8]

Another point worthy of notice is that the writer has, in certain
cases of which we are aware and doubtless in many of which we
are not, followed closely the words of some English author, evidently working over a sentence a bit but relying on the original
for vocabulary and for unusual expressions. One example will
suffice: " They may discern the Fire of that Father of Poetry,
reflected from such a polished and faithful Glass," based on a
sentence found in Pope's Preface to the translation of the *Iliad*:
" This fire is discerned in Virgil but as through a glass reflected

---

[1] P. 128, *post.*
[2] P. 145, *post.*
[3] P. 111, *post.*
[4] P. 100, *post.*
[5] P. 124, *post.*
[6] P. 94, *post.*
[7] P. 91, *post.*
[8] P. 109, *post.* Cf. *The Nation who*, pp. 133, 144, *post.* Certain expressions are
to be noted as curious rather than as corresponding directly to French usage, such
as *far enough* . . . *as to*, (pp. 90-91) *which* [what] *is more* (p. 113), etc. In the
edition of 1727 there are instances of a singular subject with a plural verb—for
example, *which the taste . . . relish* (p. 84); *their language . . . were* (p. 103).
The second of these errors was corrected, the first was not. In three cases we
find *then* instead of *than* (pp. 102, 129, 138). In each case the mistake was
corrected in 1728.

from Homer."[1]   Such borrowing is what one might expect from a person writing in a language not his own.

The amount of material within the limits of Voltaire's English writings is not large enough to make generalizations absolutely safe but a careful examination of the fifteen English letters of Voltaire belonging to the period of his residence in England helps in two ways to confirm the belief that the *Essay* was essentially his own composition—first, because the language of these letters is in all probability his independent work and is clear and expressive; secondly, because the language shows the same handling as that of the *Essay*, presenting peculiarities which correspond to those already quoted from the *Essay*.

It must be remembered that the manuscript of many of the letters has been lost and that much of the spelling has no doubt been modernized. The words *pacquet*[2] and *honnour*,[3] however, afford examples of archaic forms near the French.

There is the same confusion in the use of the article as in the *Essay*: *the fate of all the wretched books*;[4] *almost fortnight*;[4] *in the search of it*;[4] *they will give you hundred directions*;[5] *I was stranger* (corrected to read *a stranger*).[6]

Again in the letters the position of the adverb is frequently striking: *pours allways on me*;[7] *I have seen often mylord B*;[8] *I received lately two letters*;[9] *I could print secretly the Henriade*;[10] *I have thought always your's to be*.[11] It is significant that in one case the words, *I have so much written*, were later changed to read *I have written so much*.[12]

The use of tenses suggests the French as in the phrase, occurring twice, *since I am in England*, meaning *since I have been in England*.[13] The variants in the letter of October 15, 1726, indicate

---

[1] P.   89, note 4, *post*.   Cf. also p. 96, note 3; p. 99, notes 10 and 11; p. 100, notes 3 and 6; p. 101, note 3; p. 127, note 5, *post*.
[2] Foulet, *Corr.*, p. 89.
[3] *Ibid.*, p. 155.
[4] *Ibid.*, p. 89.
[5] *Ibid.*, p. 103.
[6] *Ibid.*, p. 56.
[7] *Ibid.*, p. 58.
[8] *Ibid.*, p. 60.
[9] *Ibid.*, p. 134.
[10] *Ibid.*, p. 156.
[11] *Ibid.*, p. 158.
[12] *Ibid.*, p. 62.
[13] *Ibid.*, pp. 103, 158.

an uncertainty as to the use of auxiliaries.[1] In the same letter there are two corrections which correspond exactly to one already mentioned as having been made in the *Errata* of the 1727 edition of the *Essay*. In the letter Voltaire wrote originally *a nation fond of her liberty* and *every country has his madness:* these phrases were later altered to read *their liberty* and *its madness.*[2]

Among other constructions which occur in various letters and which recall French usage may be mentioned: *obeys to the law;*[3] *all that is king;*[4] *the nation who dislikes;*[5] *at my own expenses;*[6] *answering to you,* corrected to read *answering you.*[7]

Both external and internal evidence seem to justify the conclusion that, although Voltaire probably received suggestions from English friends and relied to some extent upon English texts, the language of the *Essay on Epic Poetry,* like that of his English letters, is largely his own.

Against this evidence there stands the adverse testimony of five writers approximately contemporaries of Voltaire. Of these two were French, the Abbé Desfontaines and Mme. de Genlis, two Italian, Paolo Rolli and Giuseppi Baretti, and one an Englishman, Joseph Spence. The assertions of the Abbé Desfontaines are to be found in the *Voltairomanie,* a pamphlet of 1738. They read as follows: " Voltaire n'a point composé seul en Anglais cet écrit [the *Essay on Epic Poetry*], mais l'ayant fait d'abord en Français un Anglais l'a aidé à le traduire dans sa langue. . . . A peine est-il en Angleterre, qu'après en avoir étudié la Langue pendant trois mois, il met en Anglais un Essai sur le Poème Epique, qu'il avait composé en Français; puis ayant fait corriger cette traduction par son Maître de Langue, il la donne au Public. Il est vrai que les Anglais dirent alors que c'était un tissu de Gallicismes et de Barbarismes. Qu'importe ? Voltaire faisait voir qu'il avait un génie divin pour les Langues comme pour toutes les Sciences, et tous les beaux Arts."[8] In the *Mémoires* of Mme. de Genlis (1825) occurs the sentence: " Il ['le célèbre Wilkes du parti de l'opposition''] avait beaucoup vu Voltaire pendant son

---

[1] Foulet, *Corr.,* pp. 61, 63.
[2] *Ibid.,* p. 61.
[3] *Ibid.,* p.138.
[4] *Ibid.,* p. 61.
[5] *Ibid.,* p. 89. Cf. p. 22, note 8, *ante.*
[6] *Ibid.,* p. 60.
[7] *Ibid.,* p. 63.
[8] Pp. 45, 47.

séjour à Londres, il me dit qu'il savait très mal l'anglais et qu'il n'était pas en état de sentir la beauté des poètes." [1] Rolli remarks in his criticism of the *Essay on Epic Poetry*, in 1728, that Voltaire is proud of having learned English in so short a time and adds: " I only admire his Vanity and his pretty simile of the Nurse[2] . . . particularly when she helped him." [3] We have two statements from Baretti, the first in his *Dissertation on the Italian Poetry*, 1753, and the second in his *Discours sur Shakespeare et sur M. de Voltaire*, 1777. In 1753 he asserted that Voltaire would have done better to write his essay in French than to dishonor the English language by making it " the conveyance of his impertinence," and expressed astonishment that an author so excellent in his own language could utter so many absurdities in that of another country.[4] Here Baretti plainly takes for granted that the English is Voltaire's, but in 1777 he declares the Frenchman to be completely ignorant of English and maintains that the essays published under his name fifty years before were too correct to have been the work of a foreigner.[5] The fifth of the passages in question occurs in Spence's *Anecdotes*, first printed in 1820, although written much earlier:[6] " Voltaire, like the French in general, showed the greatest complaisance outwardly and had the greatest contempt for us inwardly. He consulted Dr. Young about his essay in English and begged him to correct any gross faults he might find in it. The Doctor set very honestly to work, marked the passages most liable to censure, and when he went to explain himself about them Voltaire could not avoid bursting out a laughing."[7]

The nature of these comments and the circumstances under which they were made deprive them of all authority. It is to be noticed that the first four of the critics in question were openly hostile to Voltaire at the time of writing and therefore incapable of impartial judgment, while the fifth was certainly not friendly

---

[1] III, p. 362.

[2] Cf. p. 89, *post*.

[3] P. 47. Rolli adds in this connection, " I have been twelve years in England and . . . I am sensible my readers will immediately find me out for a Foreigner."

[4] *Dissertation*, p. 4.

[5] *Discours*, p. 18: " La façon générale dans l'un et dans l'autre me feroit croire qu'ils sont de lui, si ce n'était que l'anglais y est trop anglais." P. 19: " Il n'y a pas le moindre mot de travers dans aucun des deux. . . . Un étranger ne s'en tire pas si britanniquement."

[6] Joseph Spence was born in 1699 and died in 1768.

[7] Pp. 374-375.

toward him. The quarrel between Desfontaines and Voltaire was approaching its height in 1738.[1] In her *Mémoires*, Mme. de Genlis herself speaks of what she calls her aversion for Voltaire.[2] As to Rolli and Baretti, they were both thoroughly angered with the French poet because of his comments on Italian literature; and Baretti, moreover, in 1777, was deeply stirred by Voltaire's attitude toward Shakespeare.[3]

Desfontaines' statement is made for the first time ten years after the publication of the *Essay* and is absurdly inaccurate and self-contradictory. Mme. de Genlis gives as her authority a person born while Voltaire was in England.[4] Rolli's remark is so vague that it counts for little. Baretti's argument in the *Discours sur Shakespeare* has to do chiefly with Voltaire's familiarity with English late in life, nearly half a century after his visit to England. As to the two reasons he gives to show that the language of the essays published in 1727 was not Voltaire's, the first, that it was too perfect to be the work of a foreigner, is, though made by a man familiar with English, merely the personal opinion of another foreigner, and an opinion which a careful study of the essay does not support; the second, that Voltaire never wrote a line in English after leaving England, is of course false. The only value of Spence's anecdote, in the form in which it has come down to us, is that it affords direct testimony that Voltaire showed his manuscript to an English friend. External evidence for so natural a precaution is superfluous.

The positive evidence of Voltaire's authorship already adduced is sufficient to outweigh adverse testimony of this kind.

---

[1] Cf. pp. 32 ff., *post.*

[2] I, p. 78.

[3] In her *Essay on the Writings and Genius of Shakespear* (1769) Mrs. Montagu ridicules Voltaire's translation of certain passages of *Julius Caesar* published in his edition of Corneille's works (1761). She acknowledges, however, (p. 236) that " Mr. Voltaire formerly understood the English language tolerably well."

[4] John Wilkes was born in 1727. In 1765 Wilkes visited Voltaire at Ferney and afterwards wrote an account of his visit. He admired Voltaire in an exaggerated fashion and spoke of him as " a divine old man." Ballantyne, pp. 80, 300.

CHAPTER III

THE FRENCH TRANSLATION OF THE ESSAY

Its publication in 1728 and later. Generally attributed to Desfontaines—His repudiation in 1738—Desfontaines and his work—His relations with Voltaire—Circumstances and value of his denial of the authorship of the translation—Comments on the translation in Voltaire's letters and in the press—The inaccuracy of the work—The text as corrected by Voltaire and reprinted in 1732.

Letters which Voltaire wrote in the spring and summer of 1728 throw light on the circumstances surrounding the first publication of the French translation of the *Essay on Epic Poetry.* In a letter of the end of March, the writer expresses his unwillingness to have his essays appear in France. He realizes that in their original form they would be displeasing to those in power. " I dare not send anything of that kind into France," he says, " before I have settled my affairs in that country. . . . I think I am not to let the French court know that I think and write like a free Englishman." [1] A few weeks later, writing to Thieriot about an " interloper " who proposes issuing in France an edition of the *Henriade,* he adds: " Tell him besides I disapprove entirely his design of translating my English essay. . . . That little pamphlet could not succeed in France without being dressed in quite another manner. . . . I know nothing so impertinent as to go about to translate me in spight of my teeth." [2] This letter was written April 21 (o. s.) and consequently too late to prevent the appearance of the translation of the *Essay on Epic Poetry,* the " approbation " for which had been obtained nine days earlier. The " privilège " was registered on May 19. The

---

[1] Foulet, *Corr.,* pp. 137-138. Voltaire did not even send a copy of his essays to Thieriot. *Ibid.,* pp. 137, note 3; 257.
[2] *Ibid.,* pp. 145-146. This letter in itself is sufficient to contradict Beuchot's statement that Voltaire " le fit traduire en français par l'abbé Desfontaines." *Oeuvres,* VIII, p. 302.

small volume appeared under the title, *Essai sur la poésie épique*,[1] *traduit de l'anglais de M. de Voltaire, par M. . . . A Paris chez Chaubert à l'Entrée du Quai des Augustins près le Pont Saint Michel à la Renomée et à la Prudence.* Since the " privilège " was not registered until May 19 and since the *Journal des Sçavans* for May, 1728, announced that the book was on sale,[2] it must have been issued late in that month. The same year it was printed, or it purported to be printed, in Holland.[3]

Strange as it may at first appear in view of Voltaire's early objections, the 1728 translation, announced as having been corrected by himself, was included in the edition of his works which was published in Amsterdam in 1732.[4] In nearly all the later editions of Voltaire's *Henriade* and of his complete works the translation was replaced by the author's own French version of the *Essay*, but the earlier form is occasionally found, as in the *Oeuvres complètes* of 1739[5] and in the edition of the *Henriade* published in Neuchâtel in 1772.[6]

Although the translation, like many others of that period, was at first published anonymously, it was at once attributed to the Abbé Guyot Desfontaines. That Voltaire himself felt no doubt as to the identity of the translator is clear from his letter to Thieriot written June 14: " I have received, by an unknown

[1] It is to be noticed that the title is less pretentious than that of the English essay. That title had been criticised by Rolli (*Remarks*, p. 37), who sarcastically remarked that he had never heard of any epic poem of Asiatic or American growth. When Rolli's book was translated into French in 1728 (par M.L.A. [Antonini]), mention was made in the preface of the change of title in the translation of Voltaire's essay and it was added: " Le traducteur Français en le changeant [le titre] a approuvé la censure que M. Rolli en a faite." Cf. Baretti, *Dissertation*, 1753, p. 70: " that contemptible Pamphlet so pompously entitled . . ."

[2] P. 319. Cf. *Mercure de France*, June, 1728, p. 1419, *Essay sur la Poésie Grecque* (sic) etc. The price is here announced as " 24 sols sans l'avertissement."

[3] A copy of the translation bearing the title, *Essai sur la Poésie Epique, traduit de l'anglois de M. de Voltaire, Par M. . . . A La Haye chez G. M. de Merville MDCCXXVIII*, is to be found in the Bibliothèque Sainte-Geneviève in Paris.

[4] *Oeuvres de M. Voltaire.* Amsterdam, 1732, p. 209.

[5] Cf. Bengesco, IV, p. 13.

[6] *Oeuvres de M. de Voltaire*, Neuchâtel, 1772. This edition, as well as that of 1739, appears to have been made without Voltaire's knowledge. Cf. also *Oeuvres*, VIII, p. 304, note by Beuchot: " La traduction de Desfontaines (et non le texte de Voltaire) se retrouve cependant dans un volume qui a ce singulier titre: *Ouvrages classiques de l'élégant poëte M. Arouel, fameux sous le nom de Voltaire . . .* ; à Oxford . . . , 1771. . . . Je ne sais si l'édition a été continuée."

hand, my English essay's translation; I suppose it came from you and I thank you for it. . . . Abbot Desfontaines has been very far from doing one justice in many passages."[1] This ascription was soon made public in the preface of the *Henriade* issued in 1730, in which the *Essay on Epic Poetry* is mentioned as having been translated by the Abbé Desfontaines.[2] And the *Journal des Sçavans*, a publication with which Desfontaines had been connected a short time before, accepted without question, in a summary of this preface, the statement regarding the authorship of the translation: " Quelques personnes, ajoute-t-on, auraient souhaité qu'au défaut d'une Dissertation plus complette sur cette matière, on eût fait imprimer ici *l'Essai sur la Poésie Epique* . . . traduit en Français par M. l'Abbé Guyot Desfontaines." As the printer of the *Journal* had issued the translation this statement may be considered reliable. At the end of the announcement quoted occur the words: " La traduction française dont on vient de parler, et qui se vend à Paris chez Chaubert, libraire du Journal." [3]

The following year, when Voltaire's works were published in Amsterdam, the translated essay was included under the title *Essai sur la Poésie épique de toutes les nations, écrit en Anglais par M. de Voltaire en* 1726 [sic] *et traduit en Français par M. l'Abbé Desfontaines.*[4] Again in 1733, when Voltaire replaced the translation by his own version, it is stated that *"L'Essai sur le Poème Epique* n'est point la traduction de M. l'Abbé des Fontaines faite sur l'original anglais de Monsieur de Voltaire." [5] In a letter of September, 1733, concerning that edition, Voltaire mentions the new version of his essay: "J'avais d'abord composé cet *Essai* en anglais, at il avait été traduit par l'abbé Desfontaines, homme fort connu dans la littérature." [6] In many of Voltaire's later letters and in all the succeeding editions of his works, the French translation is called that of the Abbé Desfontaines. It has accordingly been attributed to Desfontaines by biographers in general.

[1] Foulet, *Corr.*, p. 154.
[2] Cf. p. 11, note 1, *ante*.
[3] 1731, p. 159.
[4] Cf. p. 28, note 4, *ante*.
[5] Cf. *La Henriade*, London, 1734 (reprint of edition of 1733). Cf. Bengesco, I, p. 105.
[6] *Oeuvres*, XXXIII, p. 382.

So convincing are these statements that there would be no reason for discussing the authorship of the translation, were it not that the Abbé Desfontaines once flatly denied that it was the work of his pen. In the *Voltairomanie*, 1738, from which we have already quoted the passage casting aspersions upon Voltaire's knowledge of English, we read: "L'Abbé Des Fontaines n'a point fait à Voltaire l'honneur de traduire en Français ce malheureux essai. C'est feu M. de Plélo, ambassadeur en Danemarc et tué près de Dantzic[1] qui, pour s'amuser à Paris, fit cette traduction dans le tems qu'il apprenoit l'Anglais. Le fort de Voltaire est de se tromper en tout ce qu'il dit. Cette traduction est imprimée chez Chaubert." [2]

In order to judge concerning the authorship of the translation and the value of Desfontaines' denial, it is essential to know something of l'Abbé Desfontaines himself, of his relations with Voltaire, and of the circumstances of this denial. Pierre François Guyot Desfontaines was born in 1685 and died in 1745. After a varied career, spent partly in the provinces and partly in Paris, we find him in the summer of 1725 established in the capital as collaborating editor of the *Journal des Sçavans*. A journalist and a critic of secondary importance, he is chiefly remembered as a translator. Joseph Texte, in his discussion of the popularization of English literature in France, speaks of him as " le plus actif, sinon le plus glorieux émule que les réfugiés aient trouvé en France avant Voltaire et Prévost," whose ambition it was to be, " en quelque manière, l'introducteur attitré des productions anglaises." [3] The list of works published under his name or attributed to him by biographers includes many translations from the English, as well as critical reviews, contributions to periodicals and the like. He seems to have been very active in the years 1726, 1727 and 1728, the period with which we are concerned. In 1726 he showed his interest in English matters in general by publishing *L'Apologie du Caractère des Anglais et*

---

[1] Louis Robert-Hippolite de Bréhan, comte de Plélo, diplomat, student and poet. He became ambassador to Denmark in 1729 and died at Weichselmunde, near Dantzig, Prussia, in 1734.

[2] P. 45.

[3] P. 41. Cf. Brunetière, *L'Evolution des Genres*, I, p. 148: " Il ne se publiait pas à Londres une seule nouveauté . . . qui ne fût traduite aussitôt . . . par quelque Desfontaines."

des Français ou Observations sur le livre intitulé Lettres sur les Anglais et les Français et les Voyages. In March, 1727, a translation of the first volume of Swift's *Gulliver* appeared in Paris. A preface to this edition expresses views concerning the province of a translator.[1] Like most of Desfontaines' translations, this was published anonymously but was immediately acknowledged as his work.[2] In 1728 there was issued at Nancy a small book, *Entretiens sur les Voyages de Cyrus*, in which, as was the case more than once, Desfontaines worked in collaboration with l'Abbé Granet, the translator of Voltaire's other English essay, that upon the Civil Wars. As we examine the list of his works, it is interesting to notice that several of the publications in which he had a part were issued by Chaubert, the publisher of the *Journal des Sçavans* and of the translation of the *Essay on Epic Poetry.*

Let us now consider Desfontaines' relations with Voltaire. The latter tells us that they date from 1724. At that time the author of the *Henriade* was induced to use his influence to obtain the freedom of the Abbé who had been in prison for some months. His efforts were successful and in May of that year Desfontaines wrote him a most appreciative letter, beginning: "Je n'oublierai jamais, monsieur, les obligations infinies que je vous ai."[3] It was during the same year that an incomplete and highly unsatisfactory edition of the *Henriade*, then called *La Ligue*, for which Desfontaines is held responsible, was issued at Evreux or Rouen

---

[1] Cf. p. 36, note 8, *post.*
[2] *Voyages de Gulliver.* Tome 1, "à Paris dans la boutique de la Veuve Coutelier, chéz Jacques Guerin, Quay des Augustins," 1727. In a letter of February, 1727, Voltaire expressed great admiration for Swift's Gulliver and urged Thieriot, to whom he had previously sent a copy, to translate it, adding: "J'ai bien peur que quelqu'un plus pressé que vous ne vous ait prévenu en traduisant le premier tome." Foulet, *Corr.*, p. 78. Desfontaines' translation appeared in March. From the following passage in the translator's preface, it is evident that Thieriot had been indiscreet: " Dans ce même tems, un ami de M. de Voltaire me montra une lettre de fraîche datte de Londres, où cet illustre Poëte vantoit beaucoup le Livre nouveau de M. Swift, & assûroit qu'il n'avait jamais rien lû de plus amusant." In May Voltaire condoles with Thieriot saying: " I am afraid the abbot has outrun you " and " Take care only not to be outvied for the future by any priest: be cautious in the choice of those you will consult about your translation." Foulet, *Corr.*, pp. 95, 97. Cf. *Mercure de France*, May, 1727, p. 955: " M. l'Abbé Guyot Desfontaines, auteur de la Traduction ne s'est point asservi à son original, il a retranché beaucoup de choses, il en a aussi ajouté beaucoup, & en suivant les idées du Docteur Swift, il a métamorphosé tout son ouvrage, pour l'ajuster au goût des Français. . . . On voit à la tête une Préface modeste et judicieuse."
[3] *Oeuvres*, XXXIII, p. 110.

without the knowledge of Voltaire.[1] None the less the two seem
to have been on very amiable terms in 1725. In June, Voltaire
speaks of further good offices in behalf of " notre pauvre abbé
Desfontaines," [2] and a few months later he sends Desfontaines
a most friendly epistle. "Je ne peux pas m'accoutumer," he writes,
" à voir l'abbé Raguet dans l'opulence et dans la faveur, tandis
que vous êtes négligé." [3] Thieriot wrote Voltaire in the autumn
of 1726 warning him against Desfontaines but Voltaire merely
replied: " I have written freely to the abbot Desfontaines, it is
true, and I will allwais do so, having no reason to lay myself under
any restraint." [4] A year and a half later, in the spring of 1728,
we find Voltaire, aroused by news he has received from Thieriot,
using a different tone. He refers to " the abbot " as guilty of
the publication of the Evreux edition of the *Henriade*, calls him
an " interloper " because he proposes to publish a new edition
of the poem and characterizes as most " impertinent " his undertaking to translate the *Essay*.[5] Nevertheless in the letter written
upon the receipt of a copy of his translated essay, although he
regrets that the translation has been made, Voltaire does not
speak angrily. " I am sure," he writes, " this little pamphlet
did not at all deserve the trouble he has been at of putting it in
the French language." [6]

It is unnecessary here to recount the circumstances that led to
a violent quarrel between the two men. A clear idea of the progress of this ill-feeling may be gathered from letters of Voltaire
written between 1731 and 1738. In October, 1735, he says regarding the Abbé: " Mais son acharnement à payer par des satires
continuelles la vie et la liberté qu'il me doit est quelquechose
d'incompréhensible," [7] and again in 1736 he writes to l'Abbé
Asselin: "J'apprends que l'abbé Desfontaines continue de me
déchirer. C'est un chien poursuivi par le public, et qui se retourne,
tantôt pour lécher et tantôt pour mordre. L'ingratitude est chez
lui aussi dominante que le mauvais goût."[8] In 1738 Voltaire's
rage with the Jesuit journalist took definite form and he published

---

[1] Cf. Bengesco, I, pp. 99 ff.
[2] *Oeuvres*, XXXIII, p. 138.
[3] *Ibid.*, p. 155.
[4] Foulet, *Corr.*, p. 61.
[5] *Ibid.*, pp. 144 ff.
[6] *Ibid.*, p. 155.
[7] *Oeuvres*, XXXIII, p. 537.
[8] *Ibid.*, XXXIV, p. 51.

the *Préservatif*, containing an account of his acquaintance with Desfontaines and of the latter's " black " ingratitude, in issuing libels, satires and criticisms against his benefactor. Desfontaines' reply was the *Voltairomanie*.

In the *Préservatif*, in the course of the ironical remarks concerning a recent piece of criticism from Desfontaines' pen, Voltaire refers to the faulty translation of his essay: " Dans une traduction que ce critique fit en Français d'un Ouvrage Anglais de M. de Voltaire, il prit le mot Kake qui signifie gateau pour le Géant Cacus.[1] Il est plaisant, il faut l'avouer, qu'un pareil homme s'avise de juger les autres." [2] The calling of public attention to this absurd mistake promised to bring endless ridicule upon the accepted translator and to injure him professionally. Since the mistake really existed in the translation as it appeared in 1728, Desfontaines' only means of defense lay in denying that the work was his. That his denial was the direct result of Voltaire's ridicule is evident from the words with which it is introduced: " Le Sieur Voltaire reproche à l'Abbé Des Fontaines une méprise dans la traduction de *l'Essai sur la Poésie Epique*, composé, dit-il, par lui-même en Anglais." [3] The mere fact that this denial was made ten years after the translation was issued and at least eight years after the translation had first been publicly attributed to Desfontaines renders it well-nigh nugatory. Why, if he did not wish to be considered the translator, did he wait all this time to speak ? Moreover, Desfontaines takes the precaution to ascribe the translating of the essay to a person quite unable to deny it since he was no longer living.[4] For this ascription, which contradicts a generally accepted opinion, he gives no proof. As an episode in a literary quarrel his denial is perfectly comprehensible. The friendly terms existing between Voltaire and Desfontaines early in their acquaintance would account for the tardiness of Voltaire's public ridicule of the translation and consequently for the tardiness of Desfontaines' repudiation of the work.

[1] Cf. p. 94, *post.*

[2] P. 23. Voltaire also disputes 'Desfontaines' knowledge of English in other connections. Cf. *Oeuvres*, XXXIII, p. 530 (20 Septembre, 1735): " Ce pauvre homme [Desfontaines], qui veut se donner pour entendre l'anglais, donne l'extrait d'un livre anglais fait en faveur de la religion, comme d'un livre d'athéisme. Il n'y a pas une de ses feuilles qui ne fourmille de fautes."

[3] *Voltairomanie*, p. 45.

[4] It is difficult to account for the sentence added at the end of the denial, " Cette traduction est imprimée chez Chaubert," unless we see in it the writer's desire to advertise the translation.

Although it was not until ten years after the publication of the translation of his *Essay* that Voltaire made definite use of its inaccuracy as a means of attacking Desfontaines, his correspondence shows that he made complaints as soon as he saw the book. That these complaints became more bitter later is only natural in light of the increasing ill-feeling between the two. In the letter written in June, 1728, upon receipt of the translation, after stating that "Abbot Desfontaines" has been very far from doing him justice in many passages, Voltaire goes on to enumerate instances: " He has mistaken the West-Indies for the East-Indies;[1] he has translated the cakes, which young Ascanius takes notice of being eaten by his countrymen, for *la faim dévorante de Cacus.* So he mistakes *des assiettes* et *de la croûte de pâté* for a giant and a monster." That he does not, however, attach much importance to the matter appears from the sentence: " I have not the book by me at present, and cannot remember all his oversights." [2]   Eight years later, in 1736, when his feeling toward Desfontaines has become hostile, in a letter to the authors of the *Bibliothèque française,* he speaks more emphatically and more ironically of the incorrectness of the translation of his essay: " Il y avait autant de contresens que de lignes. Il [Desfontaines] y disait que les Portugais avaient découvert l'Amérique . . .[3] Le mot anglais *cake,* qui signifie *gateau,* fut pris par lui pour *Cacus,* et les Troyens pour des vaches." [4]   In addition to the public use made of the more striking of these mistakes in 1738, complaints of the general inaccuracy of the translation appeared in many succeeding editions of Voltaire's works. For instance, in the preface of that published in London in 1746, the year following Desfontaines' death, occurs the sentence: " Mais l'abbé sachant médiocrement l'anglais fit plusieurs fautes considérables," and at the same time in the foreword of the *Essai sur la poésie épique:* " Elle [Desfontaines' translation] fourmille de fautes et de contresens." [5]

---

[1] Cf. p. 107, *post.*
[2] Foulet, *Corr.,* pp. 154, 155.
[3] In the passage in which East Indies had been translated " Indes occidentales."
[4] *Oeuvres,* XXXIV, pp. 133-134. According to the mythological tale the giant Cacus was wont to devour whole herds of cattle in his cave.
[5] *Oeuvres diverses de M. de Voltaire,* Londres, Trévoux, Nourse, 1746.

On the other hand, in contemporary periodicals the work of the translator was highly praised. In an account of the translation in the *Mercure de France* of June, 1728, we read: " Mais elle [la langue française] n'y a rien perdu, puisque l'Ouvrage paraît aujourd'hui traduit en Français d'une manière très avantageuse, et qu'on a de la peine à s'imaginer que cette copie ne soit pas l'original même de l'auteur. . . . L'Ouvrage dont il s'agit a autant de succès icy qu'il en a eu à Londres." [1] In the *Bibliothèque française* a reviewer writes: " Nous ajouterons que la Traduction a été généralement applaudie, elle n'a rien de contraint & d'affecté, on ne sent point que ce soit une Copie, tant elle a l'air original." [2] Furthermore, in the *Preface* of the *Henriade* published in 1730 there is a flattering allusion to Desfontaines' translation; l'Abbé Desfontaines is spoken of as writing " avec plus d'élégance et de pureté que personne . . . M. de Voltaire ne se seroit pas flatté de se traduire lui-même aussi bien que M. l'abbé des Fontaines l'a traduit." [3] This praise is, however, somewhat qualified by the words " à quelques inadvertances près " added in parentheses. In view of these conflicting statements regarding the value of the translation it seems worth while to examine it in some detail. The small volume is rare[4] and, moreover, it offers a certain interest as the work of one of the most prolific translators of the early part of the eighteenth century.

A comparison of the English original with the text of the translation as it was published in 1728 gives interesting results. The errors mentioned by Voltaire exist.[5] In addition, there are numerous other mistranslations which indicate an insufficient knowledge of English or great carelessness on the part of the translator. For example, in the phrase, " longer than the other Americans," [6] Americans has been replaced by *Africains*. The adjective " hard " is translated once *hardi*[7] and again *périlleux*;[8] " anxious

[1] P. 1419.
[2] 1728, XII, p. 265.
[3] Cf. p. 11, note 1, *ante*.
[4] It was already spoken of as rare in 1772. Cf. p. 40, note 3, *post*. The copy used in this chapter was consulted in the Bibliothèque Nationale, where there are two copies, one bound with the French translation of Rolli's criticism of the essay.
[5] Pp. 94, 107, *post*.
[6] P. 124, *post*.
[7] P. 132, *post*.
[8] P. 149, *post*.

and cruel " becomes *politique et inquiet*;[1] " preposterous and aukward," *puériles et hors d'oeuvre*;[2] " insupportable and insignificant," *les plus fatigants et les plus difficiles*.[3] " Where the Bone
and the Bladder meet "[4] is translated *où les os et la vessie
s'éloignent*.

To turn to examples of the misconstruing of ideas, the sentence
" I am so far from looking upon that Liberty as a Fault that I
think it to be a great Beauty,"[5] is rendered in the French: "Je
suis aussi loin de regarder cette liberté comme une faute que de
la regarder comme une grande beauté." " The Earl of *Roscommon* and Mr. *Addison* (whose judgement seems either to guide,
or to justify the Opinion of his Contrymen),"[6] reads in the French:
" Le comte de Roscommon et M. Addison dont les sentiments
entraînent et justifient ceux de leurs compatriotes." " His Gods
are perhaps at once absurd and entertaining, as the Madness of
Ariosto amuses us with a bewitching Delight,"[7] is translated:
" Ses Dieux sont peutêtre en même tems absurdes et ridicules,
ils sont néanmoins aussi amusans que les extravagances de l'Arioste
qui nous causent une espèce d'enchantment," a rendering which
alters the meaning.

The text contains, moreover, numerous passages which are, in
their relation to the English, such as one might expect from the
author of the preface of the translation of *Gulliver*.[8] In many
cases the sentences have been translated very freely and frequently
in such a way as to affect the sense. These alterations often take
the form of making a statement more emphatic or less than in
the English. For instance, on the one hand, " disliked "[9] is

---

[1] P. 115, *post.*
[2] P. 138, *post.*
[3] P. 149, *post.*
[4] P. 146, *post.*
[5] P. 137, *post.*
[6] P. 141, *post.*
[7] P. 91, *post.*
[8] It may be well to quote passages from this preface: "Je me mis à le traduire
[Gulliver] uniquement pour ma propre utilité, c'est à dire pour me perfec-
tionner dans la connaissance de la Langue Anglaise. . . . J'apprends qu'on
en imprime actuellement une [traduction] en Hollande. Si elle est littérale
et si elle est faite par quelque Traducteur ordinaire de ce païs là, je prononce,
sans l'avoir vûë qu'elle est fort mauvaise. . . . Je puis néanmoins dire sans
trop me flatter, qu'elle [his own translation] a un certain mérite que l'original
n'a point. . . . Quoique j'aye fait mon possible pour ajuster l'Ouvrage de
Monsieur Swift au goût de la France, je ne prétens pas cependant en avoir
fait tout à fait un Ouvrage Français."
[9] P. 140, *post.*

translated *sifflé*, and " would not succeed," [1] *serait méprisé*, while, on the other hand, " could not be tolerated," [2] has become *déplairaient*, " the Taste of the Nation . . . remains in its full Force," [3] *la nation conserve en général* . . . etc. Again words, phrases and, in certain cases, whole sentences have been omitted in the translation. In the passage concerning the origin of the Romance languages omissions have altered the sense. The English reads: " In the Course of a thousand Years, the *Italians*, the *French*, the *Spaniards*, refin'd their Manners and their Idioms," [4] which has become in French: *Mais dans le cours de mille ans, ils [" les conquérants du Nord"] polirent également leurs manières et leur langage.* The expression " some little Descriptions, some obvious Similes " is changed by the omission of the adjectives when it reads, *quelques descriptions et quelques comparaisons.* In the connection in which the words are used the difference is of real importance. [5] On the other hand additions have sometimes been made, as in the clause: " who mistake commonly the Beginning of an Art, for the Principles of the Art itself, and are apt to believe that every Thing . . . ," [6] which becomes *qui par un travers ridicule, prennent communément les commencements d'un Art pour les principes de l'art même, assés peu judicieux pour se persuader* . . . " That Nation " [7] [France] is rendered *cette illustre nation* and " those Gentlemen," [8] *Messieurs les scoliastes.* In the passage concerning " the common Mass " of those who read Homer[9] the words *dans une bonne traduction* have been added.[10]

---

[1] P. 85, *post.*
[2] *Ibid.*
[3] P. 114, *post.*
[4] P. 103, *post.*
[5] P. 96, *post.* The latter part of the English advertisement, " Whosever hath the honor . . ." has been omitted in the French.
[6] P. 81, *post.*
[7] P. 132, *post.*
[8] P. 122, *post.*
[9] P. 90, *post.*
[10] Three notes have been inserted by the translator. The first occurs at the end of the advertisement and reads: " M. de Voltaire n'a point mis cet Essay à la tête de l'Edition de son Poëme qui est imprimé à Londres in-4o et qui paroît depuis quelques mois." The second concerns the gender of the word *sin*: " Les Anglais n'ont ni mots Masculins ni mots Féminins." Cf. p. 140, *post.* The third follows the passage having to do with the building of the bridge in *Paradise Lost* and is particularly interesting in view of the ignorance with regard to Dante which prevailed in France at the beginning of the eighteenth century: " Le Dante les fait aller [men's souls] en Enfer à Cheval." Cf. p. 133, note 3, *post.*

There is a third class of changes which are to be distinguished from the various kinds of free translations we have been discussing in that they have to do directly with the adaptation of the text to the French public. These changes consist largely in the omission or softening of passages which would be offensive to the Roman Catholic church or the French government. In the light of the strict censorship of the press which prevailed at the time and the difficulty often experienced in obtaining permission to print a work,[1] these suppressions were probably necessary for the publication of the essay in France as well as for its success with French people.[2] The fact that the translator was a Jesuit priest, together with the general necessity of conciliating the recognized religion, accounts for the altering of various passages. For instance: "Jesuitical Distinctions "[3] has become *distinctions sophistiques*, and the phrase: " all the Parts of *Popish* Religion which are accounted comical and mean in *England* "[4] reads *quelques autres pratiques de la Religion Romaine*. The following sentence has been omitted: " If an Author among the *French*, attempts a Poem on *Clovis*, he is allow'd to speak of the Holy Vial, brought down from Heaven, in the Bill of a Dove, into the church of *Rheims* for the Coronation of the King."[5] The translator no doubt felt that a sacred tradition of the church and of the state was spoken of too lightly. Three passages bearing on oppression in France as contrasted with English liberty have been softened or suppressed altogether. In the translation of the phrase: " To this happy Freedom that the British Nation enjoys in every Thing,"[6] the words " in every Thing " have been omit-

---

[1] Permission for printing the translation of the *Essay on the Civil Wars* in France was, as a matter of fact, refused and the work appeared in Holland. Cf. *Bibl. franç.*, XIII. Cf. Ballantyne, p. 187: " So harmless a thing as Voltaire's Essay on Epic Poetry was proscribed in France." It seems likely that Ballantyne has here confused the two English essays.

[2] Cf. Foulet, *Corr.*, p. 138: " I think I am not to let the French court know that I think and write like a free Englishman."

[3] P. 119, *post*.

[4] P. 122, *post*.

[5] Cf. p. 95, *post*. In an analysis of the translation of the *Essay on Epic Poetry*, in the *Journal des Sçavans* for September, 1728, XII, p. 165, occurs the sentence· " Le traducteur de cet ouvrage nous prie d'assurer le public que cette traduction est fidèle et qu'il n'en a retranché que trois lignes qui regardent la sainte ampoule." This assertion is remarkable in view of the inaccuracy of the work as a whole, and seems to indicate that the translator had already been criticized for inaccuracy. It is significant that he should have chosen the *Journal des Sçavans* to make his statement to the public.

[6] Cf. p. 146, *post*.

ted, making the allusion a purely literary one. This very significant sentence does not appear at all: " For it is with our heroic Poetry as with our Trade we come up to the English in neither for want of being a free Nation." [1] The allusion to the Revocation of the Edict of Nantes contained in the words " as the compelling our Protestants away hath thinned the Nation," [2] has also been omitted.[3]

All this makes clear that, even leaving out of account the concessions to French censorship, the translation can by no means be considered a satisfactory one.[4]

Why Voltaire reprinted in the edition of his works issued in 1732 the very translation which he had declared so unsatisfactory will be discussed in connection with the history of the publication of his own French version of the *Essay*. We are now concerned only with the form in which the translation appeared in 1732. In the letter to the authors of the *Bibliothèque française*[5] and at various other times Voltaire spoke of having corrected Desfontaines' text before reprinting it. In several prefaces to the *Essai* in early editions of Voltaire's works reference is made to such corrections. By comparing the translation as it was published in 1728 with the form in which it appeared in 1732, we may discover wherein those corrections consisted.

The comparison shows at once that many changes have been made in punctuation, capitalization, and spelling, although some errors are left uncorrected. There are in the course of the essay about forty variants which involve change in wording. Of these only four or five are actual corrections of inaccuracies contained in the translation of 1728. In the famous passage concerning the Cakes, " la faim dévorante de Cacus " has been replaced by *les Troyens mangeant leurs assiettes*. It is very curious that the

---

[1] P. 149, *post*.
[2] *Ibid.*
[3] Desfontaines made a change in the order in which the poets were treated, placing Tasso after, instead of before, Ercilla and therefore immediately before Milton.
[4] Bengesco (II, p. 5) speaks of Desfontaines' version of the *Advertisement* of the *Essay on Epic Poetry* as both faulty and incomplete and prints, in consequence, a translation of the *Advertisement* which he himself has made. Desfontaines' rendering of the *Advertisement* is, however, no more inaccurate than that of the essay proper and may, on the other hand, be considered typical of the whole.
[5] Cf. p. 34, *ante*.

second definite error mentioned by Voltaire is not corrected. The words, *les Indes Occidentales,* translating " East Indies," are unchanged. The error *Africains* for "Americans," also remains unchanged. The sentence: "Je suis aussi éloigné de regarder cette liberté comme une faute que de la regarder comme une grande beauté" has been changed to read: "Je suis si loin de les croire [les traits de morale] un défaut que je les regarde comme une grande beauté," which restores the sense of the English. The passage concerning the " Holy Vial " has been inserted. Voltaire was never over-cautious in remarks involving the church. In some cases a few words have been added, expressing an unimportant idea found neither in the translation of 1728 nor in the English, or slightly altering the original meaning. In several cases the same thing is simply put in a different way.[1]

It is clear that the work of revision was done hastily and with no systematic thoroughness. That Voltaire should have contented himself with comparatively few alterations, leaving the text of 1728 substantially unchanged is inconsistent with two statements with regard to Desfontaines' translation which he made some years later in the letter to the Bibliothèque française: " Il y avait autant de contresens que de lignes " and "Je corrigeai ses fautes." [2] Such inconsistency is, however, very characteristic of Voltaire.[3]

---

[1] It is interesting to notice that Voltaire has in part restored his original title, still omitting, however, the words which Rolli considered most objectionable. It is now called, *Essai sur la Poésie Epique de toutes les Nations.* Cf. p. 28, note 1, *ante.*

[2] Cf. p. 34, note 4, *ante.*

[3] In the edition of Voltaire's works published in Neuchâtel in 1772, the abbé's translation of the *Essay on Epic Poetry* appears with the explanatory note: " On n'a point répété ce que M. de Voltaire a conservé de cette traduction dans les éditions infinies de cet essai. Nous croyons que cela même rendra ce morceau précieux . . . d'ailleurs il est devenu rare. On prouve encore par là combien M. l'Abbé Desfontaines admira alors l'auteur de la Henriade quoiqu' ensuite il se soit brouillé avec lui: *ut magis inimicitus claresceret.*" A comparison of the essay as it appears in this edition of 1772 with the translation of 1728 and with Voltaire's French version shows that the note just quoted is far from accurate. It is true that many passages have been omitted, but the omissions have not been made systematically. The parts omitted are by no means always identical with passages in Voltaire's version. On the other hand certain portions of the essay have been retained which correspond to Voltaire's text as closely as others which have been omitted. Considering all the circumstances, it is remarkable that such a correspondence should exist at all. That is a question which will be discussed in the following chapter.

CHAPTER IV

Voltaire's French Version

His reasons for making such a version—Delay in the publication of it—Causes of this delay—Stages in the preparation.

Voltaire had felt from the beginning that his essays should not appear in France in the form in which they had been published in England.[1] In April, 1728, he first mentions an adaptation for the French public of the *Essay on Epic Poetry*. In a letter to Thieriot, quoted in the preceding chapter, he writes in regard to a proposed edition of the *Henriade*: "Then I will send you my plates with some sheets of a quarto edition, large paper, begun in London, with the *Essay on Epic Poetry* in French, and calculated for the French meridian."[2] In the paragraph which follows, he states as his first reason for disapproving Desfontaines' project for translating the essay that he himself has already "translated" it. In the letter of June 14 he returns to the subject of his own French version: "I told you already, and I desire you to apprize your friends of it, that the English essay was but the sketch of a very serious work which I have almost finished in French, with all the care, the liberty and the impartiality I am capable of . . . I intend to make use of your advice, and to give the public, as soon as possible, the best edition I can of the *Henriade*, together with my true *Essay on Poetry*. The printing of them both is a duty I must discharge before I think of other duties less suitable with the life of a man of letters, but becoming a man of honnour and from which you may be sure I shall never depart as long as I breathe."[3] Again, the fourth of August, writing to Thieriot in regard to the edition

---

[1] Cf. p. 27, note 1, *ante.*

[2] Foulet, *Corr.*, pp. 144-145. In a letter written in 1732, Voltaire speaks of another occasion when he had found himself under the necessity of altering what he had written in England before publishing it in France: " Il me faut déguiser à Paris ce que je ne pourrais dire trop fortement à Londres. . . . Je suis . . . obligé de changer tout ce que j'avais écrit à l'occasion de M. Locke, parcequ' après tout je veux vivre en France, et qu'il ne m'est pas permis d'être aussi philosophe qu'un Anglais." *Oeuvres*, XXXIII, p. 307.

[3] Foulet, *Corr.*, p. 155.

of the *Henriade* which he proposes to publish in the near future, Voltaire adds: "Je joindrai à cette édition un *Essai sur la poësie épique* qui ne sera point la traduction d'un embryon anglais mal formé, mais un ouvrage complet." [1]

The same reasons which had prompted the writing and publishing of the two English essays hold good, in even greater measure, for Voltaire's wish to present to the French public a suitable version of one of them. The *Essay on the Civil Wars*, furnishing the historical background for the *Henriade*, was scarcely needed in the author's own country. On the other hand, that dealing with epic poetry might be expected to have in France an influence similar to that of the two essays in England but a somewhat more serious and more lasting one. In London the small volume had served a rather ephemeral purpose, heralding the appearance of a work little known and stimulating the curiosity of the public. In France the *Essai sur la Poésie Epique* was meant to convince its readers of the permanent value of a poem which, although inaccessible, was already fairly well known. The publication of the essay would, then, quite naturally be included in the project which was still nearest Voltaire's heart, namely, the placing of a satisfactory edition of the *Henriade* within the reach of French readers. [2]

To turn to a secondary motive, Voltaire's desire in writing the English essay to contribute something to comparative literature would operate more strongly in favor of a French version, since it was evidently among the French that he felt there was the greatest need of such broadening influences. [3] The closing words of the sentence last quoted are significant in this connection: " Un ouvrage . . . très curieux pour ceux qui, quoique nés en France, veulent avoir une idée du goût des autres nations."

In view of Voltaire's statements during the year 1728, slightly inconsistent, to be sure, since he says first that he has already

---

[1] Foulet, *Corr.*, p. 175.

[2] *Ibid.*, p. 300: " Mais le fait est que la *Henriade* est introuvable en France. . . . Un Français de 1729 qui veut lire la *Henriade* doit premièrement passer la frontière."

[3] Cf. p. 70, *post.* Cf. also *Mercure de France*, June, 1728: " Il y a bien à profiter dans cet écrit [*l'Essai*]. . . . On nous donne icy une idée curieuse de tous ces Poëmes, dont la plupart sont aussi peu connus en France qu'ils sont estimez dans leurs pays." Cf. also *Bibliothèque française*, XII, 1728, Article II: " Cet ouvrage si nécessaire aux Français, pour leur donner une idée de Poëmes Epiques étrangers qu'ils ne connaissent presque pas."

made a French version and later that he has nearly completed such a version, one would certainly expect the *Essai sur la Poésie Epique* to appear with the first edition of the *Henriade* published by the poet after his return from England. There is, indeed, some reason for believing that the manuscript of the essay was submitted to the royal censor in May, 1729.[1] Yet when the promised edition of the *Henriade* appeared in France in the late months of the year 1730, no essay on epic poetry was printed with it. The matter is touched upon in the preface. We are told that there has been some question of reprinting the Abbé Desfontaines' translation with the *Henriade*, but, since " cet Essay est plutôt un simple exposé des Poëmes épiques anciens & modernes, qu'une Dissertation bien utile sur cet Art. . . . On prend le parti de renvoier ceux qui seroient curieux de lire cet Essai . . . à la traduction française de M. des Fontaines." There follows an explanation of the fact that the French version —" un plus long Ouvrage que M. de Voltaire a composé depuis " —has not been published either. The author, "ne croyant pas que ce soit à lui de donner des Régles pour courir dans une carrière dans laquelle il n'a fait peut-être que broncher," [2] dares not print it.

Nearly a year later, in August, 1731, Voltaire writes to his friend M. de Cideville in Rouen: "Jore [his publisher, also of Rouen] doit avoir reçu *l'Essai sur la Poésie épique*, que je vous supplie de lire." [3] In another letter written toward the end of the month, he asks the same correspondent to become " le tuteur de *la Henriade* et de *l'Essai sur l'Epopée*," but it appears that he had sent only a portion of the manuscript of the essay to Rouen. " Vous êtes d'étranges gens," writes Voltaire, "de croire que je m'arrête après la vie de Milton, et que je me borne à être son historien. Je vous ai seulement envoyé, à bon compte, cette partie de *l'Essai*, et j'espère, dans peu de jours, vous envoyer la fin, que je n'ai pu encore retravailler. Je vous avoue que je serai bien embarrassé quand il faudra parler de moi." In closing this letter Voltaire gives explicit directions concerning the printing of the essay, which he evidently looks upon as imminent: "A

---

[1] Foulet, *Corr.*, p. 307, note 1: " Nous croyons que c'est en effet *l'Essai* [sur la poésie épique] qui, sous le titre de 'Essai sur la Poétique par le sieur de Voltaire,' fut à la date du 22 mai 1729 présenté par l'imprimeur Sevestre et soumis au censeur Gallyot."

[2] Cf. p. 11, note 1, *ante*.

[3] *Oeuvres*, XXXIII, p. 225.

l'égard du peu de vers anglais qui peuvent se trouver dans *l'Essai sur la Poésie Epique*, Jore n'aura qu'à m'envoyer la feuille par la poste." [1]   Two months later he writes M. de Fromont: "J'ai envoyé à M. Jore *l'Essai sur la Poésie épique*, que l'on doit imprimer à la fin de *la Henriade*," [2] but that the revision of which he had spoken earlier was not yet accomplished appears from a second letter written to M. de Fromont in November: "J'ai aussi à vous consulter sur la manière dont je dois finir mon *Essai sur le Poème épique*, et mes *Lettres sur les Anglais*." [3]   And, indeed, the Jore edition of the *Henriade* and the *Essai* was not destined to appear for a year and a half.

In the meantime, in the summer of 1732, an edition of Voltaire's works, announced as corrected by himself, was issued in Amsterdam.[4]   It seems strange on the face of it that this edition did not contain the poet's own version of the *Essai sur la poésie épique* which he had begun four years before, and still stranger that it did include Desfontaines' translation of which Voltaire had spoken so slightingly.   Yet both these facts cease to appear extraordinary when one considers the circumstances.   Although the editors announced: " M. de Voltaire lui-même nous a fait souvent l'honneur de nous écrire au sujet de cette présente Edition, et a bien voulu nous envoyer les divers changements qui l'embellissent," Voltaire's attitude toward this 1732 edition was not cordial, as may be seen in a letter written to M. de Fromont shortly after its publication: " Il faut que je me disculpe un peu sur l'édition de mes oeuvres, soi-disant complètes, qui vient de paraître en Hollande.   Je n'ai pu me dispenser de fournir quelques corrections et quelques changements au libraire qui avait déjà mes ouvrages, et qui les imprimait, malgré moi, sur les copies défectueuses qui étaient entre ses mains.   Mais ne sachant pas précisement quelles pièces fugitives il avait de moi, je n'ai pu les corriger toutes.   Non-seulement je ne réponds point de l'édition, mais j'empêcherai qu'elle n'entre en France." [5]

According to Voltaire's own statements made elsewhere, the translated essay was one of these " pièces fugitives " which he did correct;[6] how very summarily has been seen from the exami-

[1] *Oeuvres*, XXXIII, pp. 225, 226.
[2] *Ibid.*, p. 234.
[3] *Ibid.*, pp. 237-238.
[4] Cf. p. 28, note 4, *ante*.
[5] *Oeuvres*, XXXIII, p. 279.
[6] *Ibid.*, XXXIV, p. 134.

nation of the text. It is entirely natural that the author should not wish to complete hastily and to publish for the first time in such an edition of his works, a piece of writing to which he had given a considerable amount of thought and which was of real importance in its connection with the *Henriade*. Moreover a part of his manuscript was at Jore's, in whose delayed edition of the *Henriade* it was to appear.[1] On the other hand the Desfontaines translation was probably already in the hands of the Amsterdam editor, especially if it had been published, as it had purported to be published, in Holland a few years before.[2] Voltaire knew that this translation had been received with favor at the time of its publication in Paris, and his hostility to Desfontaines was not yet such as to make him intolerant of the inaccuracy of his work. The embodiment of the translation in the edition in question is not, then, after all, incomprehensible, as an expedient to serve until Voltaire should have an opportunity to publish the *Essai sur la poésie épique* quite as he wished it in the long-announced edition of the summer of 1733.[3] There it was announced as " l'ouvrage de M. de Voltaire lui-même fort différent de cette esquisse qu'il donna en langue anglaise en 1728 [sic]." " Cet essai," it is added, " tel qu'il est n'a jamais été imprimé que dans cette édition."

When, now, were the various parts of the *Essai* actually written, and why did five years intervene between the first mention of the existence of the French version and its publication? Voltaire's words: " Since I have translated it myself," [4] in the letter written to prevent Desfontaines from translating his essay, must not be taken too literally. He no doubt had the project definitely in mind and he may have begun, but he certainly had not completed, his French version when he wrote this letter. We have convincing and surprising evidence to that effect. A comparison of texts shows us that numerous sentences in the latter part of the chapter on Tasso and the whole section dealing with Ercilla,

[1] *Oeuvres*, XXXIII, pp. 308, 309. " On avait commencé, il y a quelque temps, monsieur, une édition de quelques uns de mes ouvrages, qui a été suspendue."
[2] Cf. p. 28, note 3, *ante*.
[3] Cf. p. 29, note 5, *ante*. This edition issued by Jore in Rouen, appeared under the name of Innis, London. Cf. Bengesco, I, p. 104.
[4] Cf. p. 41, *ante*.

as they appeared in Voltaire's French version in 1733, were practically identical with the corresponding portions of Desfontaines' translation.[1] This discovery is doubly surprising in view of Voltaire's prompt criticism of the abbé's work and of the careful attention we know him to have given certain other parts of the essay. The passages taken from Desfontaines included one of the most striking slips in the translation, the replacing of the word "Americans" by *Africains*. *Africains* was kept by Voltaire and appears in his essay as late as 1751. The edition of 1756 corrects this error.[2]

We may surmise that Voltaire had prepared a rough French draft up to the latter part of the chapter on Tasso; then it occurred to him to use Desfontaines' translation; this he did in part for the remainder of the chapter and for that on Ercilla which follows. Since one of the changes which he had first indicated as essential to the success of his essay in France was the revision of the section on Milton,[3] he naturally ceases to borrow from Desfontaines at that point. From statements in the text we know that the beginning, and indeed the greater part of the section on Milton, cannot have been written until after the appearance of the French translation of *Paradise Lost* in 1729.[4] It seems reasonable to suppose that Voltaire was hesitating over this chapter when, in the very letter in which he acknowledged the receipt of Desfontaines' translation, he spoke of having nearly completed the French version of his essay.[5]

In 1730 it was stated that the version had been finished but that the author did not print it, fearing to appear to set down rules

[1] The few unimportant differences existing between Desfontaines' text of the chapter on Ercilla and Voltaire's in modern editions of the essay are in nearly every case due to changes made in the latter since 1733. Cf. pp. 157-159, *post*. In 1756 a note was added in the French version referring to the sentence in the chapter on Milton in which the English essay is mentioned: " C'est en partie celui-ci même, qui, en plusieurs endroits, est une traduction littérale de l'ouvrage anglais." *Oeuvres*, VIII, p. 360. We are not told, however, that the translation was in some cases Desfontaines'.

[2] Cf. p. 158, *post*.

[3] Cf. Foulet, *Corr.*, p. 145: " What I say of Milton cannot be understood by the French unless I give a fuller notion of that author." *Ibid.*, p 154: " It is but a slight performance in English [the *Essay on Epic Poetry*], but is a ridiculous one in French [Desfontaines' translation]; for the articles relating to Milton, to sir John Denham, Waller, Dryden, must needs be altogether out of the way of a French reader."

[4] P. 130, note 1, *post*.

[5] Cf. p. 41, *ante*.

in a " carrière " in which he was but stumbling himself.[1] Without seeing any undue modesty in this remark, we may, perhaps, believe that Voltaire felt that he could make his essay of more lasting use to the *Henriade* and could in particular write more tactfully of the poem, after having observed the nature of the reception accorded by French readers to the first complete edition accessible to them. It will be remembered that in the autumn of 1731, Voltaire was still uncertain and was asking advice on this point as well as concerning the chapter on Milton.[2] The fact that *Paradise Lost* had recently been translated and had enjoyed enough popularity to make it a possible rival of the *Henriade*, rendered it a live issue to Voltaire and required, in view of his chief purpose in publishing the essay, that he give a certain amount of thought to his treatment of the English poet.

But thought meant time and Voltaire's correspondence during the years following his return from England shows that he was occupied with many literary undertakings.[3] Lack of time, indeed, is the explanation which he himself gives for having reprinted Abbé Desfontaines' translation in the Amsterdam edition of his works.[4]

Whatever the cause, it appears that his own version was not complete in 1732.[5] Furthermore, it is evident that even earlier parts of the French version were rewritten in after years, if indeed a first draft of them was made in 1728.[6] A study of the subject-matter of the chapter on Homer in the French and in the English

---

[1] P. 43, *ante.*

[2] Pp. 43-44, *ante.*

[3] Cf. *Oeuvres*, XXXIII, pp. 195, 198, 214, 256, 265, 273, 274, 276, 292, 309, 312, 318, 325, 359.

[4] Cf. *Ibid.*, XXXIV, p. 134 (already quoted, p. 34, *ante*): "Je fis imprimer sa traduction à la suite de *la Henriade*, en attendant que j'eusse le loisir de faire mon *Essai sur l'Epopée* en français."

[5] Cf. Jusserand, *Shakespeare in France*, p. 209, note: "A letter to Thieriot of June 14 (1728), shows that he had already put on paper at that date the additions and corrections which he introduced later in the French text of his ' Essai ' (first published in English in an abbreviated form, and without the passage here quoted, 1727)."

[6] The study of the subject-matter will also make it seem probable either that the greater part of the French text was not written until after the appearance of Rolli's *Remarks* on the English essay or that various passages were revised in view of the content of these *Remarks*. Cf. p. 69, note 4, *post*. Rolli's book was probably published in London in the spring or early summer of 1728. It is announced in the section for London news in the *Journal des Sçavans*, June, 1728, p. 378: " Th. Edlin a imprimé les *Remarques* de M. Paul Rolli sur l'essai publié en anglais par . . . M. Voltaire sur la Poésie épique."

essays reveals such a marked change in tone and opinion[1] that, as in the case of Milton,[2] it is impossible that the two chapters should belong even approximately to the same period.

---

[1] Cf. p. 66, *post.*
[2] Cf. p. 68, *post.*

CHAPTER V

The Substance of the Essay

Voltaire's choice of poets—His knowledge of the languages represented in the poems—Substance of the English essay—The Henriade a determining influence—Passages bearing upon the quarrel of the ancients and the moderns and upon literary cosmopolitanism—Significant differences between his English and his French versions, in form and subject-matter.

Voltaire chose eight epic poets, one Greek, two Latin, two Italian, one Portuguese and one English, as representative of the European nations. Investigation bears out the natural assumption that his choice was influenced by the chief purpose of the essay, that of preparing the way for the *Henriade*.

Any adequate discussion of epic poetry would of necessity begin with Homer and Virgil, especially at a period when the rules of the type were founded on the *Iliad*, the *Odyssey* and the *Aeneid* together with Aristotle's *Poetics*, and when the writings of Greek and Latin poets were still the subject of many lively differences of opinion. It suited Voltaire's purpose to include in his list the *Pharsalia*, already known in France through Brébeuf's translation,[1] because of the similarity between Lucan's choice of subject and his own. The use of modern historical material in an epic poem was sufficiently out of the common to need defence.

As for Tasso, the *Henriade* shows that Voltaire was so familiar with the *Gerusalemme Liberata*[2] that its author was certain to find a place in the essay. Voltaire himself explains that Trissino is worthy of attention as the first to attempt an epic poem in a modern tongue, in the sense, be it understood, given to the term epic in the seventeenth and eighteenth centuries.[3] To those who

---

[1] Guillaume de Brébeuf (1618-1661), *Pharsale de Lucain*, 1655, 1657.
[2] Bouvy, *Voltaire et l'Italie*, p. 182: "Une chose certaine, c'est que sans *Jérusalem délivrée* comme sans l'*Enéide*, la *Henriade* n'existerait point, ou existerait toute différente de ce qu'elle est."
[3] Cf. Rapin, *Réflexions sur la poétique de ce temps*, p. 16: "Le premier des poètes italiens qui fît voir que l'art de la Poétique ne lui était pas tout à fait inconnu, fut Georgio Trissino dans son Poëme de *l'Italie délivrée des Gots*."

regard the *Divine Comedy* as an epic, it seems extraordinary to have included an Italian so little known as Trissino and to have passed over Dante. Such an omission was, however, quite in keeping with the time, for the *Divine Comedy*, embodying the spirit of the middle ages, was, as shown by Bouvy, almost unknown and entirely unappreciated in France in the seventeenth and early eighteenth centuries.[1] Later Voltaire, whether in adverse criticism or praise, showed considerable interest in Dante but it is likely that at the time of his visit to England he was entirely unacquainted with the *Divina Commedia*.[2]

In view of the French poet's later admiration for Ariosto one might expect the author of *Orlando Furioso* to be included in Voltaire's list. From the brief reference to that poet in the essay, it appears that although Voltaire already enjoyed the *Orlando*, he considered extravagance Ariosto's distinguishing characteristic. Indeed it was long the comic side of the *Orlando* that appealed to Voltaire most[3] and he stated repeatedly that Ariosto was not sufficiently serious to be considered an epic poet.[4] Toward the end of his life he seemed to repent of that verdict. In 1761 he wrote: " L'Arioste . . . est mon Dieu. Tous les poëmes m'ennuient, hors le sien. Je ne l'aimais pas assez dans ma jeunesse; je ne savais pas assez l'italien," [5] and in 1764 in the *Dictionnaire philosophique*: "Je n'avais pas osé autrefois le compter [Arioste] parmi les poètes épiques . . . mais en le relisant je l'ai trouvé aussi sublime que plaisant, et je lui fais très humblement réparation." [6]

It is natural, that in order to emphasize the lack of an epic in France, Voltaire should have turned from Italian to Spanish, the other modern literature best known in France. The *Araucana* seems, it is true, to have been little read beyond the peninsula[7] but Cervantes' flattering allusion in *Don Quixote*,[8] with which Voltaire was evidently familiar, would be sufficient to bring the poem to his notice. As for Camoens, it was probably in England and from an English translation that Voltaire acquired the greater

---

[1] Bouvy, pp. 37 ff., 45. Cf. also Farinelli, *Dante e la Francia*, II, pp. 158 ff.
[2] *Ibid.*, p. 40.
[3] *Ibid.*, pp. 100, 101.
[4] Cf. pp. 156-157, *post*.
[5] *Oeuvres*, XLI, p. 153.
[6] *Ibid.*, XVIII, p. 579.
[7] Cf. p. 126, note 2, *post*.
[8] Cf. p. 129, note 5, *post*.

part of what he knew about the Portuguese poem.[1] The *Lusiads* served his purpose well, showing that a literature no more abundant than the Portuguese boasted an epic poem.

The choice of Milton needs no explanation. The English were beginning to appreciate *Paradise Lost* and Voltaire, particularly desirous as he was of their good will, would have been the first to realize that it would flatter them to have a Frenchman laud Milton, and call attention to the lack of a successful modern epic in a literature so highly esteemed in England as was the French. This very insistence upon England's previous superiority in that respect would serve to advertise the *Henriade*.

A question which naturally arises at the outset is that of Voltaire's knowledge of the six languages involved in the works of these poets and of the poems he chose for discussion.

Pierron in his study of *Voltaire et ses Maîtres* shows that in the collège Louis le Grand, young Arouet received of necessity quite inadequate instruction in Greek, nor is there any reason for supposing that as he grew older he supplemented it to any extent.[2] In 1717, in the first days of his imprisonment in the Bastille, Voltaire, still François-Marie Arouet, signed a receipt for certain articles which had been sent him in prison. Along with India handkerchiefs, a small bottle of essence of cloves and the like, are mentioned two volumes of a Greek-Latin edition of Homer.[3] Further evidence of his habit of using translations, as well as of his boasted dependence upon Homer and Virgil, is found in a letter of 1722: " Et vous, mon cher Thieriot . . . Je vous demande instamment un Virgile et un Homère (non pas celui de La Motte). . . . J'en ai un besoin pressant. Envoyez-le-moi plutôt aujourd'hui que demain. Ces deux auteurs sont mes deux domestiques, sans lesquels je ne devrais point voyager." [4] The mere fact that Voltaire feels that his intimate friend may send him the French translation of Homer seems to indicate that it was not his custom to use the Greek text. Furthermore, it is perfectly clear that when he wrote the chapter on Homer in the

---

[1] Cf. Ballantyne, p. 121.
[2] Pierron, pp. 39, 212 ff.
[3] Parton, I, p. 107, quoted from *Histoire de la Détention des Philosophes*.
[4] *Oeuvres*, XXXIII, p. 64.

English essay, he had before him Pope's rendering of the *Iliad*[1] which, be it said, he praised extravagantly.

Pierron has further shown that Voltaire's early training in Latin was very thorough and that, although the numerous attempts at Latin composition and the quotations of his later years are full of inaccuracies, he preserved a lifelong familiarity with the best Roman writers as well as a great admiration for them.[2] The *Henriade* itself, in its likeness to the *Aeneid*, bears witness to the French poet's intimate acquaintance with Virgil.[3]

Although there was no thought of any courses in modern languages in the Jesuit schools of the early eighteenth century,[4] knowledge of Italian had long been considered a desirable accomplishment in France. Throughout his life Voltaire evinced an especial interest in Italy. In 1740 he undertook a systematic study of Italian.[5] Among his letters are many written in Italian to individuals and to academies of which he was a member. Bouvy feels no doubt that Voltaire was able, as a young man, to read Italian authors in the original, although he did not acquire a thorough knowledge of the language early in life.[6] The *Henriade* shows a familiarity with the *Gerusalemme Liberata* which could scarcely have been obtained from a translation. Moreover, although Tasso's poem had been translated into French, Trissino's had not.[7]

Spanish, as well as Italian, was quite generally studied in France at the period with which we are dealing. Interest in Spanish literature, very considerable in the seventeenth century, was still lively in the early part of the eighteenth.[8] Voltaire's attention could hardly have failed to turn more or less toward Spain in the years preceding his visit to England. In his letters and in his works later in life he not infrequently mentions the Spanish language, although he is less concerned with Spanish than with Italian and seems never to have attempted either to write or speak it. In his commentaries on Corneille's works, he mentions Spanish sources with apparent familiarity.[9] Toward the

---

[1] Cf. p. 127, note 5, *post.*
[2] Pierron, p. 6, pp. 36 ff., 157 ff.
[3] Cf. p. 49, note 2, *ante.*
[4] Pierron, p. 39.
[5] Bouvy, pp. 4-5.
[6] *Ibid.*, pp. 5-6, 175.
[7] *Ibid.*, p. 175 and note.
[8] Claretie, *Le Sage*, pp. 148 ff.
[9] *Oeuvres*, XXXI, pp. 171 ff.

end of his life, he played an active part in the discussion with regard to *Gil Blas*, maintaining that Le Sage had merely translated a Spanish original.[1] There is nothing, however, in either case to show that Voltaire had any accurate knowledge of Spanish.[2]

In the *Essay on Epic Poetry* he quotes in addition to Ercilla, two other Spanish authors, Cervantes and Antonio de Solis.[3] *Don Quixote* had been translated into French. Antonio de Solis' *History of Mexico* apparently had not. Nor had the *Araucana*. Although the passages of this poem which he pretends to translate are far from accurate renderings of the original, they are not such as to prevent us from supposing the Voltaire had at the time a passable reading knowledge of Spanish.

It will be remembered that, in the French version of the essay, the whole chapter concerning Ercilla was taken bodily from Desfontaines' translation.[4] These facts, in conjunction with the lack of subsequent comment on the *Araucana*, seem to indicate less active interest in the poem and therefore, very likely, less familiarity with it than with any other treated in the essay, with the probable exception of the *Lusiads*.

There is no reason to believe that Voltaire had any acquaintance with Portuguese or that he was interested in that language. It is clear that in writing the essay, he used the English translation of the *Lusiads*.[5] He makes no pretence to familiarity with the original, for he speaks of the style as very pleasing, " if we believe the Portuguese." [6]

Voltaire's knowledge of English has already been discussed.

We come now to the substance of the *Essay*. Before taking up the individual poems, Voltaire makes a number of general remarks in the introduction of the essay. He begins by saying that critics often serve only to complicate matters and that rules and definitions are useless in poetry since the country and the

[1] Claretie, pp. 203 ff.
[2] Cf. Morel-Fatio, *Etudes sur l' Espagne*, pp. 67 ff. Cf. also O. Collman, *Gil Blas*, *Arch. für das Studium der Neueren Sprachen und Literaturen*, 1870, p. 223.
[3] Voltaire's judgment of Antonio de Solis, whom he calls " the best Writer among the *Spaniards* " (p. 86, *post*), is an extraordinary one.
[4] Cf. p. 46, note 1, *ante*.
[5] Cf. p. 112, note 1, *post*.
[6] Cf. p. 109, *post*.

epoch in which a poem was written must always be taken into consideration. There follows a recognition, in itself unusual in a French classicist, of the distinct and legitimate differences in the literary tastes of different nations, with the logical conclusion that in order to have a complete knowledge of a literary type such as epic poetry we must know something of poets of different countries and of different ages. Our respect for the ancients must not lead us to a servile imitation, since our environment is entirely unlike theirs, nor to a scorn of modern writers.

The tone of this introduction is distinctly liberal. It indicates an independence of opinion which is remarkable in a person of Voltaire's training, at heart so thorough a believer in classic rules and definitions[1] and so convinced of the superiority of French literature over all others.[2] One is led to expect freedom from rules, tradition and prejudice in the criticism which follows. In many respects the essay does not fulfil these expectations nor are the ideas expressed here in accordance with what we know of Voltaire's customary theory and practice. His expression of such opinions at this particular time may be due not only to the stimulating liberalism of his environment but also to his desire to win public attention and a tolerant reception of his own poem;[3] and even in part to a real horror of all sorts of oppression, resulting from his recent experiences in his own country.

The chapter on Homer opens with two passages highly complimentary to the English, the first concerning the classic culture of the English gentlemen, the second concerning Pope's translation of the *Iliad*. A sentence which occurs at this point: " I will neither point out his [Homer's] Beauties . . . nor cavil at his Faults," is of particular interest since it is, as a matter of fact, a neat characterization of the very method of criticism followed in the entire essay, the mention of now a beauty, now a fault, with little clear presentation of the material to be judged and few convincing statements of opinion in regard to it. Although there is a certain unity in this chapter in that the general tone is extremely unfavorable to Homer, the criticism consists largely

---

[1] Cf. Faguet, *Voltaire*, p. 145: " C'est un continuateur de Boileau, plus sévère et même plus étroit que Boileau lui-même."

[2] Cf. Lanson, *Voltaire*, p. 87.

[3] Cf. *Mercure de France*, June, 1728, p. 1419: " On y apprend [in the French translation of the *Essay*] à mépriser les Règles vagues, incertaines et arbitraires de l'Epopée qui font dire aujourd'hui à tant de personnes que la *Henriade* n' est point un Poëme Epique."

in an enumeration of faults with an occasional and always casual reference to beauties. The question of the language of the poet and that of his style are practically ignored. The only definite impression received is that Voltaire himself did not at that time enjoy Homer. Among both ancient and modern writers he always found it easiest to admire those who were most regular and elegant. Furthermore his attitude in this chapter bears out the supposition that he had no intimate acquaintance with the Greek language. Then, too, Voltaire cannot have been uninfluenced by the reaction against Homer in France in the early eighteenth century[1] nor by the consideration that England's appreciation of the Greek poet made him a possible rival in England.

The section on Virgil is for the most part a defence of the poet against critics rather than a criticism. As the chapter on Homer opened with high praise of Pope, so the first sentence here is a tribute to Addison's study of Virgil. And indeed, in the opening paragraphs of this chapter as elsewhere in the essay, Voltaire follows Addison's arguments closely, without any acknowledgment of his indebtedness.[2] He departs radically, however, from Addison as well as from Pope, in his discussion of Virgil's dependence upon Homer which, in his effort to glorify the Latin poet at the expense of the Greek, he represents as quite negligible.[3] Such comparison of Homer and Virgil as occurs is greatly to the advantage of Virgil.

Voltaire's extreme partiality for Virgil is everywhere evident. Indeed the works of Virgil are characterized as " the Delight of all Ages, and the Pattern of all Poets."[4] The writer's attitude toward Virgil is entirely consistent with what we know of his preference for the regular and polished in literature and of his indebtedness to the *Aeneid*.

The short chapter on Lucan is logical, clear and fairly comprehensive. It contains a certain amount of information regarding the poet and his work and reasonably satisfactory judgments, although in each case there is something of the balancing between beauty and fault, as for instance in the sentence: " Lucan, with all the force of his Painting, with his Grandeur, with his Wit, with his political Notions is but a declamatory Gazeteer, sublime

[1] Rigault, pp. 426 ff.
[2] Cf. p. 93, note 3, *post*.
[3] Cf. p. 62, note 3, *post*.
[4] P. 97, *post*.

here and there, faulty through all the Work."[1] Striking emphasis
is laid upon Lucan's choice of a modern subject and his wisdom
in laying aside the gods of antiquity,—points of resemblance
between the *Pharsalia* and the *Henriade*. Voltaire turns the
weakness as well as the excellencies of the Latin poet to his own
advantage. Lucan's faults merely show how great are the difficulties attendant upon the use in poetry of imposing and well-
known historical facts, while the passage in his poem described
with exaggerated enthusiasm as perhaps the best " of all the
Poets "[2] is made to show that the intervention of the gods is
not necessary in an epic. This is all indirect praise for the
Henriade. The chapter closes with a compliment to Addison,
who is classed with Corneille as a man in every way superior
to Lucan. Indeed, Addison did Lucan the greatest honor in
borrowing for his *Cato* " some Strokes " from the *Pharsalia*.[3]

The discussion of Trissino is made the occasion of several digressions. The first concerns the origin of the Romance languages.
Their real formation is considered to date from the fifteenth
century, with an entire scorn of the greater part of the middle
ages quite characteristic of the seventeenth and eighteenth centuries in France. There follow further remarks on the modern
languages and the opportunity they offer for an original imitation
of the ancients. This idea, already touched upon in the introduction, has a direct bearing on the *Henriade*, which follows in
its general outlines the epics of antiquity but departs from them
in its subject-matter and in not introducing the gods of classic
mythology.

It is at this point that Voltaire begins the unfavorable observations on Italian taste which recur persistently in the course
of the essay.[4] One of his Italian critics observes acutely that
the Frenchman would have been more cautious in his remarks
concerning the Italians if he had been " about a Subscription in
Italy " at the time of writing his essay.[5]

This brief account of Trissino gives little information concerning the *Italia Liberata dai Goti*. It is chiefly interesting as the
occasion for digressions characteristic of Voltaire and of his time.

---

[1] P. 101, *post.*
[2] *Ibid.*
[3] P. 102, *post.*
[4] Baretti (*Dissertation*, pp. 12-17) explains Voltaire's prejudice as due in
part to the influence of Boileau and Bouhours.
[5] Cf. Rolli, *Remarks*, p. 119.

The chapter on Camoens is a somewhat remarkable example of the writer's disregard for accuracy. It is evident that Voltaire was very ill-informed regarding Camoens and the *Lusiads*. Some years later he himself corrected, without remark or apology, some of the errors contained in the biographical account of the Portuguese poet.[1] In the somewhat fragmentary comments on the poem, there is a certain amount of well-worded praise more than overbalanced by blame. " His Poem in my Opinion," we read at one point, " is full of numberless Faults and Beauties, thick sown near one another; and almost at every Page, there is what to laugh at and what to be delighted with." [2]

The parallel at the end between certain lines of Camoens and verses of Waller and of Denham, based, as it chanced, upon an interpolated passage,[3] is far-fetched and an obvious attempt to cater to the English public.

Voltaire's criticism of Tasso is more careful and comprehensive than that accorded any other poet except Milton, a fact to be explained no doubt by the writer's intimate knowledge of the *Gerusalemme* and by the similarity between it and the *Henriade*. His judgment of the author of the *Gerusalemme Liberata* contradicts in some measure his unfavorable observations on the Italian taste. " No Man in the World," we read, " was ever born with a greater Genius, and more qualify'd for *Epick* Poetry."[4] Compare with this Voltaire's opinion of Virgil, his other master, as " the Pattern of all Poets." [5] Again we are told that Tasso's " Excellencies challenge the unanimous Admiration of *Europe*." [6]

Filled with his subject, the author considers in a logical order, the theme of the poem, the heroes and the parts they play, the drawing of their characters, the progress of the action, the interweaving of the different adventures, and the style. This discussion includes a comparison of the characters of the *Gerusalemme Liberata* with those of the *Iliad*, greatly to the advantage of the Italian poem.

All the adverse criticism finds its place at the end of the chapter and has to do with the excesses which Tasso allowed himself in certain episodes of his poem. The episodes in question are related

---

[1] Cf. pp. 154-155, *post.*
[2] P. 111, *post.*
[3] Cf. p. 112, note 1, *post.*
[4] P. 113, *post.*
[5] P. 97, *post.*
[6] P. 116, *post.*

by Voltaire in a half-mocking tone which tends at once to prejudice the reader.[1] Thus these last pages are in harmony with the writer's judgment of Ariosto at the time as well as with his derogatory remarks concerning Italian taste.

Nearly half the article on Ercilla is given over to the comparison of a part of the Spanish poem describing a quarrel among the Araucani as to the choice of a chief, with a passage from the *Iliad* somewhat similar in its subject-matter. Voltaire naturally concludes that Ercilla's description is infinitely superior to Homer's. To this end he gives a detailed and carefully worded, although far from faithful, rendering of the stanzas from Ercilla and a very summary one of the passage in Homer.[2] He concludes with the enumeration of various defects of the Spanish poet, as if to counterbalance the high praise given the detached passage. " It is wonderful," we are told, " how he falls so low from so high a Flight." [3] The criticism here impresses one as fragmentary and shows no real familiarity with the poem. Moreover, nothing is said of the *Araucana* as representative of Spanish taste. This is rather surprising in the light of the attention the author has given to distinctions between Italian and French standards.

The early part of the chapter on Milton contains a considerable amount of dignified if sometimes slightly exaggerated praise of *Paradise Lost*. There can be no doubt that this praise rings somewhat louder because of being addressed to an English audience by a writer whose chief wish was to win favor. Moreover, it is evident, as in the case of Virgil, that the Frenchman was fresh from the reading of Addison whom, to please the British public, he called " the best Critic as well as the best Writer of his Age " [4] and whose favorable judgment of Milton he voiced in some measure.[5] On the other hand we must give Voltaire credit for a considerable degree of sincerity. He shows real independence, both in criticizing severely one or two passages of *Paradise Lost* which were among those admired most by the English[6] and in passing judgment upon the English stage.

---

[1] Cf. p. 118, note 3, *post*.
[2] Cf. *Oeuvres*, VIII, p. 351, note 1.
[3] P. 129, *post*.
[4] P. 134, *post*.
[5] Pp. 133 ff., notes, *post*.
[6] Cf. *Mercure de France*, June, 1728, p. 1419: "Au reste les loüanges que M. de Voltaire donne au *Paradis perdu* ne peuvent paroître supectes, puisqu'il a le courage de le censurer dans les endroits mêmes que les Anglais admirent e plus."

From his high praise of Milton Voltaire turns at once to the literary taste of different nations. He makes what is apparently a very liberal statement, but one which has a twofold application to his own enterprise. By no means should one nation judge its literature by the standards of another and the French least of all have a right to set up laws for epic poetry, having none of their own. On the other hand each country should pay more attention than it does to the taste and manners of its neighbors. Having laid down this principle, Voltaire proceeds at once to put it into practice. He feels that the English may be interested to hear to what points in the *Paradise Lost* the French critics would be most likely to object, although they are not, of course, to submit to the opinion of the French.[1] He places upon French critics the responsibility for his comments on the poem, unfavorable for the most part from this point on. This comparison of French and English ideas concerning epic poetry was calculated to arouse interest in a French epic. To be sure Voltaire does not succeed in preserving a consistently impersonal tone in his report of the opinion of the French. More than once the criticism is very evidently his own. Several times, too, he defends the English poet against objections he feels sure would be made in France.

The last pages of the essay contain no summary, nor are there any conclusions such as might be expected to follow the examination of poems representing five different nations, especially in the light of the questions suggested in the introduction and bearing upon comparative literature. The author dwells chiefly upon the dearth of epic poetry in France and the possible reasons for that state of affairs. His explanations include a number of bold remarks concerning the effect upon the French language of the lack of liberty in the country, the insupportable and insignificant rules to which French poets submit and the impoverishing of the language by the discarding of many old and energetic expressions, " as the compelling our Protestants away hath thinned the Nation." [2] In this arraignment of things French, England is in nearly every case held up as a shining contrast. Other explana-

---

[1] Cf. *Journal des Sçavans*, September, 1728: " M. de Voltaire qui, pour faire plaisir à la Nation Anglaise, prend sur lui-même les éloges qu'il donne à Milton, met dans la bouche des critiques français toutes les objections qu'il croit qu'on pourroit faire contre le *Paradis perdu*: il a crû apparemment se concilier par ce moyen les Anglais, & conserver chez les autres Nations la qualité de critique exact.

[2] Pp. 1 44 ff., *post*.

tions offered are still more directly arranged in the interest of the *Henriade*. The concluding sentences are, as the author himself acknowledges, naive and ingenious. "An *Epick* Poem is a harder Task in France, than in any other Country whatever. . . . The best Reason I can offer for our ill Success in *Epick* Poetry, is the insufficiency of all who have attempted it." [1]

It is clear that, as he wrote, Voltaire was never sufficiently carried away by his subject-matter to lose sight of his original purpose. He is everywhere the author of the *Henriade*, in his numerous efforts to conciliate the English and to arouse their interest, in the emphasis laid upon the poems and passages having certain points in common with his own epic. His habit of mitigating praise with much blame and thus belittling the value of existing epic poems, suggests a desire, conscious or unconscious, to glorify his own. It is consistent with this theory that Virgil and Tasso, his models, have escaped with relatively little adverse criticism, while Milton fared well as an Englishman. It is even possible to connect with this tendency, Voltaire's persistently unfavorable attitude toward Homer, due largely, to be sure, so far as the *Iliad* in the original is concerned, to his natural dislike of what seemed to him the unpolished in literature, however great, and to his inadequate knowledge of Greek, but also, it may be, to the fact that Pope's *Iliad* was of sufficiently recent publication to make it a rival of the *Henriade*. This is not inconsistent with Voltaire's high praise of Pope's rendering, which he sincerely admired and which, moreover, could not safely be depreciated in England.

It is perhaps this persistent fault-finding, the basis of which is seldom made clear to the reader and which leads to no definite or illuminating conclusions, combined with the extremely fragmentary character of certain chapters, that makes the essay as a whole an unsatisfactory piece of criticism despite its genuine interest.

Quite aside from the ever present influence of the *Henriade* and the evidence of Voltaire's greater or less degree of familiarity with the poems in question, the reader is impressed by numerous passages which give this essay a significant place in the history

[1] Pp. 149, 150, *post.*

of the author's ideas and of certain tendencies in eighteenth century literature.

A considerable number of these passages throw light upon Voltaire's attitude in 1727 toward the famous quarrel of the ancients and moderns. In regard to the general questions of relative merit and of imitation, his position is a somewhat intermediate one. In the course of the essay he shows what he himself calls a just respect for the writers of antiquity and definitely recommends the imitation of their works. He deplores, however, a slavish imitation and speaks more than once of the opportunities for independence open to modern writers. For instance: " We should be their Admirers [those of the ancients], not their Slaves." [1] " Our just Respect for the Ancients, proves a meer Superstition, if it betrays us into a rash Contempt of our Neighbors and Countrymen. We ought not to do such Injury to Nature, as to shut our Eyes to all the Beauties that her Hands pour around us, in order to look back fixedly on her former Productions."[2] Voltaire condemns " the Weakness of Men, who mistake commonly the Beginning of an Art, for the Principles of the Art itself." [3] " The best modern Writers have mix'd the Taste of their Country, with that of the Ancients." [4] " He who writes in a modern Language, hath the Ancients for his Guides, not for his Rivals." [5]

This attitude, maintained with a fair degree of consistency in the French essay and in Voltaire's later writings, is what one might expect from the author of the *Henriade*, a poem belonging to a type which had been most flourishing in ancient times, a poem which followed tradition in its general lines but was, however, distinctly modern in the choice of subject and in the rejection of the Greek and Roman gods.

To turn from the general question to phases of it peculiar to the eighteenth century in France, the original point at issue as to whether it was possible for modern authors to equal or to surpass the Greek and Latin, was now somewhat complicated by the fact that the French writers of the preceding century, the " moderns " of Perrault's time, themselves imitators of antiquity, had come to be counted more or less among the " ancients." Again,

---

[1] P. 86, *post.*
[2] P. 87, *post.*
[3] P. 81, *post.*
[4] P. 84, *post.*
[5] P. 103, *post.*

in so far as it dealt with purely ancient literature, the question was for the most part narrowed down in the early years of the eighteenth century in France to a dispute regarding the merits of Homer.[1] In connection with each of these two aspects of the question, the English essay, as distinguished from the French, has something to offer. A sentence occurring in the chapter on Tasso which does not appear in the French version, is an early expression of Voltaire's well-known belief in the superiority of the seventeenth century writers over those of his own time. " Thus in *France*," he writes, "*Corneille, Racine, Boylau* [sic], *la Fontaine, Molière* will claim forever the publick Admiration, in Defiance to a succeeding Set of Writers, who have introduced a new fangl'd Stile, kept up and cherish'd among themselves but despis'd by the Nation."[2] Here, in a sense, Voltaire is on the side of the ancients.

On the other hand, the entire essay is so anti-Homeric that it gives its author at that early period a definite place among the enemies of the Greek poet.[3] This fact has been overlooked by the best known historian of the quarrel concerning the ancients and moderns, Hippolyte Rigault. Although, in his *Histoire de la querelle des anciens et des modernes*, this writer studies fully the question of Voltaire's attitude toward Homer and evidently uses passages from the French *Essay on Epic Poetry*,[4] he entirely ignores the important testimony of the English version. It is probable that, writing in the middle of the nineteenth century, he had never seen the English essay. Even if he was aware of its existence, he must have assumed the opinions expressed there to be practically the same as those found in the French, which was, as will be shown later,[5] especially far from being the case in the chapter on Homer. " Dans sa jeunesse," Rigault writes, contrasting Voltaire's later unfavorable opinion of Homer, " il

---

[1] Rigault, pp. 353 ff. " Guerre contre Homère," etc.
[2] P. 114, *post.* Cf. p. 71, *post.*
[3] Public opinion in France in the early eighteenth century was coming to be decidedly unfavorable to Homer. Cf. p. 55, note 1, *ante.* It is interesting to note in this connection that the Jesuits of the eighteenth century were on the side of the moderns, as opposed to Homer, and in particular that Père Porée, one of Voltaire's teachers with whom he was closely associated, was a warm admirer of La Motte's modernized *Iliad.* Cf. *Rigault*, pp. 394, 427. Voltaire's chapter on Virgil in our essay also shows him to have been a lively participant in that phase of the opposition to Homer which Rigault calls " Cette interminable guerre, faite à Homère sous les drapeaux de Virgile." *Ibid.*, p. 354.
[4] Pp. 474, 475.
[5] Cf. pp. 66 ff., *post;* pp. 89 ff. and notes, *post.*

admirait Homère et l'appelait ' un peintre sublime;' il plaignait
les esprits philosophiques qui ne peuvent pardonner ses fautes en
faveur de ses beautés ' plus grandes que ses fautes.' Il prenait
la défense de ses dieux et de ses héros, parceque c'étaient les
héros et les dieux de son temps." [1] All this comes evidently
from the French version of the *Essay on Epic Poetry*. As a
matter of fact, Voltaire, hostile to Homer in 1727, an attitude
which in itself gives the English essay a tone favorable to the
moderns, appeared as the defender of the Greek poet at the time
of writing the French version, only to return before long to the
hostility of his early years, a position which he maintained during
the remainder of his life.[2]

This change of opinion together with possible reasons for it
is a subject which we shall consider later in our comparison of
the French and English essays. Suffice it to say at this point
that as regards the original question of the ancients and moderns
as well as the two aspects of it peculiar to the eighteenth century,
the English essay is an important source in a study of the opinions
of Voltaire, whom Rigault calls " l'écrivain . . . dont les
arrêts [concerning the quarrel of the ancients and moderns] ont
eu le plus d'influence sur l'opinion de la postérité." [3]

To take up another important question of the eighteenth century, that of literary cosmopolitanism in France, the *Essay on
Epic Poetry*, itself a contribution to comparative literature, shows
that Voltaire was a forerunner among his countrymen. There are
numerous passages which bear upon the benefit to be gained from
an intelligent knowledge of the literatures of other countries, the
relativity of taste and standards, and the influence of environment
which makes it essential to consider the country and the period
to which the piece of writing belongs before appraising it. All
these were distinctly new ideas in France in the eighteenth century[4] as compared with the dogmatism and the absolutism of
the classic school of the seventeenth century. Voltaire had laid
stress as early as 1722 upon the importance of judging differently
the poetry of different nations.[5] In the essay of five years later

[1] P. 474.
[2] Cf. pp. 161-162, *post*.
[3] P. 471.
[4] Cf. Foulet, *Corr.*, pp. xv-xvi.
[5] Cf. p. 7, note 5, *ante*.

there are manifold expressions of this and of similar ideas, written doubtless in part with the utilitarian purpose of paving the way for the *Henriade* but in part also expressing opinions entertained by the author before going to England. Although many of them are theories which he himself did not put into practice, the mere voicing of such theories at this early period is significant.

European travellers, he says, are inclined to bestow large praise on distant countries but to be satirical concerning those near at hand. A traveller should bring into his own country the arts of other nations. As it is, each nation shows dislike for the taste of its neighbors. " The true Love of our Country is to do good to it, to contribute to its Liberty, as far as it lies in our Power; but to contend only for the Superiority of our Authors, to boast of having among us better Poets than our Neighbors, is rather Self-love than Patriotism." [1] " Would each Nation attend a little more than they do, to the Taste and the Manners of their respective Neighbors, perhaps a general good Taste might diffuse itself through all *Europe* from such Intercourse of Learning, and from the useful Exchange of Observations." [2] " The same Fancy which hath invented Poetry, changes every Day all its Productions, because it is liable itself to eternal Vicissitudes. . . . Even a Nation differs from itself, in less than a Century. There are not more Revolutions in Governments than in Arts. They are shifting, and gliding away from our Pursuit, when we endeavor to fix them by our Rules and Definitions." [3] " Our particular Customs have introduc'd . . . a new Sort of Taste, peculiar to each Nation." [4] The reader's "Judgement will be right, if he attends without Partiality, laying aside the Prejudices of the School, or the overbearing Love of the Productions of his own Country." [5] " Those doubtful Things which are call'd Blemishes by one Nation, and stil'd Perfections by another." [6] " We do not speak the same Language. Our Religion (the great Basis of *Epick* Poetry) is the very Reverse of their Mythology: our Battles, our Sieges, our Fleets, are more different from theirs, than our Manners from those of *America*.[7] . . . An *Epick* Poet,

[1] P. 129, *post.*
[2] P. 135, *post.*
[3] P. 82, *post.*
[4] P. 84, *post.*
[5] P. 88, *post.*
[6] *Ibid.*
[7] Pp. 86-87, *post.*

being surrounded with so many Novelties, must have but a small Share of Genius, if he durst not be new himself." [1] " He [Lucan] is to be commended for having laid the Gods aside, as much as *Homer* and *Virgil* for having made use of that Machinery. Those Fables were adapted to the dark fabulous Ages in which *Priam* and *Lainust* liv'd, but in no Way suitable to the Wars of *Rome*." [2] "If the Difference of Genius between Nation and Nation, ever appear'd in its full Light, 'tis in *Milton's* Paradise lost." [3] " I am very far from thinking that one Nation ought to judge of its Productions by the Standard of another." [4] " Besides, the Force of that Idiom is wonderfully heighten'd, by the Nature of the Government, and by the Liberty of Conscience." [5]

Finally the essay has a distinct place in the history of the influence of England in France in the eighteenth century, quite apart from the fact that it represents Voltaire's contact with the country and, being written in English, is the embodiment of his interest in the language. Three important phases of English influence in France find definite expression in it. Voltaire urges his countrymen to study English as the English study French, [6] he suggests that French writers have something to learn from the English, and he draws comparisons between the lack of liberty in France and the liberty prevailing in England. [7] These comparisons, although few in number, are fully as definitely expressed as any contained in the *Lettres philosophiques*, condemned for the same offence to be burned by the public executioner in Paris in 1734.

So much for the English essay. What now are the differences between it and the French version of 1733 ?

The French essay is considerably longer than the English. The informal divisions of the earlier work appear as definite chapters. In general the tone of the French is less conversational and the whole gives the impression of a more systematic and carefully prepared piece of work, as Voltaire intended that it

---

[1] P. 87, *post.*
[2] P. 101, *post.*
[3] P. 131, *post.*
[4] P. 135, *post.*
[5] Pp. 144-145, *post.*
[6] P. 75, *post.*
[7] Pp. 144 ff., *post.*

should.[1] In one of the letters cited earlier, speaking of the changes necessary for the success in France of the *Essay on Epic Poetry*, Voltaire had written: " The style besides is after the English fashion; so many similes, so many things which appear but easy and familiar here, would seem too low to your wits of Paris." [2] In accordance with this opinion the writer made the language of the French version more formal and less figurative. Such comparisons as do appear are usually of a somewhat conventional character.[3]

Turning from form to subject-matter, we find even more striking differences. In the notes accompanying the text will be found a somewhat detailed, chapter-by-chapter comparison of the two essays. Here we shall concern ourselves only with the chief differences, classified according to the possible reasons for them. In some cases it would seem that we have to do with a real change of opinion, often influenced by circumstances, to be sure, while in many others we see efforts to interest or to conciliate the French public rather than the English.

The most conspicuous example of a fundamental change in attitude is the 1733 criticism of Homer. Little of the English chapter remains. Although at one point Voltaire says that he still considers Homer decidedly inferior to Virgil, he now enters upon a defence of the Greek poet. His criticism has become favorable in tone and shows a certain spontaneous appreciation and enthusiasm which were entirely lacking in the English. Here the writer seems to have laid hold of a new conception of the power of real genius: " Tel est le privilége du génie d'invention: il se fait une route où personne n'a marché avant lui; il court sans guide, sans art, sans règle; il s'égare dans sa carrière, mais il laisse loin derrière lui tout ce qui n'est que raison et qu'exactitude. Tel à peu près était Homère: il a créé son art, et l'a laissé imparfait: c'est un chaos encore; mais la lumière y brille déjà de tous côtés." [4] Twelve beautiful lines of Homer, he goes on to say, surpass a mediocre although perfectly regular piece of writing as an uncut diamond a carefully wrought tin trinket.

The beauty of the Greek language and Homer's masterly use of it had been entirely passed over in the English essay but are

[1] Cf. p. 41, *ante.*
[2] Foulet, *Corr.*, pp. 145-146.
[3] Cf. *Oeuvres*, VIII, pp. 329, 359-360.
[4] *Ibid.*, p. 318.

recognized with concrete examples in the French. It follows naturally enough that the author's ideas concerning the value of translations have undergone a radical change since the days of the English essay when he had spoken of Pope's *Iliad* as a version in which none of the beauties of the original were lost and most of the faults lessened. He now says: " Qu'on ne croie point encore connaître les poëtes par les traductions; ce serait vouloir apercevoir le coloris d'un tableau dans une estampe. Les traductions augmentent les fautes d'un ouvrage, et en gâtent les beautés." [1] Such contradictory statements cannot be explained wholly by the writer's early desire to flatter Pope.

For his marked change of opinion in regard to Homer, Voltaire himself gives an explanation. He had never been able, he says, to reconcile the gross defects and the greater beauties of Homer's work, a contrast found in no classic or French writer, until he became thoroughly acquainted with the plays of Shakespeare. He found these plays more popular than any others in London play-houses and yet they were filled with absurdities, "des monstres en tragédie." [2] When he came to a more thorough understanding of English, he realized that the English were right and that the marvelous beauties of Shakespeare's dramas were the more remarkable because of their very defects, as a bright light shines brighter in a dark night. In addition to this clearer recognition of the superiority of true genius to exactness and regularity, the French chapter, in its sympathy and appreciation and in its scorn of translations, seems to show greater familiarity with the *Iliad* in the original. It is very possible that the second of these changes like the first was the direct result of the author's years in England and of his intimate friendship with Pope and other English classical scholars. It is also to be remembered that in France, where Homer was in quite general disfavor, he had no reason for decrying the Greek poet as a possible rival. That his favorable attitude toward Homer was the outcome of a passing influence seems probable from the fact that in after years he returned to his former dislike of the Greek poet. [3]

The liberal spirit which pervades this chapter is seen also in the belief occasionally expressed that great writers are superior

---

[1] *Oeuvres*, VIII, p. 319.
[2] *Ibid.*, p. 317.
[3] Concerning Voltaire's later opinion of the poets treated in his French and English essays cf. pp. 161 ff., *post*.

to rules and in the digressions on the stage which occur in the introduction. The first of these digressions recognizes the possibilities of English drama: " Si les auteurs de ce pays joignaient à l'activité qui anime leurs pièces un style naturel, avec de la décence et de la régularité, ils l'emporteraient bientôt sur les Grecs et sur les Français." ¹ The other is a plea for tolerance in literature, looking toward cosmopolitanism: " Irai-je refuser le nom de comédies aux pièces de M. Congrève ou à celles de Calderon, parcequ'elles ne sont pas dans nos moeurs?" ²

The French and English chapters on Milton form nearly as striking a contrast as those dealing with Homer, but here it is difficult to feel certain to what extent we have to do with a real change in opinion and to what extent with concession to circumstances. Much is evidently a genuine change of opinion. In the English essay Voltaire's judgment of Milton was on the whole favorable, his adverse criticism having to do with details. The spirit of the French is cold and for the most part hostile.³ In 1727 he expressed himself as quite unable to understand how Dryden could praise Milton so highly at one time, and rate him so low at another. In 1733 he explains Dryden's inconsistency without hesitation as due to the existence in *Paradise Lost* of a great number of defects.

The radical difference between Voltaire's two judgments of the English poet may be seen from the comparison of sentences, French and English, in which he briefly describes Milton's epic. In 1727 he called *Paradise Lost* " the noblest Work, which human Imagination hath ever attempted . . . the only Poem wherein are to be found in a perfect Degree that Uniformity which satisfies the Mind and that Variety which pleases the Imagination." ⁴ The French chapter ends with the statement that the English epic is " un ouvrage plus singulier que naturel, plus plein d'imagination que de grâces, et de hardiesse que de choix, dont le sujet est tout idéal, et qui semble n'être pas fait pour l'homme." ⁵ This is laid at the door of the French critics, to be sure, but is

¹ *Oeuvres*, VIII, p. 307.
² *Ibid.*, p. 308.
⁰ He devotes less than a page to the enumeration of the beauties of the poem which have found favor with the French and over two pages to the parts which have been disapproved by French critics. The latter are in most cases passages which he had touched upon in the English essay as unlikely to please the French.
⁴ Pp. 131, 132-133, *post*.
⁵ *Oeuvres*, VIII, p. 360.

the logical conclusion of Voltaire's own arguments. The marked change is no doubt due partly to altered circumstances. The translated *Paradise Lost* had become a serious rival of the *Henriade* and there was no longer the need to conciliate the English.

In the case of the four great writers, Homer, Dante, Shakespeare and Milton, all of them, according to pseudo-classic taste, majestic and powerful rather than polished and elegant, Voltaire's opinion underwent notable changes. At heart he was radically opposed to their irregularity and his favorable opinion of them seems in each case to have been a passing one, due to external influences and temporary conditions. This explains in the *Essai sur la poésie épique* his favorable attitude toward Homer, a passage regarding Shakespeare which a well-known critic[1] has called the most appreciative in all Voltaire's works,[2] and at the same time his hostility to Milton.

There is, in the course of the essay, still another apparent change of opinion which may, however, be largely due to external influences. The unfavorable allusions to Italian taste in the English essay had at once brought a bitter retort from the pen of Rolli.[3] In the French these unpleasant comments were in most cases either suppressed or ingeniously altered so as to lose their venom.[4]

As the natural result of the author's change in attitude and of his failure to revise the whole, the French essay presents some marked inconsistencies, especially between the revised chapter on Homer and comparisons of Homer with other poets, Virgil, Tasso, Ariosto and Ercilla, the decision being always unfavorable to the Greek poet. Two brief sentences may be quoted as examples, the first occurring in the chapter on Virgil, the second in that on Tasso. "*Homère a fait Virgile*, dit-on; si cela est, c'est sans doute son plus bel ouvrage." [5] " Si on lit Homère par une espèce de devoir, on lit et on relit l'Arioste pour son plaisir." [6]

We may also see some discrepancy between the unfavorable

[1] Lounsbury, *Shakespeare and Voltaire*, p. 52.
[2] *Oeuvres*, VIII, pp. 317-318.
[3] Cf. p. 9, note 3, *ante*.
[4] Cf. pp. 84, note 4; 107, note 1; 116, note 5; 118, notes 1, 2, 3; 130, note 3; 144, note 3, *post*. One of these changes (p. 157, *post*) was not made until later than 1742.
[5] *Oeuvres*, VIII, p. 323.
[6] *Ibid.*, p. 337.

tone of the French chapter on Milton and the sentences in the introduction: "Beaucoup de personnes le préfèrent [*Paradise Lost*] à Homère avec quelque apparence de raison," [1] and " Milton fait autant d'honneur à l'Angleterre que le grand Newton." [2]

The changes due to the fact that the writer is now addressing himself to a French and not an English public are of two kinds. The first are those which show that he has become more didactic and in a mild way more polemic in the presence of his own countrymen. He gives biographical information which he had not thought necessary in England, concerning not only Milton,[3] but also Homer, Virgil and Tasso. He makes a plea for a broad-minded study of the language of other countries: " Celui qui ne sait que la langue de son pays est comme ceux qui, n'étant jamais sortis de la cour de France, prétendent que le reste du monde est peu de chose, et que qui a vu Versailles a tout vu." [4]

The discussion of the simplicity of Homer's heroes is made the occasion of two sharp comments upon the evil effects of French court life. These comments, like those contained in the *Lettres philosophiques*,[5] may well be the result of the writer's stay in England, although in the second, Saint James is mentioned with Versailles as a concession to the French public.

A second class of changes is due to the fact that the writer's efforts are now to conciliate the French. The excessive praise of Pope and Addison and the far-fetched allusions to Denham and Waller are omitted. On the other hand, in the later chapter on Milton, Voltaire speaks of " les poésies efféminées et la mollesse de Waller." [6] In the same chapter the English imagination is mentioned as having a grewsome quality.

Conversely, the author has added allusions to matters interest-

---

[1] *Oeuvres*, VIII, p. 306.

[2] *Ibid.*, p. 313.

[3] Cf. Foulet, *Corr.*, p. 145: " What I say of Milton cannot be understood by the French unless I give a fuller notion of that author."

[4] *Oeuvres*, VIII, p. 308.

[5] Cf. Lanson, *Lettres phil.*, I, p. 122. As an example of the simplicity of life of certain great heroes, Voltaire, ever mindful of his own interests, cites Charles XII of Sweden. He had published the history of Charles XII in 1731.

[6] Cf. Foulet, *Corr.*, p. 154: " The articles relating to Milton, to Sir John Denham, Waller, Dryden, must needs be altogether out of the way of a French reader." Cf. p. 111, note 3, *post*.

ing to the French, to the disputes regarding Homer between Perrault and Boileau and between La Motte and Mme. Dacier as well as to Boileau's criticism of Tasso. There are other more definite if sometimes more trivial appeals to the French public. In the section on Camoens a passage describing the death of Inez de Castro, a subject which had inspired a play of La Motte presented in Paris in 1723, is spoken of as the most beautiful in the *Lusiads*.[1] It had not even been mentioned in the English essay. The sentence: " L'exactitude française n'admet rien qui ait besoin d'excuse,"[2] had read in the English: ". . . whose Exactness is often called in *England* Timidity." [3] Again " Tous les critiques judicieux, dont la France est pleine " [4] are pleasant words but singularly inconsistent with certain of the author's remarks concerning critics in both the English and French version.

On the other hand important concessions to the French public and to French authorities are to be seen in the omission of passages occurring in the English essay which would have been offensive to men of letters in France, to the church or to the state. Such are the passages alluding to the inferiority of " new-fangled " French writers as compared to those of the century of Louis XIV and to the " insupportable and insignificant " rules to which French poets submit,[5] the statement that the *"Popish* religion " is accounted mean and low in England [6] and that the general public has a mocking attitude toward sacred history, as well as all the significant sentences contrasting France and England.

The conclusion of the French essay, like that of the English, contains no general deductions such as one might expect. Here, too, the author is occupied with the question as to why the French have no epic poem, though the discussion takes a different form. The lack of liberty in France as well as in the French language and versification, an idea which had such a prominent place in the English, is not touched upon in the French version. It is shameful, Voltaire says, that the French should be reproached with having no epic poem; as a matter of fact no great French

---

[1] Cf. *Oeuvres*, XXXIII, p. 89: "J'ai été à *Inès de Castro*, que tout le monde trouve mauvaise et très-touchante." *Ibid.*, p. 98: " Il pleut des critiques *d'Inès*, où il est parlé de moi, tantôt en bien, tantôt en mal, et toujours assez mal à propos."

[2] *Oeuvres*, VIII, p. 311.

[3] P. 86, *post*.

[4] *Oeuvres*, VIII, p. 357.

[5] Pp. 114, 149, *post*.

[6] P. 122, *post*.

writer has ever attempted that type; *Télémaque* is by no means an epic. The French language is, however, quite capable of flights of imagination, nor does the necessity of rime in French make epic poetry impossible, though the unimaginative spirit of the times makes it more difficult for a Frenchman to produce an epic than for a writer of any other nationality. Indeed an eminent authority whom Voltaire had consulted some years before concerning the *Henriade* had discouraged him, saying: " Vous entreprenez un ouvrage qui n'est pas fait pour notre nation; *les Français n'ont pas la tête épique.* . . . Quand vous écririez aussi bien que MM. Racine et Despréaux, ce sera beaucoup si on vous lit." [1] It is to conform to the prevailing spirit of the century, Voltaire tells us, that he has chosen an historical and not a fabulous hero and has used no " fiction " other than personifications of realities. Here, as elsewhere, we note an evident effort to establish the position of the *Henriade* in the author's own country. As in the English conclusion, the closing words are significant: " C'est à *la Henriade* seule à parler en sa défense, et au temps seul de désarmer l'envie." [2]

---

[1] *Oeuvres*, VIII, p. 363.
[2] *Ibid.*

AN
ESSAY UPON THE CIVIL WARS OF FRANCE.
Extracted from curious MANUSCRIPTS.

AND ALSO UPON
THE EPICK POETRY OF THE EUROPEAN NATIONS.
FROM HOMER DOWN TO MILTON.
By Mr. de VOLTAIRE.

LONDON; Printed by SAMUEL JALLASON, in
Prujean's Court Old Baily, and sold by the Booksellers of
London & Westminster.
MDCCXXVII.

ADVERTISEMENT TO THE READER.[1]

It has the Appearance of too great a Presumption in a Traveller, who hath been but eighteen Months in England *to attempt to write in a Language, which he cannot pronounce at all, and which he hardly understands in Conversation.* But I have done what we do every Day at School, where we write Latin *and* Greek, *tho' surely we pronounce them both very pitifully, and should understand neither of them if they were uttered to us with the right* Roman *or* Greek *Pronunciation.*

I look upon the English *Language as a learned one, which deserves to be the Object of our Application in* France, *as the* French *Tongue is thought a kind of Accomplishment in* England.[2]

Besides, I did not learn English *for my Private Satisfaction and Improvement only, but out of a kind of Duty.*

I am ordered to give an Account of my Journey into England.[3]

---

[1] The text followed is that of 1727. Changes, other than those in capitalization and punctuation, found in the 1728 edition which was announced as corrected by Voltaire himself, will be indicated in the notes, as well as variants of any interest occurring in the editions of 1731 and 1760.

The *Advertisement* preceded the first of the essays, that on the Civil Wars. The *Essay on Epic Poetry* occupied pp. 37-130.

[2] Cf. Lanson, *Lettres phil.*, II, p. 257. (It will be remembered that this edition reproduces a text which was, in point of date, very near our essay, that of the *Lettres philosophiques* as they first appeared in 1734): " Un ambassadeur de France en Angleterre est toute autre chose. Il ne sait pour l'ordinaire pas un mot d'anglais." Cf. also Addison in the *Spectator*, ed. Morley, London, 1891, III, p. 195: "And perhaps the Balance of Fashion in *Europe*, which now leans upon the side of *France*, may be so alter'd for the future, that it may become as common with *Frenchmen* to come to *England* for their finishing Stroke of Breeding, as it has been for *Englishmen* to go to *France* for it." That already in 1727 Frenchmen were beginning to turn their attention to the learning of English appears from certain of Voltaire's own letters of that year (cf. p. 18, *ante*) as well as from a passage contained in the preface of the translation of *Gulliver* (cf. p. 31, note 2, and p. 36, note 8, *ante*) in which the translator speaks of " la langue anglaise qui commence à être à la mode à Paris et que plusieurs personnes de distinction et de mérite ont depuis peu apprise."

[3] It is here that Voltaire first refers to his intention of setting down his impressions of England which were to form one of his most important works. Cf. Lanson, *Lettres phil.*, I, p. xxxvi; Bengesco, II, p. 9. His use of the word *ordered* in this connection seems to indicate that a definite request led him to undertake the work.

ii *Such an Undertaking can no more be attempted without un|der-
standing the Language, than a Scheme of Astronomy could be laid
without the help of Mathematicks. And I have not a Mind to imitate
the late Mr. Sorbieres, who having staid three Months in this Country
without knowing any Thing, either of its Manners or of its Language,
thought fit to print a Relation which proved but a dull scurrilous
Satyr[1] upon a Nation he knew nothing of.*[2]

Our European *Travellers for the most Part are satyrical upon
their neighboring Countries, and bestow large Praises upon the* Per-
sians *and* Chineses;[3] *it being too natural to revile those who stand
in Competition with us, and to extol those who being far remote from
us, are out of the reach of Envy.*

iii *|The true Aim of a Relation is to instruct Men, not to gratify their
Malice. We should be busied chiefly in giving faithful Accounts
of all the useful Things and of the extraordinary Persons, whom to
know, and to imitate would be a Benefit to our Countrymen. A
Traveller who writes in that Spirit, is a Merchant of a nobler Kind,
who imports into his native Country the Arts and Virtues of other
Nations.*[4]

I will leave to others the Care of describing with Accuracy, Paul's
Church, *the* Monument,[5] Westminster, Stonehenge, &c. *I consider* England *in another View; it strikes my Eyes as it is the Land
which hath produced a* Newton, *a* Locke, *a* Tillotson, *a* Milton,
a Boyle, *and many great Men either dead or alive, whose Glory in*

---

[1] 1728 Satire.

[2] Samuel Sorbières, *Relation d'un Voyage en Angleterre*, Paris, 1664. Cf.
Texte, p. 27: "Voltaire est ici aussi inexact qu'injuste. La *Relation d'un
voyage en Angleterre* n'est nullement une satire et elle est—si l'on regarde à
la date òu elle parut—l'une des premières appréciations motivées de l'esprit
anglais qu'il y ait dans notre langue. Même, cette appréciation est généralement favorable."

[3] For the interest in Persia and China felt in France in the early eighteenth
century cf. P. Martino, *L'Orient dans la littérature française au XVIIe et au
XVIIIe siècle*, Paris, 1906, pp. 176 ff. Voltaire himself not infrequently uses
an oriental setting. Cf. *Zadig, L'Orphelin de la Chine*, etc.

[4] The comparison is significant. Voltaire was greatly impressed by the dignity of the position of merchants in England. Cf. Lanson, *Lettres phil.*, I,
pp. 121-122 and *Oeuvres*, II, pp. 537, 547: *Zaïre, Epître dédicatoire*, 1733 and 1736.

[5] Cf. Lanson, *Lettres phil.*, I, p. 23: "Celle [la chapelle des Quakers] où
j'allai est près de ce fameux pilier qu'on appelle le Monument," and *Commen-
taire*, p. 26: "Ce qu'on appelle le *Monument* à Londres est une très haute
colonne (100 pieds du rez-de-chaussée à la sommité) que le roi Charles II fit
ériger dans l'endroit où commença le grand embrasement qui réduisit la plus
grande partie de la ville en cendres, l'an 1666. Les inscriptions qui sont sur
cette colonne contiennent l'histoire de cet incendie." Quoted from Misson,
Mémoires et Observations faites en Angleterre, 1698, p. 303.

War, in State-Affairs, or in Letters, will not be confined to the Bounds of this Island.[1]

Whosoever had the Honour and the Happiness to be acquainted with any of them, and will do me the Favour to let me know some notable (tho' [2] *perhaps not enough known) Passages of their Lives, will confer an Obligation not only upon me, but upon the Publick.*

|Likewise if there are any new Inventions or Undertakings, which iv *have obtained or deserved Success, I shall be obliged to those who will be so kind as to give me an* [3] *Informations of that Nature. And shall either quote my Authors, or observe a religious Silence, according as they think it proper.* [4]

As to this present Essay, it is intended as a kind of Preface or Introduction to the Henriade, *which is almost entirely printed, nothing being wanting but the printing of the Cuts which I must recommend here as particular: Master-Pieces of Art in their Kind: 'tis the only Beauty in the Book, that I can answer for.* [5]

---

[1] Cf. Lanson, *Lettres phil.*, I, pp. 152-153: " Puis donc que vous exigez que je vous parle des hommes célèbres qu'a porté l 'Angleterre, je commencerai par les Bacons, les Lockes, les Newtons, &c," and II, p. 110: (Variant first occurring in the edition of 1752) "C'est pourtant là le païs qui a produit des Addissons, des Popes, des Lokes, et des Newtons." Of the *Lettres philosophiques*, one is devoted to Locke and several to Newton. Tillotson, Milton and Boyle, however, are not discussed. Voltaire's feeling toward Milton had undergone a change (cf. p. 68, *ante*) and, moreover, the author of *Paradise Lost* had been treated at length in the *Essai sur la poésie épique* published the year before.

In the letter to Swift written in December, 1727, (cf. p. 6, note 2, *ante*) to ask help in gathering subscriptions for the *Henriade* Voltaire turns this passage of his essay to good account. " You will see by the Advertisement," he writes, " that I have some designs upon you, and that I must mention you for the honour of yr country and for the improvement of mine. Do not forbid me to grace my relation with yr name. Let me indulge the satisfaction of talking of you as posterity will do." As a matter of fact, Swift was given scant space although a certain amount of warm praise in the *Lettres philosophiques*.

[2] 1728 though.

[3] 1728 any.

[4] This passage indicates one way in which Voltaire may have gathered information for his work, at the same time arousing the interest of the English public in it. An English translation of the *Lettres philosophiques* appeared in London in 1733 before the original French version had been published. Cf. Bengesco, II, p. 11.

[5] In the edition of 1731 " which is . . . answer for " has been omitted and replaced by " the Octavo edition whereof is sold by N. Prevost; as also the French tragedy of Brutus." Voltaire's *Brutus* was first presented in Paris in December, 1730. Because of its connection with Shakespeare's *Julius Caesar* it was of particular interest to the English public as was the *Discours sur la tragédie*, containing a comparison between the French and the English stage and printed as an introduction to *Brutus* when the play was published in 1731. An English translation of this *Discours* was issued with Voltaire's essays that year in London (cf. p. 9, note 3, *ante*). It is natural that, at the same time, the tragedy should have been put on sale in London book-shops and that it should have been announced together with the *Henriade* in the *Advertisement*

preceding the essays. Yet Churton Collins (*V.M.R.*, p. 95) in an attempt to explain Parton's statement (*Life of Voltaire*, I, *Appendix*) that *Brutus* was published in London in 1727, suggests that he may have been "misled by an ambiguous paragraph at the end of the preface to the fourth edition of the *Essay on Epic Poetry*." There is nothing in this paragraph itself to give rise to Parton's mistake which, however, becomes clear when we investigate, as Churton Collins evidently did not in this connection, the chapter in which Parton mentions the English essays (I, pp. 220-221). There he quotes a part of the *Advertisement* of what he calls the 1727 edition but of what is in reality that of 1731 and therefore contains the allusion to *Brutus*. As a result of this misapprehension, he concludes that the tragedy which did not appear in Paris until several years later had already been published in London in 1727.

Voltaire's correspondence for several years preceding his stay in England shows that he gave particular attention to the illustrations of the *Henriade*. Cf. *Oeuvres*, XXXIII, pp. 78, 83, 89-90, 108, etc.; VIII, p. vi.

It is in this ingeniously modest sentence that Voltaire first states the purpose of the essays which is to be so evident throughout.

ERRATA

pag.	46	lin. last but one	raising	*read*	rising
pag.	51	lin. 1	rouse her	"	rouse it
pag.	53	lin. 7	Minds	"	Mind
pag.	65	lin. 24	*Northen*	"	*Northern*
Ibid.		lin. 25	were	"	was
pag.	66	lin. 2	*Italian*	"	*Italians*
pag.	68	lin. 24	put on	"	puts on
pag.	75	lin. 9	to the *Christ*	"	to *Christ*
pag.	83	lin. 2	*Olinda*	"	*Olindo*
pag.	89	lin. 6	Shake of	"	Shake off
pag.	99	lin. 9	*Piritous*	"	*Pirithous*
pag.	103	lin. 24	the last	"	the first
pag.	124	lin. 10	are infinite Things	"	is an infinite Number of Things
Ibid.		lin. 12	Paraphrase	"	Periphrase
Ibid.		lin. 26	Skin	"	Chin

We have in every Art more Rules than Examples, for Men are more fond of teaching, than able to perform; so there are more Commentators than Poets, and many Writers who could not make two Verses, have over-charg'd us with voluminous Treatises of Poetry.[2] All those Teachers seem[3] to have much labour'd by their Definitions, Distinctions, &c. to spread a profound Obscurity over Things in their own Nature clear and perspicuous; and 'tis no wonder if such Lawgivers, unequal to the Burthen which they took upon themselves, have embroil'd the States which they intended to regulate.

|The greatest Part of the Criticks have fetch'd[4] the Rules of 38 *Epick* Poetry from the Books of *Homer*, according to the Custom, or rather, to the Weakness of Men, who mistake commonly the Beginning of an Art, for the Principles of the Art itself, and are apt to believe, that every Thing must be by its own Nature, what it was, when contriv'd at first.[5] But as *Homer* wrote two Poems

---

[1] In the French essay (*Oeuvres*, VIII, pp. 305 ff. All references to the *Essai* in these notes are to *Oeuvres*, Garnier frères, VIII.) this introduction has become Chapitre I, with the title: " Des différents goûts des peuples." Nearly twice as long as the English, the French chapter contains practically all the ideas of the English, further developed and more definitely and more systematically expressed. Examples intended to show the uselessness of rules as well as the difference between the standards of different nations and taken from fields other than literature have been inserted in the French. The idea of comparative literature is further emphasized by an added appreciation of the superiority of real genius and a more concrete expression of the necessity of a broad-minded attitude toward the literature of other nations. Cf. p. 68, *ante*.

[2] Cf. Lanson, *Lettres phil.*, II, p. 81: "Je vous répondrai qu'il est bien aisé de raporter en prose les erreurs d'un poëte. . . . Tous les grimauds qui s'érigent en critiques des Ecrivains célèbres, compilent des volumes . . ." Cf. Addison in *Spectator*, II, p. 148: "As there are many eminent Critics who have not writ a good Line . . ."

[3] 1728 seem'd.

[4] Churton Collins, quoting this passage, reads *filched* for fetched, an error not corrected in his revised edition. (*V.M.R.*, p. 66.)

[5] Cf. Le Bossu, *Traite du Poème épique*, I, p. 2: "C'est donc dans les excellens ouvrages des anciens qu'il faut chercher les fondemens de cet Art." Le Bossu was considered an authority on the rules of epic poetry. His work was well-known and greatly admired in England as well as in France. Cf. Dryden, ed. Scott-Saintsbury, XIV, p. 210; Pope, *Iliad*, ed. Chalmers, p. 11; John Sheffield, Duke of Buckinghamshire, *An Essay upon Poetry*, 1682, ed. Spingarn, *Critical Essays of the Seventeenth Century*, II, pp. 295-296.

of a quite different Nature, and as the *Eneid*[1] of *Virgil* partakes of the *Iliad*, and of the *Odissey*, the Commentators were forc'd to establish different Rules to reconcile *Homer* with himself, and other new Rules again to make *Virgil* agree with *Homer*: Just as the Astronomers labour'd under the Necessity of adding to, or taking from their Systems, and of bringing in concentric, and excentric Circles, as they discover'd new Motions in the Heavens.

The Ignorance of the Astronomers[2] was excusable, and their Search after the unfathomable System of Nature, was to be commended; because it is certain, that Nature hath its own Principles unvariable, unerring, and as worthy of our Search, as remote from our Conceptions.

But it is not with the Inventions of Art, as with the Works of
39 Nature. The same Fancy which hath invented Poe|try, changes every Day all its Productions, because it is liable itself to eternal Vicissitudes. The Poetry and Musick of the *Persians*, differ as much from ours, as their Language. Even a Nation differs from itself, in less than a Century.[3] There are not more Revolutions in Governments, than in Arts. They are shifting, and gliding away from our Pursuit, when we endeavour to fix them by our Rules and Definitions.

If I am to give a Definition of a Suit of Cloaths[4] I ought not to describe any particular one. Neither the *Roman* nor the *Greek*, nor the *French* ought to be set up for a Pattern. A Suit of Cloaths[5] in itself, is the covering of the Body, that is all that is essential to it. The rest is but accessary Ornament, which Fancy and Custom create, preserve and destroy at their Will; and if we like one Fashion best, we are not to exclude every other.

So 'tis perhaps with *Epick* Poetry. The Word *Epick* comes from *Epos*, which signifies Discourse. An *Epick* Poem is a Discourse in Verse. Use alone has prefix'd the Name of *Epick*, particularly to those Poems which relate some great Action. Let the Action be single or complex, let it lie in one single Place, as
40 in | the *Iliad*, or let the Hero wander all the World over, as in

---

[1] 1728 Æneid.
[2] Churton Collins (*V.M.R.*, p. 67.) has " The ignorance of the Ancients."
[3] Cf. *Essai*, p. 307: La même nation n'est plus reconnaissable au bout de trois ou quatre siècles." Cf. Lanson, *Lettres phil.*, II, p. 265: "C'est à-peu-près ainsi qu'il faudrait juger des nations, et surtout des Anglais; on devrait dire: 'Ils étaient tels en cette année, en ce mois.' "
[4] 1728 Clothes.
[5] 1728 Clothes. This comparison criticized by Rolli (*Remarks*, p. 39) was omitted in the French version.

the *Odissey*; let there be one single Hero, or a great many; happy, or unfortunate; furious as *Achilles*, or pious as *Æneas*; let them be Kings, or Generals, or neither of them; let the Scene lie upon the *Indian* Ocean, as in the *Lusiada* of *Camouens*;[1] in the *West-Indies*, as in the *Araucana* of *Alonzo* of *Ereilla*;[2] in Hell, in Heaven, out of the Limits of our Nature, as in *Milton*; the Poem will equally deserve the Name of *Epick*, unless you have a Mind to honour it with another Title proportionable to its Merit.[3]

In so boundless a Career, the Point of the Question, and of the Difficulty, is to know what all polite Nations agree upon, and in what they differ.

An *Epick* Poem ought to be grounded upon Judgement, and embellish'd by Imagination; what belongs to good Sense, belongs to all the Nations of the World. The *Greeks*, the *Romans*, the *Italians*, *French*, *English* and *Spaniards*, tell us in all their Works, that they chiefly like *Unity of Action*, because the Understanding is better satisfy'd when it reposes upon a single Object, adequate to our View, and which we may take in easily, than when it is lost in the Hurry of Confusion.

|They tell us, that such an *Unity* ought to be attended with 41

---

[1] Don Luiz de Camoëns, 1524-1580. His *Lusiads* was published in 1572. The spelling Camouens is followed throughout and preserved in all editions of the English essay, as well as in early editions of Voltaire's French version. In the French translation the form Camoëns appears.

In a dissertation preceding Mickle's translation of the *Lusiads*, 1776, Voltaire's remarks on Camoens in the *Essay on Epic Poetry* are quoted and severely criticized. It is stated there that no other author ever spelled Camoens as Voltaire did. (*The Works of the English Poets from Chaucer to Cowper*, XXI, London, 1810. *The Lusiad*, translated by W. J. Mickle. *Dissertation on the Lusiad*, p. 607, note.)

The tone of Mickle's comments may be seen from a brief quotation: "Such is the original criticism of Voltaire on the Lusiad. And never, perhaps, was there such a random reverie, such a mass of misrepresentations and falsities as the whole of it exhibits. The most excusable parts of it are superficial in the highest degree."

[2] Alonso Ercilla y Zuñiga, (or Çuñiga), 1533-1596, *Araucana*, 1569-1590. Written Ereilla throughout the essay and in 1728, 1731 and 1760. In the French translation, we find both Ereilla and Ereylla, corrected in two cases to read Ercilla when Voltaire made use of that translation in 1732, but in one case left Ereilla. The cedilla is everywhere omitted from the C in Çuñiga.

[3] Cf. La Motte, *Discours sur Homère* (*L'Iliade*, 1714), p. xxvii: "Pourquoi lui refuseroit-on le nom de Poëme épique, à moins que ce ne fût pour lui en trouver un plus honorable ?" A sentence in the introduction of the *Essai* serves to connect this idea with a somewhat similar passage in the *Spectator*: "Si vous vous faites scrupule, disait le célèbre M. Addison, de donner le titre de poëme épique au *Paradis perdu* de Milton, appelez-le, si vous voulez, un poëme divin, donnez-lui tel nom qu'il vous plaira, pourvu que vous confessiez que c'est un ouvrage aussi admirable en son genre que *l'Iliade*."

Variety, as a Body is made up of Members,[1] all different, and all conducive to the same End; That the Action should be *great*, to strike us with Awe, *interesting*, because we delight in being mov'd;[2] *entire*, that our Minds may be wholly satisfy'd.

These, and the like, are a Kind of eternal Laws, submitted to by all Nations, because enacted by Nature. But the *Machinery*, the *Episodes*, the Stile itself, and all that depends upon that Instinct call'd *Taste*, and upon the Tyranny of Custom, that is the Point in which there are too many Opinions and no Rules.

It is true, there are Beauties which the Taste of every Nation equally relish. Since all *Europe* hath set up the *Greek*, and *Roman* Authors for Models of Writing, *Homer* and *Demosthenes*, *Virgil* and *Tully*, have in some Measure united under their Laws our *European* Nations, and made of so many and different Countries, a single Commonwealth of Letters. But still our particular Customs have introduc'd among them all, a new Sort of Taste, peculiar to each Nation.

The best modern Writers have mix'd the Taste of their Country, 42 with that of the Ancients. Their Flowers and their | Fruits, warm'd and matur'd by the same sun, yet draw from the Soil they grow upon, their different Colours, their Flavours and their Size. It is as easy to distinguish a *Spanish*, an *Italian*, or an *English* Author, by their Stile, as to know by their Gate,[3] their Speech, and their Features, in what Country they were born.

The *Italian* Softness, their Witticism, so often degenerating into Conceit,[4] the pompous and metaphorical Stile of the *Spaniard*, the Exactness and Perspicuity of the *French*,[5] the Strength peculiar to the *English*,[6] their Fondness of Allegories, their running into Similes,[7] are so many distinguishable Marks, which do not escape the Observation of proper Judges.

---

[1] Cf. Le Bossu, I, p. 142: "Alors on les considère comme un corps qui ne devoit pas avoir des membres de natures différentes et indépendans les uns des autres." *Ibid.*, p. 119: " Mais cela ne sera pas deffendu si un Poëte est assez adroit pour les réunir [les Episodes] toutes en un seul corps comme des membres et des parties, dont chacune à part seroit imparfaite." *Ibid.*, II, p. 14: " Les Poëtes ont tout réduit à une seule action, sous un seul & même dessein & en un corps qui ne reçoit point de membres & de parties étrangères."

[2] 1728 moved.

[3] 1728 Gait.

[4] Cf. *Essai*, p. 309: " La douceur et la mollesse de la langue italienne s'est insinuée dans le génie des auteurs italiens."

[5] *Ibid.*, p. 310: " Les Français ont pour eux la clarté, l'exactitude, l'élégance."

[6] *Ibid.*, " La force, l'énergie, la hardiesse, sont plus particulières aux Anglais."

[7] Regarding the free use of similes in the *Essay*, wherein Voltaire feels that he is conforming to English taste (cf. p. 66, note 2, *ante*) Rolli says (*Remarks*,

From their different Characters flows that dislike that[1] every Nation shows for the Taste of its Neighbour. Hence it is that the Battle of the Angels in *Milton*, would not succeed among the *French*. Hence it is that the long, but noble Speeches of *Cinna*, and *Augustus*, in *Corneille*, could not be tolerated upon the *English* Stage.

|These following Lines of *Tasso*,[2] are admired in *Italy*, learnt 43 by Heart, and in every Body's Mouth.

> *Colei* Sophronia, *Olindo egli S'apella,*
> *D'una cittade entrambi, e d'una fede.*
> *Ei che modesto e si com' essa e bella,*
> *Brama assaï, poco Spera, e nulla chiede,*
> *Ne sa Scoprirsi, o non ardisce; e ella,*
> *O lo Sprezza, o no'l vede, o non s'avede;*
> *Cosi fin hora il misero ha servito,*
> *O non visto, o mal noto, o mal gradito.*[3]

There is nothing in these Lines that offends against good Sense; but such a gingling[4] of Words, that overnice Symmetry of Expression, that curl'd Thought revolving on itself, won't methinks be applauded by a *French*, or an *English* Reader, who requires[5] a more serious and more majestick Simplicity in *Heroic* poetry.

Among many Passages of *Milton*, which every *French* Reader

---

p. 92): " The Reader should take notice how M. Voltaire embellishes his Essay with pretty similes. I own I am delighted with them and expect them as I do songs in an Opera...they belong besides very well to an Essay of so great a subject as Epick Poetry, & to so grave an Author as M. Voltaire."

[1] 1728 which.

[2] Torquato Tasso, 1544-1595.

[3] *Gerusalemme liberata*, Canto II, stanza 16. Rolli (*Remarks*, p. 43) says that these lines of Tasso were never admired by the Italians. In the *Essai* this extract was replaced by two other passages of Tasso from the *Gerusalemme liberata*. Rolli criticized severely various parts of the Essay but it was naturally the slurs cast upon Italian taste which he resented most. Cf. *Ibid.*: " Mr. Voltaire does perhaps understand but I am sure he has read but three or four Italian authors, he never was in Italy, he never perhaps conversed with any Italian of true learning, yet he, either by a superior Genius or de gaîté de coeur ventures at this most bold and inconsiderate Blow against no less than a whole Nation, a Nation who, in matter of Epick Poetry had Ariosto and Tasso almost twenty years before France had Mr. Voltaire." *Ibid.*, p. 119: " The whole Italian Nation is most injuriously used by this great author." It is significant that the comments on the Italians have been in several cases made more favorable in the French version. Cf. p. 69, note 4, *ante.*

[4] 1728 jingling.

[5] 1728 require.

would startle at, I beg leave to quote one, which has here more
Partizans[1] than Criticks; 'tis in the first *Canto*,—

> *At once as far as Angels Ken he views*
> *The dismal Situation, waste and wild,*
44 > *|A Dungeon horrible, on all Sides round,*
> *As one great Furnace flam'd; yet from those Flames*
> *No Light, but rather a Darkness visible*
> *Serv'd only to discover Sights of Woe.*[2]

Antonio de *Solis*, in his excellent History of *Mexico*,[3] hath
ventur'd on the same Thought, when speaking of the Place wherein
Montezuma was wont to consult his deities: " 'Twas a large dark
subterraneous Vault, says he, where some dismal Tapers afforded
just Light enough to see the Obscurity."

Such daring Thoughts would be look'd upon as Nonsense by
a *French* Critick, whose Exactness is often call'd in *England* Timidity. And since the greatest Poet among the *English*, and the
best Writer among the *Spaniards*, have not scrupl'd[4] to indulge
now and then such Flights bordering on Bombast, that proves
at least that in their Countries, the Authors have a more free
Scope than in *France*.

I need no more Examples to demonstrate, that there is such
a Thing as a National Taste.

This once granted, if we have a Mind to get a true Knowledge
of *Epick* Poetry, it would be worth our while to take a Survey
45 of all the different Poems of that | Kind, which have succeeded
in different Ages, and in different Countries.

'Tis not enough to be acquainted with *Virgil*, and *Homer*. As
in regard to Tragedy, a Man who has only perus'd[5] *Sophocles*
and *Euripides* could not have an entire Notion of the Stage. We
should be their Admirers, not their Slaves. We do not speak the
same Language. Our Religion (the great Basis of *Epick* Poetry)
is the very Reverse of their Mythology: Our Battles, our Sieges,
our Fleets, are more different from theirs, than our Manners from

---

[1] 1728 Partizans.
[2] *Paradise Lost*, I, ll. 59-04. L. 03 reads: " No light; but rather darkness
visible."
[3] Antonio de Solis y Ribadeneyra, Spanish poet, dramatist and historian,
1610-1686. *Historia de la Conquista de Méjico* (1684), *Biblioteca de Autores
Españoles*, XXVIII, 205-387.
[4] 1728 scrupled.
[5] 1728 perused.

those of *America*.[1] The Invention of Gun-Powder, that of the Compass, that of Printing, so many Arts besides newly emerg'd[2] into the World, have alter'd[3] the Face of the Universe; and an *Epick* Poet, being surrounded with so many Novelties, must have but a small Share of Genius, if he durst not be new himself.[4]

We send our Children to travel into neighboring Countries, after they have read *Virgil* and *Homer* at School. Should their Time be ill employ'd in getting a thorough Knowledge of *Milton* in *England*, or of *Tasso* in *Italy*? Where are Monuments to be found which better deserve the Observation of a Traveller?

|Our just Respect for the Ancients,[5] proves a meer Superstition, if it betrays us into a rash Contempt of our Neighbors and Countrymen. We ought not to do such an Injury to Nature, as to shut our Eyes to all the Beauties that her Hands pour around us, in order to look back fixedly on her former Productions.[6]

'Tis a pleasure, no doubt, and a great Improvement of our Mind, to survey all the *Epick* Writers in their respective Countries, from *Homer* down to *Milton*, and to observe the different Features, and the various Dresses of those great Men.

'Tis a task beyond the Reach of my Capacity, to give a full Prospect of them. I shall but faintly touch the first Lines of

46

---

[1] We have here an interesting example of the use of America, prevalent among French writers of the seventeenth and eighteenth centuries, as typical of what is most remote and most unlike France. Cf. Montesquieu, *Lettres persanes*, 1721, *Oeuvres*, V, p. 205: " Le fils méconnoît le portrait de sa mère tant l'habit avec lequel elle est peinte lui paroît étranger; il s'imagine que c'est quelque Américaine qui y est représentée, ou que le peintre a voulu exprimer quelqu'une de ses fantaisies."

Fontenelle, *Digression sur les anciens et les modernes*, 1688, *Oeuvres*, IV, p. 251: " Dieu sait avec quel mépris on traîtera en comparaison de nous les beaux esprits de ce temps là, qui pourront bien être des Américains." Cf. Chinard, *L'Amérique et le rêve exotique dans la littérature française au* XVIIe *et au* XVIIIe *siècles.*

[2] 1728 emerged.

[3] 1728 altered

[4] This sentence, at first translated rather literally in the *Essai*, was changed between '51 and '56 to read; " Il faut peindre avec des couleurs vraies comme les anciens mais il ne faut pas peindre les mêmes choses." P. 152, *post*. Cf. André Chénier, *L'Invention, Oeuvres*, II, p. 9:
  " Changeons en notre miel leurs plus antiques fleurs,
  Pour peindre notre idée empruntons leurs couleurs;
  Allumons nos flambeaux à leurs feux poétiques;
  Sur des pensers nouveaux faisons des vers antiques."

[5] 1728 Antients.

[6] Cf. Perrault, *Paralelle des Anciens et des Modernes*, Préface: "Il m'a paru tant d'aveuglement dans cette prévention et tant d'ingratitude à ne pas vouloir ouvrir les yeux sur la beauté de nostre Siècle,à qui le Ciel a départi mille lumières qu'il a refusées à toute l'Antiquité."

their Pictures.   Some abler Hand will add the finishing Strokes
to this imperfect Drawing.

The judicious Reader will supply the Defects, and inforce the
feeble Hints he will find in this Essay.   My part is to propose,
his to judge; and his Judgement will be right, if he attends without
Partiality, laying aside the Prejudices of the School, or the overbearing Love of the Productions of his own Country.

He will mark the Progresses, the Sinking of the Art, its Rais-
47 ing[1] again, and pursue it through its various Changes. | He
will distinguish the Beauties, and the Faults which are such,
every where, and in all Ages, from those doubtful Things which
are call'd Blemishes by one Nation, and stil'd[2] Perfections by
another.   He will not be tyranniz'd[3] by *Aristotle, Castelvetro,
Dacier, Le Bossu,*[4] but he will extract his own Rules from the
various Examples he shall have before his Eyes, and governed
by his good Sense alone, be a Judge between the Gods of *Homer,*
and the God of *Milton,* and between *Calipso, Dido, Armida* and *Eve.*

But if the Reader be so just, as to make Allowances for the
Time, in which those different Authors have writ, it is to be hoped,
he will look with some Indulgence on the Diction of this Essay
and pardon the failings of one who has learn'd[5] *English* but this
Year of one who has drawn most of his Observations from Books
written in *England,*[6] and who pays to this Country but Part of

---

[1] 1728 Rising.   Cf. *Errata.*
[2] 1728 stiled.
[3] 1728 tyrannized.
[4] Each of the critics mentioned here was either the translator of Aristotle's
Poetics or the author of a work based on Aristotle: Lodovico Castelvetro, 1505-
1571, *La Poetica d'Aristotile;* André Dacier, 1651-1722, *Poétique* (d'Aristote);
René Le Bossu, 1631-1680, *Traité du Poème épique,* (based on Homer and Virgil
and the theories of Aristotle). Cf. Spingarn, *A History of Literary Criticism
in the Renaissance,* and Saintsbury, *A History of Criticism,* II.
[5] 1728 learned.
[6] Although it is not claimed that the notes given here contain an exhaustive
study of sources, they are sufficiently full to show how remarkably true is this
statement of Voltaire's and in particular to what an extent he "drew his observations" from Addison's *Spectator.* Cf. pp. 93, 94, 95, 115, 133, 136, 138,
139, 140, 143, 145, *post.* We have seen that at some time early in his stay
in England, probably during the spring of the year 1727, Voltaire formed the
habit of reading aloud from the *Spectator* for practice in pronunciation (cf.
p. 18, *ante*). At the time of writing his essay not only does he pay Addison
the subtle compliment of borrowing much from him, but definitely calls him
the best writer and the best critic of his age (p. 58 note 4, *ante*) " whose Judgment seems either to guide or to justify the Opinion of his Countrymen." P.
141, *post.*
    Again, with his easy use of superlatives, Voltaire had in the autumn of
1726 spoken of Pope as " the best poet of England and at present of all the
world " (Foulet, *Corr.,* p. 54), and his admiration for the author of the *Essay* on

what he owes to her. A Nurse is not displeased with the stammering Articulations of a Child, who delivers to her with much ado his first undigested Thoughts.[1]

|*Homer.*[2]   **48**

It would seem too assuming, and prove very useless, to expatiate upon *Homer* and *Virgil*, especially in *England*, where there is scarce a Gentleman unacquainted with *Latin* and *Greek*.

As to *Homer*, those who cannot read him in the Original have Mr. *Pope's* Translation;[3] they may discern the Fire of that Father of Poetry, reflected from such a polish'd and faithful Glass.[4] I will neither point out his Beauties, since none of them are lost

Criticism is well-known. It is therefore not surprising that the text of our essay should show that the writer kept Pope's *Iliad* (and its Preface) before his eyes and in some cases made a curious use of sentences found there.

Voltaire must also have owed much to conversations with men of letters, with classical scholars, and with Englishmen in general. (Cf. Lanson, *Lettres phil., Introduction,* p. li, note 1.) Among others, he doubtless talked with the French refugees who met and discussed literature and diverse topics at the Rainbow Coffee House. Cf. Texte, p. 18.

As a concrete example of the use of an oral source, we have the account of Camoens contained in the essay, if we accept what seems fairly authentic testimony. Cf. Dr. Joseph Wharton: note to *Dunciad,* iv, 560, quoted in the *Parliamentary History,* VII, 459, note and thence by Ballantyne, p. 121: "I remember Collins told me that Bladen had given to Voltaire all that account of Camoëns inserted in the Essay on the Epic Poets of all Nations; and that Voltaire seemed before entirely ignorant of the name and character of Camoëns."

[1] This passage bearing directly upon the English of the essay was naturally omitted in the French. It was replaced by a paragraph found in the English chapter on Milton (cf. p. 135, *post*) concerning the benefits one nation might derive from a better knowledge of the literatures of others.

[2] Cf. *Essai,* Chapitre II, *Homère,* p. 314. The French chapter is nearly twice as long as the English. It is, as has been shown, the part of the French essay which deviates most widely from the original, differing from it radically in plan, detail and spirit. It will be remembered that various reasons for this change have been suggested: Voltaire's desire while in England to praise Pope but to decry Homer in whom he no doubt saw a rival, and the tendency of the France of his youth to scorn Homer, combined with his own natural preferences in literature and his insufficient knowledge of Greek probably determined the tone of the English chapter; the fact that Homer was unpopular in France and not to be considered as a rival in that country, together with the impress of the years in England and a better knowledge of the Iliad in the original Greek may have determined the tone of the French.

Of the numerous points treated in the English, only three or four appear in the French at all, and then in quite a different light,—the force of Homer's painting, the extravagance of his gods and his combats, and the fact that he has been at the same time worshipped and neglected. The French chapter on the other hand contains information about Homer and the literature of his times, a defence of his gods and his heroes, an account of the disputes concerning the Greek poet which had taken place in France and a statement of Voltaire's own position. Cf. pp. 66 ff. *ante.*

[3] Pope's *Iliad* was published between 1715 and 1720.

[4] Cf. Pope, *Iliad,* ed. Chalmers, preface, p. 3: "This fire is discerned in Virgil, but discerned as through a glass, reflected from Homer."

in the Translation, nor cavil at his Faults, which are for the most part lessen'd or embellish'd.[1]

Let every Reader consult himself, when he reads *Homer*, and reflect how that Poem works upon his Mind; then he will judge if *Homer* hath reach'd to the utmost Pitch of the Art,[2] in any Thing else but in that predominant Force of *Painting* which makes his peculiar Character.[3]

Notwithstanding the Veneration due, and paid to *Homer*, it is very strange, yet true, that among the most Learn'd,[4] and the greatest Admirers of Antiquity, there is scarce one to be found, who ever read the *Iliad*, with that Eagerness and Rapture, 49 which a Woman feels when she reads the Novel | of Zaïda;[5] and as to the common Mass of Readers, less conversant with Letters, but not perhaps endow'd[6] with a less Share of Judgment and Wit, few have been able to go through the whole *Iliad*, without strugling[7] against a secret Dislike, and some have thrown it aside after the fourth or fifth Book. How does it come to pass that *Homer* hath so many Admirers, and so few Readers? And is at the same time worshipp'd[8] and neglected?

I'll endeavour to give some Reasons for this Paradox. The common Part of Mankind is aw'd[9] with the Fame of *Homer*, rather than struck with his Beauties. The judicious Reader is pleas'd[10] no doubt with the noble Imagination of that great Author, but very few have command enough over their own Prejudices, and can transport themselves far enough into such a remote An-

---

[1] Cf. Lanson, *Lettres phil.*, II, p. 136 :"Vous pouvez plus aisément vous former quelqu'idée de Mr. Pope; c'est, je crois, le poëte le plus élégant, le plus correct, & ce qui est encore beaucoup, le plus harmonieux qu'ait l'Angleterre." Cf. Foulet, *Corr.*, pp. 53-54: " I intend to send you two or three poems of Mr. Pope, the best poet of England, and at present of all the world."

[2] Cf. p. 99, *post*, where the words "reached to the utmost Pitch of the Art" occur again. This coincidence is perhaps worth noticing in connection with the study of the language of the essay.

[3] Cf. *Essai*, p. 318: " Le grand mérite d'Homère est d'avoir été un peintre sublime."

[4] 1728 Learned.

[5] Mme. de La Fayette's *Zaïde* was published in 1670.

In the account of the French translation of the Essay in the *Journal des Sçavans* (Sept. 1728, pp. 517 ff.) there occurs a curious misprint in connection with this passage: "Notre Auteur supposant qu'il n'y a point de Sçavans qui ayent lû Homère avec autant de plaisir qu'en ressentent les femmes qui lisent Ovide [sic] . . ."

[6] 1728 endowed.

[7] 1728 struggling.

[8] 1728 worshipped.

[9] 1728 awed.

[10] 1728 pleased.

tiquity, as to become the Contemporaries of *Homer* when they read him:[1] Good Sense bids them to make Allowances for the Manners of his Time, but 'tis almost impossible to bring themselves to a quick Relish of them. The Rays of his Light transmitted to their Eyes through so long a Way, afford them but a feeble glimmering Twilight, and no Warmth. They are like the old Counsellors of | *Priam*, who confess'd without any emotion 50 of Heart, that *Helena* was a Beauty.

A second Reason of their Dislike, is that Uniformity which seems diffused through all the Work. The Battles take up three Parts of the whole *Iliad*. The Reader is more likely to be disgusted by the continual Glare of that predominant Colour which is spread over the Poem, than to be pleased with the Variety of Teints, and Shades, which require a refin'd Sight to perceive them.

Thirdly, the Poem is certainly too long, and 'tis an Exception that all *Epick* Poets are liable to; for there is no *Epick* Poetry without a powerful Imagination, and no great Imagination without over-flowing.

I wave here all the Quarrels rais'd[2] by the Enemies of *Homer*, to such Parts of his Poems, as may be the Objects of our Criticism, but never the Cause of our Sleep.

His Gods are perhaps at once absurd and entertaining, as the Madness of *Ariosto*[3] amuses us with a bewitching Delight. And for his other Faults, the Majesty, and the Fire of his Stile, brightens them often into Beauties.

But in my Opinion, the best reason for that Languour[4] which creeps upon the Mind of so many Readers, in Spight[5] of | the 51 Flashes which rouse her[6] now and then, is, that *Homer* interesses[7] us for none of his Heroes. *Achilles* is too boisterous to inspire us with a tender Concern for him. And suppose his very Fierceness could extort from us that favourable Disposition which the over-powering Idea of Valour generally forces us into, his long Idleness wears away the Thought of him, and as the Poet lays him aside, so does the Reader.

---

[1] Cf. La Motte, *Discours*, p. cxxxvii: "Il y a au contraire des Lecteurs dégoûtez, qui trop pleins de nos usages, & de nos goûts, ne sçauroient se transporter à des tems si différents des nôtres."

[2] 1728 raised.

[3] Lodovico Ariosto, 1474-1533, *Orlando Furioso*, 1532.

[4] 1728 Languor.

[5] 1728 Spite.

[6] 1728 it. Cf. *Errata*, p. 79, *ante*.

[7] 1731 interests.

Menelaus, who is the only Occasion of the War, and in whom of Course our Affections ought to center, is very far from being a shining Character. *Paris,* his Rival, excites our Contempt. *Menelaus* is in the Poem, but the Brother of *Agamemnon,* and *Paris* the Brother of *Hector.* *Agamemnon,* King of Kings, shocks us with his Pride, without giving us any great Idea of his Conduct. I do not know how it comes to pass, but every Reader bears secretly an ill Will to the wise *Ulysses.* The fair *Helena,* the Cause of so great Mischiefs, is insignificant enough. Nobody cares whose Share she will fall to, since she seems herself indifferent between her two Husbands.

When two Warriors fight in the *Iliad,* we are aw'd[1] indeed 52 with the Description, nay often transported with their | Fury, but we feel neither Hope nor Fear for any of them.

We are like *Juno* in the *Æneid, Tros rutulus ve fuat, nullo discrimine habebo.*[2]

We pity indeed the Misfortunes of *Priam,* nor will I quarrel with the Tears that we give to his Afflictions. I wish only that *Homer* would have interested us for the *Greeks,* throughout all the Poem, since he intends to praise them, and since they are the Heroes of the Poem; but I'll go no further than to observe, that if we are mov'd[3] with the Sorrow of *Priam,* at the very End of the Poem, we are indifferent towards him in the Course of the Action.

Of all the Warriors, the couragious,[4] the tender, and the pious *Hector,* deserves most our Affections. He hath the best Character, though he defends the wrong Cause; and he is betray'd by the Gods, though he has so much Virtue.

But our Concern for him is lost, in the Crowd of so many Heroes. Our Attention is divided and lessen'd, like a Stream cut into many Rivulets.

Thus the Reader's Imagination is often fill'd[5] with great and 53 noble Ideas, while the Affections of the Soul stag|nate; and if in any long Work whatever, the Motions of the Heart do not keep Pace with the Pleasures of the Fancy, 'tis no Wonder if we may at once admire and be tir'd.

[1] 1728 awed.
[2] *Aeneid,* X, l. 108.
[3] 1728 moved.
[4] 1728 courageous.
[5] 1728 filled.

If all these Reasons are contested (for what Assertion of our Minds is undisputable?) I must add a further Observation, which is a Matter of Fact out of the Reach of Dispute. Many of the Books of the *Iliad* are independent from one another; they might be transpos'd without any great Alteration in the Action. And perhaps, for that Reason, they were call'd Rapsodies. I leave to the Judgement of the Reader, if such a work, let it be never so well written, never so teeming with Beauties (can be interesting) and win our Attention.[1]

VIRGIL.[2]

Mr. *Addison* was the first who considered in their proper View the Materials which compos'd the Structure of the *Æneid.*[3]

It is certain *Virgil* fram'd his Poem out of many Fables concerning the Settlement of *Æneas* in *Italy*, handed down to his Time, which were credited by the People, with a Kind of superstitious Belief.[4]

|In the like Manner, it is probable, *Homer* founded his *Iliad*, 54 upon the Tradition of the *Trojan* War.

For to believe *Homer* and *Virgil* submitted before-hand, to the Rules laid down by *Le Bossu*, who bids an *Epick* Poet invent, and dispose the Constitution of his Fable, before he thinks of the

[1] Rolli reproaches Voltaire with having "so ill-used" Homer (*Remarks*, p. 37)· Cf. Marais, *Journal*, III, p. 554, ed. Lescure, quoted by Foulet, *Corr.*, p. 160, note: "Voltaire a fait en anglais un *Essai sur le poëme épique*; il est traduit en françois; s'il ne parloit pas si mal d'Homère, je trouverois l'ouvrage très bon."
In view of the tone of the English chapter, it is interesting to notice a sentence occurring toward the end of the French, p. 319: "Ceux qui ne peuvent pardonner les fautes d'Homère en faveur de ses beautés, sont la plupart des esprits trop philosophiques, qui ont étouffé en eux-mêmes tout sentiment."
[2] Cf. *Essai*, p. 320, Chapitre III, V*irgile*. The substance of the English chapter appears in the French which is noticeably longer. The reference to Addison has been omitted as have the allusions to critics who have accused Virgil of copying Pisander and Apollonius. Cf. p. 96, note 5, *post*.
The French chapter opens with a considerable amount of biographical information. Virgil's superiority to Homer is emphasized and the discussion of the last six books of the *Aeneid* is expanded. In this connection an interesting sentence has been added at the end of the chapter, p. 325: " Mais ma présomption va trop loin, ce n'est point à un jeune peintre à oser reprendre les défauts d'un Raphaël; et je ne puis pas dire, comme le Corrége: *Son pittore anch' io.*"
[3] There is nothing here to indicate that the paragraphs which follow are based directly on Addison's work. Indeed in the French version, the allusion to Addison is omitted while the ideas taken from the *Spectator* are retained.
[4] Addison in *Spectator*, II, pp. 519 ff: " We find, however, that he [Virgil] has interwoven, in the course of his Fable, the principal Particulars, which were generally believed among the *Romans*, of *Aeneas* his Voyage and Settlement in *Italy*."

Name of his Heroes, is not indeed natural.[1] In all likelihood they did not cut the Coat, without knowing whose shape it could fit. Such a Rule may be observ'd[2] in Comedy, which deals cheifly in the Exposition of the Manners, and of the Ridicule of the Age; or Delights in a Plot, made up of surprising,[3] but little Incidents, which never require the Testimony of History, or the Weight of any celebrated Name.

But the *Epick*, as well as the *Tragick* Poets, generally pitch upon a Subject, and a Hero well known, whose single Name must strike the Reader with Awe, and command his Attention. They adapt their Invention to the History, for if one should begin by laying down a Fable intirely of his own Imagination, all the Records in the Universe could not afford him an Event, adequate to his Plan; he must needs alter it. And I cannot apprehend 55 why Mr. *Le Bossu* | advises to build what must necessarily be destroy'd.

Whatever it be, Part of the Events included in the *Æneid*, are to be found in *Dionysius Halicarnassus*. He mentions with Accuracy, the Course of the Navigation of *Æneas*. He does not omit the Fable of the *Harpies*, the Predictions uttered by *Celaeno*, the eating up of the Cakes, &c.[4]

As to the Metamorphose of the Ships into Nymphs, if *Dionysius* does not mention it, *Virgil* himself takes care to justify such

---

[1] Cf. Le Bossu, II, p. 36: " Le Poëte doit feindre une action générale, . . . il doit ensuite chercher dans l'histoire ou dans les Fables connuës, les noms de quelques personnes, à qui une action pareille soit arrivée véritablement ou vraisemblablement, et . . . il doit mettre enfin son action sous ces noms. Ainsi elle sera feinte vraisemblablement, & inventée par l'Auteur; et elle paroîtra prise dans l'Histoire ou dans une Fable plus ancienne." *Ibid.*, p. 84: "Aristote ordonne de faire une action générale qui ne soit d'aucun particulier; d'imposer les noms aux Personnes, après cette première Fiction & de former ensuite les Episodes." *Ibid.*, p. 92: " Il [Homère] a fait la Fable et le dessein de ses Poèmes sans penser à ses Princes; et ensuite il leur a fait l'honneur de donner leurs noms aux Héros qu'il avait feints." Cf. Addison in *Spectator*, II, p. 592: " Though I can by no means think, with the last mentioned *French* author [Le Bossu], that an Epick Writer first of all pitches upon a certain Moral, as the Ground-Work and Foundation of his Poem, and afterwards finds out a Story to it." Cf. also Pope, ed. Elwin and Courthope, X, p. 402, *Receipt for making an Epic Poem, For the Fable*. Voltaire cannot fail to have been acquainted with Le Bossu's work before coming to England.

[2] 1728 observed.

[3] 1728 surprizing.

[4] Cf. Addison in *Spectator*, II, p. 520: " The Reader may find an Abridgement of the whole Story as collected out of the ancient Historians, and as it was received among the *Romans*, in *Dionysius Halicarnasseus* . . . The Historian above mentioned acquaints us, a Prophetess had foretold *Aeneas* that he should take his Voyage Westward, till his Companions should eat their Tables."

an Absurdity, by telling us, that it was an ancient[1] Tradition;
Prisca fides facto, sed fama perennis.[2]

It seems that *Virgil,* asham'd of such a fairy Tale, hath a Mind
to excuse it by the common Belief.[3]

Many passages of *Virgil* considered in this View, are intirely
vindicated against his Criticks, whose good Sense was misled in
that Particular by their Inattention.[4]

If an Author among the *French,* attempts a Poem on *Clovis,*[5]
he is allow'd to speak of the Holy Vial, brought down from Heaven,
in the Bill of a Dove, into the Church of *Rheims,* for the Corona-
tion of the King.[6] If an *English* Wri|ter takes King *Arthur* for 56
his Subject, he may without Censure bring in the Incantations
of *Merlin,* it being the Fate of all those antient Fables, which
the Beginning of every Nation is involv'd in, to be rever'd for
their Antiquity, when they are laugh'd at for their Absurdity;
but upon the Whole, it would be better to omit them, though
we are allow'd to mention them; for a single Reader of Sense,
who will be shock'd at such Stories, deserves more Respect, than
the Crowd which gives them Credit.

As to the Construction of his Fable, he is accus'd by some,
and commended by others, for having follow'd *Homer* closely;
but if I dare speak my Opinion, he deserves neither such an
Injury, nor such a Compliment.[7] He could not avoid introduc-

---

[1] 1728 antient.

[2] *Aeneid,* IX, l. 79.

[3] Cf. Addison in *Spectator,* II, p. 521: " I am apt to think that the changing
of the *Trojan* Fleet into Water-Nymphs, which is the most violent Machine
in the whole *Aeneid,* and has given offence to several Criticks, may be accounted
for the same way. *Virgil* himself, before he begins that Relation, premises,
that what he was going to tell appeared incredible, but that it was justified
by Tradition."

[4] Cf. *ibid:* "None of the Criticks I have met with having considered the Fable
of the *Aeneid* in this Light, and taken notice how the Tradition, on which it was
founded, authorizes those Parts in it which appear the most exceptionable . . . "
Voltaire's sentence is not clear until one reads Addison's. The phrase
"considered in this View," one of those which makes for vagueness since there
is nothing to which it can refer directly, corresponds to Addison's "considered
. . . in this Light." Cf. *Essai,* pp. 322-323: " Si on considérait dans cette
vue plusieurs en droits de Virgile qui choquent au premier coup d'oeil, on serait
moins prompt à le condamner."

[5] Jean Desmarets, sieur de Saint Sorlin, was the author of an epic poem called
Clovis ou la France chrétienne, 1654-57, while another epic likewise called *Clovis*
and never finished appeared in 1725, the work of Ignace François Saint-Didier.

[6] This passage, dropped by Desfontaines and restored by Voltaire when he
reprinted the Abbé's translation in 1732, also found a place in the French version
of 1733. His persistency in mentioning among absurd fables a legend of the
church is characteristic of Voltaire.

[7] The form of this sentence seems a reminiscence of Racine's: "Ni cet excès
d'honneur ni cette indignité." *Britanicus,* II, 3, l. 84.

ing the Gods of *Homer*, who were the *Roman* Gods too, nor talking
of the Siege of *Troy*, since *Æneas* was a *Trojan* Hero.

Those Things were common to the *Greek* Author and to him.
He draws his Richesses from the same Source, but not at the
Expence of his Predecessor.

Virgil, 'tis[1] true, hath translated some Passages of the *Iliad*
and of the *Odissey*; he hath borrow'd some little Descriptions,
57 some obvious Similes, which sure|ly his great Genius did not
want, by which but a little Glory could acrue[2] to him, and which
are rather an Honour paid by him to *Homer*, than a Proof of his
standing in Need of Help.

'Tis[1] pleasant to see how some Criticks have triumph'd in
the Discovery of those Trifles. Those who take up Arms for
Homer, against *Virgil*, and who sacrifice the Pleasure of being
pleas'd with both, to the chimerical Fancy of raising the Glory
of the one, at the Expence of the other, pretend that *Dido* is the
Copy of *Calipso*. That *Æneas* is sent to the Shades after *Ulysses*,
and the like.[3] Let the Readers compare those pretended Copies
with the suppos'd Original, they will find a wonderful Difference.

The Passion of *Dido*, her Misfortune, her Death, brought in
as the Cause of that everlasting Hatred between *Carthage* and
Rome; and *Anchises* calling forth from the Womb of Time, the
Fate of the *Roman* Empire, all these Beauties are not certainly
owing to *Homer*.

It is not in the Nature of a Genius, to be a Copist. Wherever
Virgil is great, he is himself; but in those little Passages borrow'd
from *Homer*, he commonly falls short of the Original; and 'tis a
58 just Punishment for having clogg'd the | Liberty of his Genius,
with the Fetters of Imitation.[4]

Some Criticks proceed further, they tell us, *Virgil* has copied
his second Book from *Pisander*, and the fourth after *Apollonius*.[5]

---

[1] 1760 it is.
[2] 1728 accrue.
[3] Cf. Pope, *Iliad*, preface, p. 4: " If Ulysses visit the shades, the Aeneas of
Virgil, and Scipio of Silius, are sent after him."
[4] Certain passages from the *Spectator* and from Pope's preface form an interesting contrast to Voltaire's opinion concerning Virgil's debt to Homer. Cf.
Addison in *Spectator*, II, p. 255: " [Virgil] seldom elevates and transports us
where he does not fetch his Hints from *Homer*." *Ibid.*, p. 478: " There are
a thousand shining Passages in *Virgil*, which have been lighted up by *Homer*."
Cf. Pope, *Iliad*, preface, p. 5: "And it is evident of Virgil especially, that he
has scarce any comparisons which are not drawn from his master."
[5] Pisander, poet of Camirus in Rhodes, flourished about B. C. 650, author
of the *Heraclea*. Apollonius Rhodius, flourished B. C. 222-181, author of the

If he has stolen from them, then hath he not robb'd *Homer*. But all that ought to be flatly deny'd; and the only Answer which is to be made to such Discoveries, is, that the second and fourth Book of *Virgil*, are too great Master-Pieces of Art to be but Copies. 'Tis just as some People say *Milton* hath stolen his Poem from an *Italian* Stroller call'd *Andreino*.[1]

And after all, what avails such a trifling Enquiry? 'Tis not the Person of *Virgil*, 'tis the *Æneid* which we admire; let the second and the fourth Book belong to *Pisander*, to *Apollonius*, or to *Virgil*, or to any-body else, the Name of the Author does not alter the Beauties of the Book. Let *Macrobius*[2] and the other Criticks, detract from the six Letters which make up the Name of *Virgil*, his Works will nevertheless be the Delight of all Ages, and the Pattern of all Poets.

Argonautica. Cf. Pope, *Iliad*, preface, p. 4: " Thus the story of Sinon, and the taking of Troy was copied (says Macrobius) almost word for word from Pisander, as the loves of Dido and Aeneas are taken from those of Medea and Jason in Apollonius, and several others in the same manner."

Voltaire's allusion to Apollonius gave rise to a discussion, curious in that no one of the three persons contributing to it had ever seen the text he was discussing. This fact shows how soon the English essays became rare. Cf. *Preface*.

In 1778, only fifty years after the first edition of Voltaire's essays had appeared and in the very city in which they had been published, Edward Harwood printed the following paragraph in the article Apollonius Rhodius in his *Biographia Classica*, I, p. 161: " It is somewhat remarkable that Voltaire in one of his critical essays, after affirming that critics have generally been of the opinion that in the most splendid part of the *Aeneid*, the Intercourse between Dido and Aeneas, the Roman Poet had largely borrowed from Apollonius of Rhodes adds, ' it is greatly to be lamented that we have not the *Argonautica* now remaining that by instituting a Collation we might see how much the Roman has been indebted to the Grecian poet.' " About twenty years later Chardon de la Rochette (*Magasin Encyclopédique*, 1807, II, p. 320) refers to Harwood's assertion saying that he was at first inclined to believe it, although such an error regarding Apollonius, whose *Argonautica* is still preserved, would be " peu excusable dans un disciple du Père Porée." He has not been able to procure a copy of the English *Essay on Epic Poetry* but since the sentence quoted by Harwood did not occur in Desfontaines' translation and was not mentioned by Rolli in his criticism of the essay, la Rochette concludes that Harwood's assertion must be counted among the " mensonges imprimés."

Again, twenty years later, Beuchot refers to the matter in his edition of Voltaire, quoting from Harwood and from la Rochette. He, too, has not been able to consult the English essay but the fact that Voltaire's French version, which he evidently considers to be very like the English original, does not contain the statement regarding the *Argonautica* leads him to accept la Rochette's conclusion. Cf. *Oeuvres*, Garnier Frères, VIII, p. 304. A knowledge of the English text, of course, shows that this conclusion was correct but it throws no light upon the source of Harwood's " mensonge."

[1] Cf. p. 130, note 2, *post*. This sentence does not appear in the French chapter.

[2] Macrobius, Latin grammarian of the fifth century, the author of the *Saturnales*. Cf. Pope, *Iliad*, preface, p. 4, cited above.

Another Objection against him, is, that he hath not crowded[1] in his Poems so many Heroes as *Homer* hath done. That *Ajax,* 59 *Diomedes, Idomeneus,* &c., | are all shining Characters; whereas the faithful *Achates,* the strong *Gias,* and the magnanimous *Cloanthus,* are of no Manner of Use, and serve only but to fill now and then the Gap of a Verse or two.

I am apt to think, that such an Objection turns a great deal to the Advantage of the *Æneid. Virgil* sung the Actions of *Æneas,* and *Homer* the Idleness of *Achilles.*

The *Greek* Poet lay under the Necessity of supplying the Absence of his first *Hero,* with some other Warriors; but what was judicious in *Homer,* would have been preposterous in *Virgil:* He knew too much of his Art, to drown his principal Character in the Crowd of many other Heroes, indifferent to the main Action.

Thus he found the Way to center our Concern in *Æneas,* he interesses us for him, by never losing Sight of him, while *Homer* presenting us with the shifting Scene of so many shining Characters, interesses us for none.

Mr. *De St. Evremont*[2] says, *Æneas* is fitter to be the Founder of an Order of Monks, than of an Empire.[3] 'Tis true, *Æneas* hath the Misfortune to pass generally under the Notion of a 60 pious Man, and not a great Warrior; the | Fault is not in *Virgil,* it lies in the wrong Notions which the Generality of Mankind entertains of Courage. Our Eyes are dazzl'd with the boisterous Fury of a wild Hero. Had *Virgil* been less wise, had the Courage of *Æneas* been a barberous Rashness, instead of a sedate, and calmly-daring Valour, perhaps he might please better, but surely he would deserve it less.

It is a just Criticism on *Virgil,* that the latter part of his Poem is less animated than the first, not that the six last Books are intirely languishing, but their milder Light is overpowered by the Lustre of the others.

That great Defect is owing to the Disposition of the Poem, and to the Nature of the Things. The Design of a Match between *Æneas* and *Lavinia* unknown and indifferent to each other, and a War rais'd about a Stag wounded by a young Boy, could not

[1] 1728 crouded.
[2] St. Evremont was an exile in England from 1661 until the time of his death in 1703.
[3] Cf. Lucan's *Pharsalia,* translated by Nicholas Rowe, preface, p. xxxiii: "In short, it's St. *Evremont's* Opinion, he [Aeneas] *was fitter to make a Founder of an Order than a State.*"

indeed command our Concern as well as the burning of *Troy*, and the Love of *Dido*.

'Tis a great Mistake to believe an Author can soar, when the Subject sinks. All the Art he employs, shews[1] only that he till'd with Labour and Skill an ungrateful Soil. If the natural Chain of Events in the *Æneid* could have allow'd *Virgil* to rise by Degrees in point of Sen|timents and Grandeur; his Poem had 61 been as unexceptionable as the Bounds of human Talent[2] will permit.[3] In short his Fault lies in having reach'd to the utmost Pitch of the Art[4] in the middle of his Course.

LUCAN.[5]

After we have lifted up our Eyes toward *Virgil*, and *Homer*, we need not look down on the other *Roman* Authors who have been stumbling in the same Carrier.[6] Let us lay aside their mean and monstrous Mimicks, *Statius*,[7] and *Silius Italicus*;[8] but we ought not to overlook *Lucan*, who took entirely a new Course, and whose free Genius borrow'd neither its Beauties, nor its Faults.

He was of an ancient[9] equestrian Family, born at *Cordova* in *Spain* under *Caligula*;[10] he was brought to *Rome* when Eight Month's old, and educated there, under the Influence of his Uncle *Seneca*, with the nice Care that his Birth, his opulent Fortune,[11] and especially the Pregnancy of his early *Genius* deserved. I mention this, only to silence those Criticks who have call'd in question the Purity of his Language; they took him for a *Spaniard*, who wrote *Roman* Verses; and prepossess'd[12] with that Notion,

---

[1] 1728 shews.

[2] 1728 Talents.

[3] This sentence does not appear in the French but on the other hand the *Aeneid* is spoken of as " le plus beau monument qui nous reste de toute l'anti-quité." *Essai*, p. 322.

[4] Cf. p. 90, note 2, *ante*.

[5] M. Annaeus Lucanus, A. D. 39-65, author of the *Pharsalia*. Cf. *Essai*, p. 326, Chapitre IV, *Lucain*. The French chapter is slightly longer than the English but is in no way radically different from it.

[6] 1728 Career.

[7] P. Papinius Statius, about A. D. 61-96, author of the *Thebaid*.

[8] Silius Italicus, about A. D. 25-100, author of the *Punica*.

[9] 1728 antient.

[10] Cf. Rowe, *Pharsalia*, preface, p. iii: " *Lucan* was of an Equestrian Family of *Rome*, born at *Corduba* in *Spain*, . . . in the Reign of *Caligula*." This preface appears to be the source of various ideas expressed by Voltaire in his chapter on Lucan as well as of his phraseology in several cases.

[11] *Ibid.*, p. v: " Thus he set out in the World, with the greatest Advantages possible, a Noble Birth, an Opulent Fortune . . . the . . . Protection of an Uncle, who . . .was Favorite . . . to the Emperor."

[12] 1728 prepossessed.

62 they fancied they discover'd[1] in his Language | some Faults which do not really exist; and which if they did exist, could not be perceiv'd by any Modern.

He was at first a Favourite to *Nero*,[2] till he had the noble Imprudence to contend with him for the Prize of Poetry,[3] and the dangerous Honour of carrying it.

He praised that Emperour in his *Pharsalia*, while Nero was yet the Delight of the Empire; he conspir'd[4] against him when the Emperor became a Tyrant. All the World knows he was sentenced to die, and the Choice of the manner of his Death being left to him, he chose to have the Veins of his Arms and Legs open'd in a hot Bath; and dy'd[5] with that Tranquillity, which in those Moments is the true greatness of Soul.[6]

He was not the first who thought a recent History the proper subject of an *Epick* Poem, for *Varius*[7] had ventur'd before him (and with Success) on such a dangerous Undertaking.

The Proximity of the Times and the Notoriety of the Events which he took for his Theme, were certainly a great Clog to his Poetical Invention, (if he had any).

The greater his Subject was, the greater the Difficulty. *Cesar* 63 and *Pompey* were no doubt Men of higher Impor|tance than *Agamemnon*, or *Æneas*; and the War wag'd[8] before the Walls of *Troy*, and before *Latium*, were but Frays of Children in comparison of the *Roman* Civil War in which the greatest Men of *Rome* fought for the Empire of the World.[9]

Lucan could hardly give any Scope to his Imagination on a Subject so well known, and with more Difficulty come up to its Grandeur.[10] On these Accounts the frame of his Poem is dry

---

[1] 1728 discovered.

[2] Cf. p. 99, note 11, *ante*.

[3] Rowe, pp. viii-ix: "*Lucan* . . . had the Imprudence to dispute the Prize of Eloquence with *Nero* . . ."

[4] 1728 conspired.

[5] 1728 died.

[6] Rowe, p. xi: "*Lucan* had the Choice of the Manner of his Death," and p. xii: "having chose to have the Arteries of his Arms and Legs open'd in a hot Bath . . . then taking leave of them with the greatest Tranquillity of Mind."

[7] L. V. Varius Rufus, epic poet of the Augustan age.

[8] 1728 waged.

[9] These words have been rendered in the French (*Essai*, p. 327): "L'empire de la moitié du monde connu." Cf. p. 153, note 1, *post*.

[10] Cf. Le Bossu, II, p. 14: "Cette seconde raison exclut encore du nombre des Epopées une Morale écrite en vers, une simple Histoire comme la *Pharsale* de Lucain."

and tedious, because he dares not deviate from the History; and his Stile swells too often into *Fustian*, when he endeavours to raise it to the Actions of his Heroes.

So *Æneas* and *Achilles*, who were inconsiderable in themselves, are for ever great in *Homer* and *Virgil*. While *Cesar* and *Pompey* sink under the Bombast of *Lucan*. 'Tis a great Pity that the Pictures of his Heroes being drawn with such masterly Strokes, their Actions are so little affecting.

Nothing is more beautiful than the Character of *Cato*, of *Cesar* and of *Pompey*, but nothing more languishing than the part which they act. *Lucan* with all the force of his Painting,[1] with his Grandeur, with his Wit, with his political Notions is but a declamatory Gaze|teer:[2] Sublime here and there, faulty through 64 all the Work.

He is to be commended for having laid the Gods aside, as much as *Homer* and *Virgil* for having made use of that Machinery.[3] Those Fables were adapted to the dark fabulous Ages in which *Priam* and *Latinus* liv'd,[4] but no Way suitable to the Wars of *Rome*. What brightens the Character of *Æneas* and confers a Majesty on the inconsiderable Beginnings of *Rome*, would have debas'd[5] the Character of *Cesar* and drawn a Ridicule upon him. What a poor Figure would that Conqueror make in the Field of Pharsalia, should he be assisted by *Iris* or by *Mercury* ?

Methinks that shows evidently that the Intervention of the Gods is not absolutely requir'd[6] in an *Epick* Poem. They are so far from being necessary, that the best Passage of *Lucan* (and perhaps of all the Poets) is the speech of *Cato* in the Ninth Book,[7] when he scorns to consult *Jupiter*. 'Tis not for want of Gods, but for want of managing with Art the Affairs of Men, that *Lucan* is inferior to *Virgil*.[8] The Judgement of the World is justly passed upon him. He is look'd[9] upon as a strong Genius, tho'

---

[1] Cf. *Essai*, p. 327: " Il n'y a dans son poëme aucune description brillante comme dans Homère." *"Force of Painting"* are the very words used in connection with Homer earlier. Cf. p. 90, *ante*.

[2] 1728 Gazetteer.

[3] Cf. Pope, *Iliad*, preface, p. 4: " It then became as reasonable in the modern poets to lay it [allegorical fable] aside, as it was in Homer to make use of it."

[4] 1728 lived.

[5] 1728 debased.

[6] 1728 required.

[7] *Pharsalia*, IX, ll. 954-1005 (Rowe's translation). In the French chapter Voltaire quotes the passage in question from Brébeuf's translation, " malgré ses défauts," as he tells us.

[8] Throughout this discussion it is clear that Voltaire has his own poem in mind.

[9] 1728 looked.

not as a good Poet; and the precious Stones which shine in the
65 | *Pharsalia* (tho' ill set), yet dazzle and shine in our Eyes. Mon-
sieur *de Corneille* was us'd[1] to say, that he was more indebted
to *Lucan* than to *Virgil*.[2] Not that he was so unjust, and of so
injudicious a Taste as to prefer the *Pharsalia* to the *Æneid*. But
an Author who brings real Heroes upon the Stage, has but little
to do with Poetical Fictions, and will be better help'd by the
vigorous Thoughts of *Lucan*, than by the elegant Narration of
Virgil. Mr. *Addison* borrowed from the *Pharsalia* some Strokes,
in the drawing of his *Cato*.[3] That Ancient[4] Poet never received
a greater Honour then[5] when he was imitated by Mr. *de Corneille*
and by Mr. *Addison*, two Men every way superior to him.[6]

TRISSINO.[7]

After the Fall of the *Roman* Empire in the *West*; several Kingdoms rose out of its Ruins, and many Languages were form'd

---

[1] 1728 used.

[2] Cf. Voltaire's Commentaries on Corneille where numerous passages of the
Pharsalia are indicated as sources. *Oeuvres*, XXXI, pp. 171 ff.

[3] *Cato* (tragedy), 1713. Cf. Lanson, *Lettres phil.*, II, pp. 84-85: " Le premier
Anglais qui ait fait une pièce raisonnable & écrite d'un bout à l'autre avec
élégance, est l'illustre Mr. Adisson. Son Caton d'Utique est un chef-d'oeuvre
pour la diction, & pour la beauté des vers. . . . Le Caton de Mr. Adisson me
paroît le plus beau personnage qui soit sur aucun théâtre."
Cf. *Discours sur la tragédie*, *Oeuvres*, II, p. 322: "Aussi la tragédie de *Caton*,
qui fait tant d'honneur à M. Addison, votre successeur dans le ministère, cette
tragédie, la seule bien écrite d'un bout à l'autre chez votre nation, à ce que je
vous [Bolingbroke] ai entendu dire à vous même, ne doit sa grande réputation
qu'à ses beaux vers . . ."
Cf. *Essai*, p. 317: "Je n'ai jamais vu à Londres la salle de la comédie aussi
remplie à *l'Andromaque* de Racine, toute bien traduite qu'elle est par Philips,
ou au *Caton* d'Addison, qu'aux anciennes pièces de Shakespeare."

[4] 1728 Antient.

[5] 1728 than.

[6] The indebtedness of Addison to Lucan is not mentioned in the French,
nor is that of Corneille save for an indirect allusion. The closing words of
the French chapter are expressive and characteristic of the conventional comparisons mentioned earlier. *Essai*, p. 329: "Ce n'est presque plus [*The Pharsalia*] qu'une gazette pleine de déclamations: il me semble que je vois un por-
tique hardi et immense qui conduit à des ruines."

[7] Giovanni Georgio Trissino, 1478-1550, *L'Italia liberata dai Goti*, 1547-48.
Cf. *Essai*, p. 329, Chapitre V, *Le Trissin*. As in the English, the chief interest
of this chapter lies in the digressions. The brief pages concerning Trissino
are much the same in French and in English but the digressions are somewhat
different. The French chapter is rather shorter than the English. The passage concerning the possible use of Latin by modern writers has been omitted.
Other alterations and additions will be indicated in the notes.

out of the remains of the *Latin* Tongue.[1] The *Northen*[2] Invaders brought everywhere their Roughness and their Ignorance. Their Language made up at first of a corrupted *Latin*, and of irregular *Gotick*,[3] were[4] as uncouth as their Manners, and as destitute of Words as their Minds of *Ideas*.[5]

|In the Course of a thousand Years, the *Italian*,[6] the *French*, 66 the *Spaniards*, refin'd their Manners and their Idioms, and learning spreading itself by Degrees almost over all *Europe*, enlarg'd the Sphere of every Language.

Many Writers complain now-a-days, that the *Latin* is us'd[7] only in the Schools, and in the *Romish* Churches; they upbraid the Insufficiency of modern Languages; they say that their own Idioms sink under their Imagination. But they would have more to complain of, if according to their Desires the *Latin* was still the Language of *Europe*; for in that Case, very little Room would be left for their Labours. A Multitude of ancient Authors more generally read and better understood would shut up all the Avenues to the Ambition of the Modern. To imitate *Virgil* or *Tully* would be a Plagiarism, to deviate from them, an Affectation. The World overstocked with Models of Writing would discountenance any new Endeavour, and the greatest Genius would be discouraged.

On the contrary, he who writes in a modern Language, hath the Ancients for his Guides, not for his Rivals; when he imitates them, he enriches his own Country; the particular Cast of his Mother-tongue awakens his Imagination into new Turns, and bestows an air of Novelty | on some Conceptions which otherwise 67 would have appear'd too common. In short every new Language occasions some new Productions.

The *Italian* Tongue was at the end of the fifteenth Century brought to the Perfection in which it continues now, and in which

---

[1] Cf. *English Review*, Feb. 1914, p. 318 (Note-book of Voltaire): "From the rubishes of the roman empire several kingdoms are formed and grounded upon its ruines; in the same manner, italian tongue, the french, the spanish arose from the ruines of the roman language."

[2] 1728 *Northern*. Cf. *Errata*, p. 79, *ante*.

[3] 1728 Gothick.

[4] 1728 was. Cf. *Errata*.

[5] In the French version (p. 329) a sentence even more scornful with regard to the middle ages, and therefore very characteristic of French classicism, has been added: "Ce qui nous reste malheureusement de l'architecture et de la sculpture de ces temps-là est un composé bizarre de grossièreté et de colifichets. Le peu qu'on écrivait était dans le même goût."

[6] 1728 Italians. Cf. *Errata*.

[7] 1728 used.

it will remain as long as *Tasso* in Poetry, and *Machiavel* in Prose shall be the Standart[1] of the Stile.[2]

Tasso was in his Childhood, when *Trissino* (the Author of the first Tragedy written in a modern Language[3]) lanch'd[4] out into the attempt of an *Epick* Poem.[5] His Subject was *Italy* deliver'd from the *Goths* by *Belizarius*[6] under *Justinian*. The Subject was noble, the Performance was mean, but still succeeded, and this Dawning shone a little in a time of Darkness, till it was absorb'd in the broad Day of *Tasso*.

Trissino was a Man of great Parts, and of extensive Learning, he was employ'd by *Leo* the Tenth in many great Affairs, and had succeeded very well in his Embassy to the Emperor *Charles* the Fifth. But at last he sacrificed his Ambition, and worldly Affairs, to his Passion for Letters, which at that Time were reputed honourable, because they were newly reviv'd in *Europe*, and in 68 the Glo|ry of their Prime.[7] He was justly fond of *Homer*, and yet his great Fault is to have imitated him; for Imitation requires more Art than is generally believed. The Flowers of the ancient[8] appear but wither'd when gather'd by unskilful Hands.[9] This I insist upon, because nothing is more common than Authors who mangle *Homer* and *Virgil* in their own Productions, and screen themselves under those great Names, without suspecting that the

[1] 1728 Standard.

[2] Rolli (*Remarks*, p. 67) objects to this sentence and speaks of Dante, Petrarch and Boccacio, belonging to the late thirteenth and the fourteenth centuries, as the " first, best, never-interrupted standards of style." In the French essay this sentence was omitted and replaced by a paragraph beginning: " La poésie fut le premier art qui fût cultivé avec succès. Dante et Pétrarque écrivirent dans un temps où l'on n'avait pas encore un ouvrage de prose supportable." *Essai*, p. 330. There follows a digression on poetry as preceding prose.

[3] *Sophinisba* written 1515, printed 1524.

[4] 1728 launch'd.

[5] This statement must be understood to refer to the completion of Trissino's poem in 1548. He began the writing of it in 1527. Tasso was not born until 1544.

[6] Belisarius.

[7] The respect due the profession of letters was a favorite subject of Voltaire's. Cf. Lanson, *Lettres phil.*, Letter 23.
   In the *Essai* an interesting addition has been made at this point (p. 330): " Bien différent en cela de quelques hommes célèbres que nous avons vus quitter et même mépriser les lettres, après avoir fait fortune par elles." Voltaire no doubt had Congreve in mind. Cf. Lanson, *Lettres phil.*, II, p. 108: "Il [Congreve] avoit un défaut, c'étoit de ne pas assez estimer son premier métier d'auteur, qui avoit fait sa réputation & sa fortune."

[8] 1728 Ancients.

[9] Cf. p. 84, *ante*. Cf. also Steele in *Spectator*, III, p. 119: " The Antients had a Secret to give a lasting Beauty, Colour, and Sweetness to some of their choice Flowers, which flourish to this Day, and which few of the Moderns can effect."

very Things which are to be admired in *Virgil*, may be ridiculous in them.

Thus *Trissino*, for Example, endeavours to imitate that beautiful passage of *Homer*, where *Juno* having summon'd all her Charms, and adorn'd with the Girdle of *Venus*, deludes her Husband into an unusual Fondness.

The Wife of *Justinian* hath the same Design upon her Husband. First she washes herself in her fine Closet, she put[1] on a clean Shift, and after the long enumerations of all the Trinkets of her Toilette,[2] she comes alone into a little Garden where the Emperor was sitting down: She coins a Lie,[3] she allures him by some Coquettries, and at last the Emperor—

> Le Diede un Bacio
> Suave; e, le getto le braccia all collo.
> |E ella stette e sorridendo disse.   69
> Signor mio dolce or che volete fare ?
> Che se venisse alguno in questo luogo
> E ci vedesse, havrei tanta vergogna
> Che piu non ardirei levar la fronte;
> Entriamo nelle nostre usate stanze,
> Chiudamo li usci, e sopra il vostro letto
> Ponianci, e fate poi, quel che vi piace.
> L'imperador rispose; alma mia vita,
> Non dubitate dela vista altrui:
> Che qui non puo venir persona humana,
> Senon per la mia Stanza.   E io la chiusi
> Come qui venni, e ho la chiave a canto;
> E penso che ancor vi chiudeste l'uscio
> Che vien in esso dele Stanze vostre;
> Perche giamai non lo lasciaste aperto:
> E detto questo, subito abbraciolla;
> Poi se colcar ne la minuta herbetta,
> La quale allegra lii fioriva d'intorno, &c.[4]

" The Emperor gave her a Kiss, and folded her tenderly in his Arms. She paused a little, and said, O my Sweet Lord, what will you do ! should any body come hither and spye[5] us, I could

[1] 1728 puts. Cf. *Errata*.
[2] 1728 Toilet.
[3] 1728 Lye.
[4] Cf. *L'Italia liberata da' Goti*, Parigi, 1729, I, pp. 102-103.
[5] 1728 spy.

never show my Face, for Shame. Let us step into our Bed-
Chamber, let us lock up all the Doors, and when we are together
70 upon our Bed, you may do with me what you please. The | Em-
peror answered, My Dear, my Soul ! do not lie under any fear
of being discovered: For not one living Soul can arrive at us
but through my Chamber; I took care to shut the Door as I came
hither, and I have the Key in my Pocket; I suppose too you have
the Key of the Back-Door which opens from your Apartment
intô mine, for you never leave it open: he said, and hugged her.
The tender Grass on which they dallied, rejoiced at their Pleas-
ures, and shot forth into tender Flowers."

Thus what is beautiful and noble between *Jove* and *Juno*, becomes as low and distasteful between the old *Justinian* and *Theo-
dora;* as when among us a Man and Wife caress one another before
Company.

Trissino hath especially endeavour'd to follow *Homer* in the
Detail of the Descriptions; but he is very accurate in describing
the Furniture of the Houses of his Heroes: He does not omit a
Button, or a Garter in their Dresses; and does not say a Word of
their Characters.

However, I do not mention him only to point out his Faults,
but to give him the just Praise he deserves; for having been the
71 first in *Europe*, who attempted | an *Epick* Poem, in a vulgar
Tongue, and in blank Verse; for not having been Guilty of a single
Quibble in his Works, though he was an *Italian*;[1] and for having
introduc'd less Magicians, and fewer inchanted Heroes, than any
Author of his Nation.

CAMOUENS.[2]

While *Trissino* was clearing away the Rubbish in *Italy*, which
Barbarity and Ignorance had heap'd up for ten Centuries, in the

---

[1] Cf. *Essai*, p. 332: " Il est le seul des poëtes italiens dans lequel il n'y ait
ni jeux de mots ni pointes." Unlike most of the allusions to Italian taste and
Italian literature this one has not become more favorable in the French. Cf.
also pp. 109, note 2; 116, note 6, *post.*

[2] Cf. *Essai*, p. 332, Chapitre VI, *Le Camoëns.* This chapter is remarkably
inaccurate, showing a very superficial knowledge of the poem in question and
no acquaintance whatever with the original. As it appeared in 1733, the French
version differs considerably less from the English than does the form in which
we now know it, important corrections and additions having been made in
1742. Cf. pp. 154-156, *post.* When this section was put into French the
allusions to Waller and Denham were omitted. On the other hand further
biographical information was added, as was the passage extolling a part of the
Lusiads sure to interest the French which is not even mentioned in the Eng-

Way of the Arts and Sciences,[1] *Camouens* in *Portugal* steer'd a new Course, and acquir'd a Reputation which lasts still among his Countrymen, who pay as much Respect to his Memory, as the *English* to *Milton*.[2]

He was a strong instance of the irresistable Impulse of Nature, which determines a true Genius to follow the Bent of his Talents, in Spight of all the Obstacles which could check his Course.

His Infancy lost amid the Idleness and Ignorance of the Court of *Lisbon*; his Youth spent in romantick Loves, or in the War against the *Moors;* his long Voyages at Sea, in his riper Years; his Misfortunes at Court, the Revolutions of his Country, none of all these could suppress his Genius.

Emanuel the second King of *Portugal*,[3] | having a mind to 72 find a new Way to the *East-Indies* by the Ocean,[4] sent *Velasco de Gama*[5] with a Fleet in the Year 1497, to that Undertaking, which being new was accounted rash and impracticable, and which of Course gain'd him a great Reputation when it succeeded.

Camouens follow'd *Velasco de Gama* in that dangerous Voyage, led by his Friendship to him, and by a noble Curiosity, which seldom fails to be the Character of Men born with a great Imagination.[6]

lish—the episode of Inez de Castro (cf. p. 71, note 1, *ante*). At the end of the chapter as it now reads the lack of connection between the various parts of the poem, a point which had not been touched upon in the English, is called the gravest defect. This passage was added between 1738 and 1742.

[1] The opening words of the French chapter on Camoens are quite different in tone: " Tandis que le Trissin, en Italie, suivait d'un pas timide et faible les traces des anciens . . ." *Essai*, p. 332.

[2] Cf. *ibid.*: " Une réputation qui dure parmi ses compatriotes, qui l'appellent le *Virgile portugais*."

[3] There has been no Emanuel II of Portugal. It was Emanuel I (1469-1521) who sent Vasco da Gama on his famous expedition in 1497. *Emanuel the second* remains uncorrected in the English editions of the essay. In the French the Portuguese king is called *Emmanuel-le-Grand*.

[4] A criticism from Mickle's pen occurring at this point seems far-fetched and is based upon an unnecessary interpretation of Voltaire's words. " ' That Gama went a new way to the East Indies by the ocean,' " we read, " though corrected in the edition of 1768, affords a most striking proof of Voltaire's very careless perusal of the Lusiad, at the time when he first presumed to condemn it. For it is often repeated in the poem, there was no way to India by the ocean before." Mickle, p. 607, note.

[5] This incorrect form appears in all the English editions. The name was written Verasco de Gama in the French translation and that spelling was not corrected by Voltaire when he republished the translation. In the first editions of the French version we find Velasco which was changed to Vasco between 1742 and 1746.

[6] Since the date of Camoens birth is 1524,* this is obviously an incorrect statement. As a matter of fact Camoens' grandfather accompanied da Gama. In a comparatively early edition of the French version Voltaire acknowledged

He took his Voyage for the Subject of his Poem; he enjoy'd the sensible Pleasure, which no-body had known before him, to celebrate his Friend, and the Things which he was an Eye-Witness of. He wrote his Poem, Part on the *Atlantic Sea*, and Part on the *Indian Shore;* I ought not to omit, that in a Shipwrack[1] on the Coasts of *Malabar*,[2] he swam a Shore, holding up his Poem in one Hand, which otherwise had been perhaps lost for ever. Such a new Subject, manag'd by an uncommon Genius, could not but produce a Sort of *Epick* Poetry unheard of before.

There no bloody Wars are fought, no Heroes wounded in a 73 thousand different Ways; no Woman enticed away, and | the World overturn'd for her Cause; no Empire founded; in short nothing of what was deem'd before the only Subject of Poetry.

The Poet conducts the *Portugese* Fleet to the Mouth of the *Ganges*,[3] round the Coasts of *Africk*. He takes Notice in the Way, of many Nations who live upon the *African* Shore. He interweaves artfully the History of *Portugal*. The Simplicity of his Subject, is rais'd by some Fictions of different Kinds, which I think not improper to acquaint the Reader with.

When the Fleet is sailing in the Sight[4] of the *Cape of Good-Hope*, call'd then the *Cape of the Storms*, a formidable Shape appears to them, walking in the Depth of the Sea; his Head reaches

his mistake† (pp. 154, 155, *post*), but in all the French editions we are told that Camoens came to Lisbon during the first year of the reign of Emanuel the Great, that is in 1495 or 1496. Again, in the French as in the English, Camoens is spoken of as a contemporary of Trissino who was born in 1478 and who died in 1550, his poem dating from 1547 and 1548. (The *Lusiads* was published in 1572 and Camoens died in 1580.) In referring to the Portuguese poet's " noble curiosity " Voltaire may have had himself in mind.

* Until recent years authorities differed as to this date, some giving 1517, others 1524.

† Mickle (p. 607, note) speaks of this correction as dating from 1768. As a matter of fact it had been made over twenty-five years earlier. It appears that Mickle consulted only two editions of the French version of the Essay, that of 1738 and that of 1768, and drew his conclusions from them. This critic (p. 608, note) calls attention to the fact that even in the edition of 1768, in an essay called " Idée de la Henriade," Voltaire repeats the assertion that Camoens " a célébré un évènement dont il avait été témoin lui-même."

[1] 1728 Shipwreck.

[2] This wreck, that of the annual ship from China to India, occurred, not off the coast of Malabar, but at the mouth of the Mekong or Cambodia river which flows through southeastern Asia into the China Sea. (Cf. Mickle, p. 607, note.) In the French version of the essay the disaster is spoken of as having taken place " sur les côtes de la Chine." (P. 333.)

[3] As a matter of fact Gama's voyage did not extend to the mouth of the Ganges but only to Calicut on the southwest coast of India (the coast of Malabar). Cf. *The Lusiads*, Cantos VI, VII, VIII, IX and X. Cf. also Mickle, p. 607, note.

[4] 1728 in Sight.

to the Clouds, the Storms, the Winds, the Thunders, and the Lightnings hang about him; his Arms are extended over the Waves. 'Tis the Guardian of that foreign Ocean unplough'd before by any Ship. He complains of his being oblig'd to submit to Fate, and to the audacious Undertaking of the *Portugese*, and fortels them all the Misfortunes which they must undergo in the *Indies*.[1]

I believe, that such a Fiction would be thought noble and proper, in all Ages, and in all Nations.

|There is another, which perhaps would have pleas'd the *Italians* 74 as well as the *Portugese*, but no other Nation besides:[2] It is an inchanted Island, call'd the Island of Bliss, which the Fleet finds in her Way home, just rising from the Sea, for their Comfort and for their Reward: *Camouens* describes that Place, as *Tasso* did some Years after, his Island of *Armida*. There a supernatural Power, brings in all the Beauties, and presents all the Pleasures which Nature can afford, and which the Heart may wish for; a Goddess enamour'd with *Velasco de Gama*, carries him to the Top of an high Mountain, from whence she shows him all the Kingdoms of the Earth, and foretells[3] the Fate of *Portugal*.

After *Camouens* hath given loose[4] to his Fancy, in the lascivious Description of the Pleasures which *Gama* and his Crew enjoy'd in the Island, he takes care to inform the Reader, that he ought to understand by this Fiction, nothing but the Satisfaction which the virtuous Man feels, and the Glory which accrues to him by the Practice of Virtue; but the best Excuse for such an Invention, is, the charming Stile in which it is deliver'd (if we believe the *Portugese*) for the Beauty of the Elocution makes sometimes amends for the Faults of the Poets,[5] | as the colouring of *Rubens* 75 make Defects in his Figures pass unregarded.

There is *another* Kind of *Machinery* continued throughout all the Poem, which nothing can excuse, in any Country whatever; 'tis an unjudicious[6] mixture of the Heathen Gods with our Reli-

---

[1] This rather picturesque description of the phantom which appeared to the Portuguese is far from following the original closely. Cf. *The Lusiads*, Canto V and Mickle, p. 617, note.

[2] In the French, Voltaire still considers this Fiction "conforme au génie italien."

[3] 1728 foretels.

[4] 1728 hath given a loose to. Cf. *Spectator*, II, p. 434: " . . . have given a Loose to their Imaginations."

[5] 1728 Poet.

[6] 1728 injudicious.

gion. *Gama* in a Storm addresses his Prayers to the *Christ*,[1] but 'tis *Venus* who comes to his Relief; the Heroes are *Christians*, and the Poet *Heathen*. The main Design which the *Portugese* are suppos'd to have (next to the promoting of their Trade) is to propogate *Christianity*; yet *Jupiter*, *Bacchus*, and *Venus*, have in their Hands, all the Management of the Voyage. So incongruous a *Machinery*, casts a Blemish upon the whole Poem; yet shows at the same Time, how prevailing are its Beauties, since the *Portugese* like it with all its faults.[2]

Camouens hath a great deal of true Wit, and not a little Share of false; his Imagination hurries him into great Absurdities. I

---

[1] 1728 to Christ. Cf. *Errata*, p. 79, *ante*.

[2] Cf. Rapin, *Réflexions sur la poétique*, p. 100: " Le Camoëns qui parle sans discretion de Vénus, de Bacchus & des autres divinités profanes dans un poème chrétien."

Voltaire no doubt felt that his repeated criticism of the mixture of heathen and Christian ideas emphasized a good point of his own poem in which he was proud to have "laid aside the gods of antiquity." Rolli's opinion in regard to this point is interesting. Remarking that the mixture of pagan and Christian ideas is "granted by custom to all great poets" he goes on: "It is indeed the first time I have heard a Poet, who out of Eagerness of disparaging the greatest Poets, would destroy all Poetical Licences & even the most allowed which are the greatest Beauties of Poetry and then to be guilty himself of what he blamed others for." *Remarks*, p. 92. " It is singular to see in Voltaire Lewdness, Religion, Discord, Love, Pope, Prophecy, Witchcraft, Inquisition, Heaven and Hell . . . Saints & Visions heaped together." *Ibid.*, p. 85.

In regard to the sentence: " 'Gama in a storm addresses his prayers to Christ, but it is Venus who comes to his relief,' " Mickle attempts to break down this criticism of Voltaire's by saying "but there is no such passage in the Lusiad" (p. 609), basing his assertion apparently on the fact that the name of Christ does not appear in the Portuguese. He himself, however, translates certain lines of the passage in question as follows:

" 'Oh Thou!' he cries 'whom trembling Heaven obeys,
Whose will the tempest's furious madness sways,
Who, through the wild waves, ledds't thy chosen race,
While the high billows stood like walls of brass:
. . . . . .
Oh! save us now, be now the Saviour God!' "
Pp. 697-698, ll. 647 ff.

It matters little whether this prayer, which is followed by the intervention of Venus, was addressed to God or Christ. The incongruity remains the same. Like Rolli, Mickle sees in the *Henriade* a mixture of Christian ideas and of allegorical characters created in imitation of heathen machinery (p. 615). As regards the general acceptance of Voltaire's estimate of Camoens, Mickle says (p. 607): " Yet this criticism, though most superficial and erroneous, has been generally esteemed throughout Europe, as the true character of that poem." And indeed in many encyclopedia articles, reference is still made to Voltaire's criticism of the Portuguese poet.

In this connection there occurs in the French a sentence indicative of Voltaire's feeling for local-color, corresponding to one found elsewhere in the English essay but suppressed at that point in the French: "De même que les beautés de l'exécution ont placé Paul Véronèse parmi les grands peintres, quoiqu'il ait placé des pères bénédictins et des soldats suisses dans des sujets de *l'Ancien-Testament*." *Essai*, p. 335. Cf. p. 123, note 4, *post*.

remember,[1] that after *Velasco de Gama*, hath related his Adventures to the King of *Melinda*, now says he, O *King, judge if* Ulysses, *and* Aeneas *have travell'd so far, and undergone so many Hard|ships.* 76 As if that barberous *African*, was acquainted with *Homer* and *Virgil.*[2]

His Poem, in my Opinion, is full of numberless Faults and Beauties, thick sown near one another; and almost in every Page there is what to laugh at, and what to be delighted with. Among his most lucky Thoughts, I must take Notice of two for the Likeness, which they bear to two most celebrated Passages of *Waller* and Sir *John Denham*.[3] *Waller* says, in his Epistle to *Zelinda*;

> *Thy matchless Form will Credit bring,*
> *To all the Wonders I can sing.*[4]

Camouens says, in speaking of the Voyages of the *Argonautes*, and of *Ulysses*, that the Undertaking of the *Portugese* shall give Credit to all those Fables, in surpassing them.

Sir *John Denham*, in his Poem on *Coopers-Hill*, says to the *Thames*:

> *O could I flow like thee, and make thy Stream,*
> *My great Example, as it is my Theme;*
> *Tho' deep, yet clear, tho' gentle, yet not dull,*
> *Strong without Rage, without o'erflowing full.*[6]

Camouens addresses the Nymphs of *Tagus* in the like Manner; "O Nymphs, if ever I sung of you, inspire me now | with new 77

---

[1] This word is interesting in the light of Voltaire's evident lack of familiarity with certain events of the poem.

[2] Mickle (p. 609, note) objects at this point that the Melindians are, according to history, "a humane and polished people."

[3] Edmund Waller, 1605-1687; Sir John Denham, 1615-1669. Cf. Lanson, *Lettres phil.*, II, p. 126: "On a beaucoup entendu parler du célèbre Waller en France." But in 1728 Voltaire had written: "The articles relating to Milton, to sir John Denham, Waller, Dryden must needs be altogether out of the way of a French reader." Cf. p. 70, note 6, *ante*. Cf. Pope, *Essay on Criticism*, II, ll. 360, 361:
> " And praise the easy vigour of a line,
> Where Denham's strength, and Waller's sweetness join."

[4] Waller, *Works*, ed. Fenton, p. 163. The second line reads: " To all the wonders I shall sing."

[5] 1728 *Argonots*.

[6] *The Works of the English Poets*, ed. Chalmers, VII, pp. 236-237 (*Denham's Poems*). Cf. Dryden, ed. Scott–Saintsbury, XIV, p. 207, *Dedication of the Aeneis*, 1697: "I am sure there are few who make verses, have observed the sweetness of these two lines in *Cooper's Hill*—
> ' Though deep, yet clear; though gentle, yet not dull;
> Strong without rage; without o'erflowing full.'
and there are yet fewer who can find the reason of that sweetness."

and strong Lays; Let my Stile flow like your Waves; let it be deep and clear as your Waters, &c." [1]

It is not to be inferr'd from thence, that *Waller* and Sir *John Denham* have imitated *Camouens*; we must only conclude, that Wit is of the Growth of every Country. It is very unjust, and very common, to call Plagiarism what is but Resemblance.

TASSO. [2]

Torquato Tasso began his *Jerusalem*, when *Camouens* was finishing his *Lusiada*. [3] He us'd to say that the only Rival he fear'd in *Europe* was *Camouens*. [4] His Fear (if sincere) was very ill-

---

[1] This passage translated literally from the Portuguese of Camoens reads:
"And you, my nymphs of Tagus, since you have created in me a new ardent genius, if your stream has always been joyfully celebrated by me in humble verse: grant me now a lofty and sublime note, an eloquent and high sounding style; for of your waters Phoebus ordains that they shall not envy those of Hippocrene." (For this translation I am indebted to Supt. G. W. Barwick of the British Museum). In the English translation of the Lusiads made in 1655 by R. Fanshawe the passage is rendered:
" And you my Tagus' Nymphs, since ye did raise
My Wit to more than ordinary flame:
If I, in low, yet tuneful Verse, the praise
Of your sweet River always did proclame:
Inspire me now with high and thundering lays:
Give me them cleer and flowing like his stream;
That to your Waters Phoebus may ordaine
They do not envy those of Hyppocrane."
In 1753 Baretti (*Dissertation*, p. 71) merely says that Voltaire has endeavored to impose on the reader by translating falsely some lines of Camoens to create a resemblance between them and a passage of Denham. Mickle points out (p. 610, note) that the idea Similar to that of Denham was not contained in the original but was added by Fanshawe.

[2] Cf. *Essai*, p. 336, Chapitre VII, *Le Tasse*. Here again the French chapter is several pages longer than the English. Various parts of the English, however, have been omitted, for instance that regarding the inscription on Tasso's tomb, the unfavorable comment upon modern French writers, and several passages which will be indicated in the notes, three concerning religion, the criticism of Tasso's commenting upon himself, including the anecdote of the ambassador and the sentence at the end of the chapter having to do with local color. We shall also see that one of the episodes of the poem is related in much less detail and that remarks concerning Italian taste have been made less offensive.
On the other hand comments on Ariosto, varying considerably in earlier editions of the *Essai* (cf. pp. 156, 157, *post*), have been added at the beginning and the biographical information has been greatly elaborated. Certain sentences appear in the French which seem to make the chapter still more definitely anti Homeric and others which emphasize the idea of comparative literature. A characteristic comment on the folly of the crusades has been inserted.

[3] The *Gerusalemme Liberata* was begun in 1575 and published in 1581. The *Lusiads* appeared in 1572.

[4] Cf. Fanshawe, *Lusiad, Dedication*: " He [Tasso] was heard to say (his great Jerusalem being then an embrio) he feared no man but Camoëns."

grounded; for he was as far superior to him, as that *Portugese* excell'd the Poets of his own Country.

No Man in the World was ever born with a greater Genius, and more qualify'd for *Epick* Poetry.[1] His Talents which gain'd him so great a Reputation, were the Cause of his Misfortunes. His Life prov'd a Chain of Miseries and Woes. Banish'd from his own Country, he was reduc'd to the grievous Necessity of having a Patron. He suffer'd Want, Exile, and Prison; and which is more intolerable, he was oppress'd by Calumny.

|Even his poetical Glory, that chimerical Comfort in real Calami-78 ties, was contested. The Number of his Enemies eclips'd for a long while his Reputation.[2] And at last when his Merit began to overcome Envy, when he was ready to receive the Honour of Triumph in *Rome*, which *Petrarch* had formerly enjoy'd (though with less Merit) and which was at that Time as glorious as it is now ridiculous, he dy'd[3] the very Day before the design'd Solemnity.[4]

Nothing discovers more plainly the high Sense which *Rome* entertain'd of his Merit, than the Inscription on his Tomb.

The *Pope*, who order'd him a magnificent Funeral, as if it were to atone for the Misfortunes of his Life, propos'd a Reward for the best Epitaph which should be written in his Honour.

Many were brought to him, all full of the just Praises of *Tasso*. The Judges appointed to chuse the Epitaph, were divided in their Opinions, when a young Man came to them with this Inscription,

Torquati Tassi ossa.

The Judges immediately agreed in giving the Preference to it, being persua|ded that the name of *Tasso* was his greatest Encom-79 ium.[5]

---

[1] In the preface of the fifth edition of his translation of *Jerusalem Delivered*, 1783, John Hoole refers to Voltaire's favorable opinion of Tasso, expressed in his *Essay on Epic Poetry*. From his summary of Voltaire's comments, it is evident that, although writing in London, Hoole was using the French version of the essay. Cf. *The Works of the English Poets*, Chalmers, XXI, pp. 389 ff.

[2] Voltaire never fails to think of himself. There can be no doubt that he has in mind the similarity between his own misfortunes and Tasso's.

[3] 1728 died.

[4] Modern authorities agree that arrangements had been made for the crowning of Tasso with the laurel wreath when he died, April 25, 1595. The statement that his death occurred the day before he was to have been crowned is open to question.

[5] It is significant that this interesting piece of information, which it seems difficult to substantiate, has been omitted in the French version of the essay.

Time, which undermines the Reputation of indifferent Authors, hath stamp'd the Character of Immortality upon his Works. His Poem is sung now-a-days in many Parts of *Italy*, as the Poems of *Homer* were in *Greece;* and if the Poets, his Successors, have degenerated from him, if *Italy* is now over-grown with pitiful Sonnets and Conceits; still the Taste of the Nation form'd after his Poems remains in its full Force: He is admir'd by the Readers, though not imitated by the Writers. Thus in *France, Corneille, Racine, Boylau,*[1] *la Fontaine, Molière*, will claim for ever the publick Admiration, in Defiance to a succeeding Set of Writers, who have introduc'd a new fangl'd Stile, kept up and cherish'd among themselves, but despis'd by the Nation.

The *Jerusalem liberata*, is in some Parts an Imitation of the *Iliad*. The Subject of *Tasso* is nobler than that of *Homer*, in as much as all *Europe*, rising up in Arms for the Recovery of the Land which is consecrated by the Birth and Blood of their God, strikes the Mind with a more awful Idea, than *Greece* fighting against *Troy*, for *Helena*.

80 |As to the Disposition of so great a Work, the impartial Reader may judge if *Tasso* is above, or under his Master, in what he copies from him.

Goffredo acts methinks the Part of *Agamemnon*, with as much Grandeur, less Pride, and more Wisdom.

The Hermit *Piero* is the *Calcas;* and if I dare speak my Opinion, I find nothing very shining nor defective in either.

Rinaldo, is among the *Christian* Princes what *Achilles* is among the *Grecian* Heroes. His Courage is full as boisterous, but his Character more amiable. The Fall of *Jerusalem* is reserv'd to his Sword, as that of *Troy* to the Arms of *Achilles*. The Absence of the one from the Camp, is borrow'd from the Inaction of the other; but certainly *Rinaldo* employs his Leisure more to the Satisfaction of the Reader, than the Heroe[2] of *Homer* does.

As a matter of fact, it appears that it was Tasso's protector, Cardinal Cinzio, who intended erecting a magnificent monument to his memory but it was not until thirteen years later that this intention was carried out by Cardinal Boniface Bevilacqua. It is also stated that Tasso himself had directed that his epitaph should be, " Hic jacet Torquatus Tassus." Cf. Boulting, *Tasso and his Times*, pp. 302, 303. The inscription on the monument of 1608 reads: "D. O. M. Torquati Tassi Ossa illic jacent. Hoc ne nescius Esses, hospes, Fratres hujius eclesiae posuerunt." Cf. *Biographie Générale*, Paris, 1864.

[1] 1728 Boileau. This passage does not appear in the French. Cf. p. 71, *ante*.

[2] 1728 Hero.

Aladino, Sultan of *Jerusalem,* is in nothing like *Priam,* but in his being the King of the Town beseig'd; and *Argante* bears no other Resemblance to *Hector,* but in his being the firmest Bulwark of the City.

Certainly the Character of *Hector* is every way above that of *Argante,* and the grandeur of *Priam* more majestick, and his Misfortunes more touching than those of *A|ladin.*[1]   I will not 81 decide, if *Homer* hath done right or wrong, in gaining upon our Affections towards *Hector,* and in moving our Pity for *Priam;* but sure it is, that if *Tasso* had not represented *Aladin* and *Argante* rough and unamiable, if he had not skilfully created an Aversion to them, in the Mind of the Reader, he had defeated his own Intention; for in that Case, instead of being concern'd for the Cause of the *Christian* Princes, we should look upon them as Plunderers, united together to lay waste a foreign Country, and to massacre in cold Blood, an old venerable *Eastern* Monarch, together with his innocent Subjects.[2]

Tasso hath learn'd from *Homer,* the Art of marking the different Shades of the same Colour, I mean the different *Kinds* of the same *Virtue,* of distinguishing the *Valiant* from the *Valiant,* and the *Prudent* from the *Prudent,* &c.[3]   Thus *Goffredo* is sedate and wise, *Aladin* anxious and cruel.   The generous Valour of *Tanerede,*[4] shines in Opposition to the brutal Impetuosity of *Argante.* Love in *Armida* is a Mixture of Coquettry and Rage, in *Herminia* a gentle Tenderness.   Every one of his Actors is to be known by some distinguishable Mark, | as in the *Iliad,* and everyone of them 82 acts always suitable to his Character, which is not always to be found in *Homer;* and in that respect methinks he hath improv'd the Art which *Homer* taught him, but an Art which he learn'd

---

[1] Written *Aladino* at the bottom of p. 80 and *Aladin* at the top of p. 81.

[2] In the *Essai* a paragraph has been added which is very characteristic of Voltaire.   He seldom lost an opportunity to inveigh against fanaticism in any form.   The opening sentence reads (p. 341): "C'était une chose bien étrange que la folie des croisades." The writer goes on to speak of the evils attendant upon the crusades.

[3] Cf. Addison in *Spectator,* II, p. 233: "His [Homer's] Princes are as much distinguished by their Manners, as by their Dominions; and even those among them, whose Characters seem wholly made up of Courage, differ from one another as to the particular kinds of Courage in which they excel."

Cf. Pope, *Iliad,* preface, p. 5: "Nothing can be more exact than the distinctions he has observed in the different degrees of virtues and vices. The single quality of courage is wonderfully diversified in the several characters of the Iliad."

[4] 1728 Tancrede.

from no body.[1] 'Tis that inchanting Way of interresting[2] us for his Heroes, 'tis that unexpressible[3] Address in interweaving the different Adventures of the Poem, in leading us from the Alarms of Wars, to the Allurements of Love, and from Love to War again; in working up our Concern by Degrees, and in rising above himself from Book to Book.

As to his Style, it is perspicuous and elegant through all the Poem; and when he enters into Descriptions which require Strength and Majesty, it is wonderful how the natural Effeminacy of the *Italian* Language soars up into Sublimity and Grandeur, and assumes a new Character in his Hands, if we except about an hundred Lines[4] in which he flattens into pitiful Conceits, but I look on these Errors as a kind of Tribute, which his Genius condescended to pay to the *Italian* Taste.[5]

If his Excellencies challenge the unanimous Admiration of 83 *Europe*, there are Faults in him which methinks are cen|sur'd everywhere.[6]   The episode of *Olinda*[7] and *Sophronia* in the beginning of the Action seems defective in all respects.

The Poet introduces a *Mahometan* Magician call'd *Ismeno*, who against the strict and never violated Laws of the *Mahometan* Religion, carries an Image of the Virgin *Mary* into the principal *Mosquee*,[8] in order to make it by the Force of his Enchantments the Pledge and Security of the Town, as formerly the Fate of *Troy* depended upon the *Palladium*. It happens one Night that the Image is stol'n[9] away, the Christians of *Jerusalem* being

---

[1] The comparison between Homer and Tasso, although briefer in the French, is more distinctly favorable to Tasso: "J'ose dire que le Tasse a été bien au delà de son modèle. Il a autant de feu qu'Homère dans ses batailles, avec plus de variété. Ses héros ont tous des caractères différents comme ceux de *l'Iliade;* mais ses caractères sont mieux annoncés, plus fortement décrits, et mieux soutenus; car il n'y en a presque pas un seul qui ne se démente dans le poëte grec, et pas un qui ne soit invariable dans l'italien. Il a peint ce qu' Homère crayonnait . . ." (p. 340).

[2] 1728 interesting.

[3] 1728 inexpressible.

[4] Cf. *Essai*, p. 342: " Environ deux cents vers."

[5] Cf. *ibid.*: " Mais ces faiblesses étaient une espèce de tribut que son génie payait au mauvais goût de son siècle pour les pointes, qui même a augmenté depuis lui, mais dont les Italiens sont entièrement désabusés." The significant phrase " mais dont les Italiens etc.," was added between 1742 and 1746. Cf. p. 157, *post.*

[6] Cf. *ibid.*: " Il y a aussi bien des endroits qu'on n'approuve qu'en Italie, et quelques uns qui ne doivent plaire nulle part."

[7] 1728 *Olindo.* Cf. *Errata.*

[8] 1728 Mosque.

[9] 1728 stolen.

suspected of the Theft, the *Sultan* incens'd, sentences them all to Death, that he might be sure to punish the guilty in the common Slaughter. Meanwhile *Sophronia*, a Pious Christian Virgin, comes before the *Sultan*. She saves her Countrymen by a generous Lie,[1] she declares that she hath stol'n[2] the Image, the King condems[3] her to be burnt. *Olindo* her Lover endeavours to save her Life by another noble Lie,[1] he takes the Guilt upon himself, and claims the Pile prepar'd for her. At last both are sentenced to die, both are ty'd to the same stake, when of a sudden arrives *Clorinda* from *Persia*. She mov'd | with Pity towards them, and 84 looking with Scorn upon the Sorcery of *Ismeno*, asks and obtains their Pardon. *Olindo* and *Sophronia* go from the Pile to their Church, Marry, and are no more heard of in the Poem.

Tasso adorn'd that useless Episode with all the Pomp of Poetry, nay he is not sparing of *Italian* Conceits in it. He dwells with so much Complacency upon the Description of *Sophronia*, he speaks of the Love of *Olindo* with so much Warmth, he excites so much Pity for them both, that every Reader cannot but believe that both are principal Characters in the Poem. He is amaz'd and angry afterward to see them as useless to the Affairs of the Christians, as the Image of Virgin *Mary*[4] to the Infidels. All the Embellishments which *Tasso* lavishes upon such a needless piece of Enchantment, and upon so preposterous an Episode serve but to render the Fault more conspicuous.[5]

All the World owns with the *Italians*, that nothing is so artfully describ'd as the Coquettry of *Armida*, nothing so tender as her Love, nothing so animated and so moving as her Complaints. The Taste of the *English* and of the *French*, tho' averse to any Machinery grounded | upon Enchantment, must forgive, 85 nay commend that of *Armida*, since it is the Source of so many Beauties. Besides she is a *Mahometan*, and the Christian Religion allows us to believe that those Infidels are under the immediate Influence of the Devil.[6]

---

[1] 1728 Lye.

[2] 1728 stolen.

[3] 1728 condemns.

[4] 1728 of the Virgin Mary.

[5] Rolli (*Remarks*, p. 84) accuses Voltaire of having overlooked an important detail of this episode. As to its uselessness he writes: " What is a useless Episode . . . according to Voltaire an Episode must not be an Episode." In the *Essai* the incident in question is merely mentioned, not related.

[6] Here we see Voltaire the apostle of tolerance. This sentence does not appear in the French.

But indeed no body but an *Italian* can bear with the wild Excess, to which *Tasso* hath carried that Machinery.[1] Ten Christian Princes turn'd into Fish in the Ponds of *Armida*, and a Parrot singing amorous Songs of his own making, are very strange Things in the eyes of a serious Reader, tho' one is precedented by the Story of *Circe* in *Homer*; and tho' the Parrots are thought among us to mimick now and then human Voices.

Still we should easily forgive such poetical Extravagancies for the sake of the Beauties which are mingled with them. Let the Devils (since they are admitted) have a free Scope to play their wild Pranks, especially in *Italy*, where the Superstition of the People brings Credit to no less strange Tales.[2]

But it is unaccountable how Men of Sense can approve of Christian Magicians, who help *Rinaldo* out of the Hands of the *Mahometan* Wizards. It is singular to see in *Tasso* Lewdness, 86 Mass, Confessi|on, the Litanies of the Saints, and pieces of Witchcraft heap'd together.[3]

What strange Fancy! to send *Ubaldo* and his Companion to an old *holy Conjurer*, who carries them *just into the Center of the Earth*. The two Knights walk there on the Banks of a Rivulet cover'd with precious Stones of all Kinds. From that Place they are sent to *Ascalon* to an old Woman who carries them swiftly in a little Ship to the *Canary Islands*.[4] Thither they arrive in the Name of God, holding in their Hands a magick Wand, they perform their Ambassy, they carry *Rinaldo* back with them to the Camp of the Christians; for the Army was in need of him. But what was the great Exploit which must necessarily be performed by *Rinaldo*, and by him only?

---

[1] Cf. *Essai*, p. 342: " Il y a dans l'épisode d'Armide. . . des excès d'imagination qui assurément ne seraient point admis en France ni en Angleterre. . . . Les enchantements ne réussiraient pas aujourd'hui avec des Français ou des Anglais. . . . Sans doute un homme qui vient de lire Locke ou Addison sera étrangement révolté de trouver dans *la Jérusalem* un sorcier chrétien."

[2] Cf. *ibid.*: " Mais du temps du Tasse ils étaient reçus dans toute l'Europe, et regardés presque comme un point de foi par le peuple superstitieux d'Italie."

[3] This sentence is omitted in the French, very likely because of a comment of Rolli's. Cf. p. 110, note 2, *ante*. Cf. also Rolli, *Remarks*, p. 86: " M. Voltaire writ those three following Paragraphs in the Stile of Scarron . . . with the intent of writing il Tasso travestito by which anyone may ridicule all the best poetical works."

[4] Cf. Baretti, *Dissertation*, p. 70: " Ubaldo and his Companion spied a Little Bark, and seated in the Stern a Maid ordained to guide it. Her Hair hung in loose curls upon her Forehead. A soft Complacency sparkled in her Eyes. The shining Lustre of her Face expressed angelic Beauty. This is the old Woman of Ascalon that M. de Voltaire takes notice of."

He was destin'd by Providence, and brought by Enchantment from the Pic [1] of *Teneriff* to *Jerusalem*, in order to cut down some Trees in a Forest inhabited by Elves and Hoggoblings.[2] That Forest is the great Machinery of *Tasso*. It is remarkable that in the former Books God almighty orders His Archangel *Michael* to drive down into Hell the Devils who were let loose in the Air, raising Storms, and managing his Thunders against the Christians in Favour of the *Mahometans*. *Michael* forbids them strictly to meddle | any more in those Affairs. They obey and plunge into 87 Hell immediately; but soon after the Enchanter *Ismeno* recalls them out, they find Means to elude the Orders of God, and under the pretence of some *Jesuitical* Distinctions, they take Possession of the Forest, wherein the Christians intended to provide the Timber necessary to build a wooden Tower.

There they assume innumerable Shapes to frighten away those who come to cut the Trees. There *Tancred* finds his *Clorinda* after her Death shut up in a Pine, and bleeding for the Blow which he strikes at the Root. There *Armida* peeps out of a Mirtle,[3] while she is some Miles off, in the Ægyptian Army, totally unappris'd of her being in two Places at once, tho' she is the best Sorceress in the World. At last the Prayers of the *Hermit* and the Merit of *Rinaldo's* Contrition after his Confession, break the Enchantment.

Methinks it is not very foreign to the Purpose to see how differently *Lucan* hath handled in his *Pharsalia* a Topick pretty much of the same Nature. 'Tis when *Cesar* orders his Troops to cut down some Tres[4] in the sacred Forest of *Marseilles*, to have them made into warlike Instruments. The Passage deserves to be | set in its full Length, as it is translated by the late Mr. *Rowe*.[5] 88

> *Not far away, for Ages past had stood*
> *An old inviolated sacred Wood;*
> *Whose gloomy Boughs, thick interwoven, made*

---

[1] 1728 Pike, 1731 Pic.
[2] 1728 Hobgoblings.
[3] 1728 Myrtle.
[4] 1728 Trees.
[5] Nicholas Rowe, 1674-1718, made poet laureate in 1715. His translation of the *Pharsalia* was published shortly after his death.

In the French version Voltaire quotes from Brébeuf's *Pharsalia* (cf. p. 49, *ante*) which he characterizes as " comme toutes les autres traductions . . . au dessous de l'original." *Essai*, p. 343. This accords with his attitude toward translations in the French chapter on Homer. Cf. p. 67, note 1, *ante*.

A chilly chearless everlasting Shade,
There, nor the rustick Gods, nor Satyrs Sport,
Nor Fauns[1] *and Syluans*[2] *with the Nymphs resort;*
But barb'rous Priests some dreadful Pow'r adore,
And lustrate ev'ry Tree with human Gore.
If Mysteries, in times of old receiv'd,
And pious Ancientry be yet believ'd,
There nor the feather'd Songster builds her Nest,
Nor lonely dens conceal the savage Beast:
There no tempestuous Winds presume to fly,
Ev'n Lightnings Glance aloof, and shoot obliquely by,
No wanton Breezes toss's[3] *the dancing Leaves,*
But shiv'ring Horror in the Branches heaves.
Black Springs with pitchy Streams divide the Ground
And bubbling tumble with a sullen Sound.
Old Images of Forms mis-shapen stand,
Rude and unknowing of the Artist's Hand;
With hoary Filth begrim'd each ghastly Head
Strikes the astonish'd Gazer's Soul with Dread.
No Gods, who long in common Shapes appear'd,
Were e'er with such Religious Awe rever'd:
But zealous Crouds in Ignorance adore;
And still the less they know, they fear the more.

The pious Worshippers approach not near,
But shun their Gods, and kneel with distant Fear:
The Priest himself, when, or the Day, or Night,
Rowling have reach'd their full meridian height,
Refrains the gloomy Paths with wary Feet,
Dreading the Daemon *of the Grove to meet;*
|Who, terrible to Sight, at that fix'd Hour,
Still treads the ground[4] *about his dreery*[5] *Bow'r.*
This Wood near neighb'ring to th' encompassed Town,
Untouch'd by former Wars remain'd alone;
And since the Country round it naked stands,
From hence the Latian *Chief Supplies demands.*
But lo ! the bolder Hands that should have struck,

89

---

[1] 1728 Fawns.
[2] 1728 Sylvans.
[3] 1728 toss.
[4] Rowe's translation reads *Round.*
[5] 1728 dreary.

With some unusual Horror trembling Shook;
With silent Dread and Rev'rence they survey'd,
The Gloom Majestick of the sacred Shade:
None dares with impious Steel the Bark to rend,
Least [1] *on himself the destin'd stroke descend.*
Caesar *perceiv'd the spreading Fear to grow,*
Then Eager caught an Ax and aim'd a Blow:
Deep sunk within a violated Oak
The wounding Edge, and thus the Warrior spoke.
Now, let no doubting Hand the Task decline:
Cut you the Wood, and let the Guilt be mine.
The trembling Bands unwillingly obey'd;
Two various Ills were in the Ballance laid,
And Caesar's *Wrath against the Gods was weigh'd.* [2]

I confess that the whole *Pharsalia* is not to be compar'd to the *Jerusalem* of *Tasso*. But at least that particular Passage shows how the true Grandeur of a real Hero is above the Romantick,[3] and how solid and strong Thoughts excell [4] those Inventions, which the Crowd calls poetical Beauties, and on which wise Men look down as Tales fit for Children.

The *Virtuosi* in *Italy* have disputed for a long while and still contest which of the two *Ariosto* or *Tasso* deserves the Precedency. But every where else the chief|est Exception that Men 90 of Understanding take to *Tasso*, is that of having too much of *Ariosto* in him. *Tasso* seems to have been conscious of this Fault. He could not be unsensible that such wild fairy Tales, at that Time so much in the Fashion not in *Italy* only but in all *Europe*, were altogether inconsistent with the Gravity of *Epick* Poetry: In order to cover this Defect he printed a Preface, in which he pretends that all his Poem is but a Shadow and a Type.

The Army of the Christian Princes, says he, represents the Body and the Soul. *Jerusalem* the figure of true Happiness, which cannot be obtain'd but by Labour and Difficulties. *Goffredo* is the Mind, *Tancredo*, *Raimondo*, &c. are the faculties of

---

[1] 1728 Lest.
[2] Rowe, *Pharsalia*, Bk. III, ll. 591-617 and 623-649.
[3] It is evident that this passage has been quoted and praised with a view to the interests of the *Henriade*. Voltaire's use of the work *romantick* is interesting in connection with the history of the term *romantique* in France. Cf. A. François, *Annales J. J. Rousseau*, V, pp. 199 ff., also *Rev. d'Hist. litt.*, 1911, pp. 440, 940.
[4] 1728 excel.

the Mind. The common Soldiers make up the Limbs of the Body. The Devils are at once figur'd, and figures (*figura è figurato*). *Armida* and *Ismeno* are the Temptations which besiege our Souls. The Spells and the Illusions of the inchanted Forest shadow out the false reasoning (*falsi sillogismi*)[1] into which our Passions are apt to mislead us.

Such is the Key that *Tasso* thinks fit to give us of his Works. He deals with himself as the Commentators have done with *Homer* and *Virgil*. Those Gentlemen are like speculative and
91 dully wise | Politicians, who construe the most insignificant Actions of great Men, into Designs of the greatest Depth and Importance. But *Tasso* was like that Ambassador, who having spent all the Time of his Ambassy in Debauchery and Riot, wrote to his Master that he was whoring and drinking for the Service of his Majesty.[2]

However, the ridiculous Explanation which *Tasso* gives with so much Gravity of his Extravagancies, cannot impose upon Mankind; for we no more allow an Author to comment upon himself, than a Priest to prophecy[3] of himself.[4]

If the Devils act in *Tasso*, the insipid part of despicable Jugglers, on the other Hand what is relating to Religion, is writ with Majesty, and I dare say in the Spirit of Religion itself. Nay Processions and Litanies, and all the Parts of *Popish* Religion, which are accounted comical and mean in *England*, appear in a reverend Awfulness in that Poem. So prevalent is the Art of Poetry when it exerts itself in its full Force, and so peculiar to it is the Power of raising what is low, and of enlarging the Sphere of all Things.

He is guilty of indulging the inaccurate Custom of calling the
92 evil Spirits by the Names of *Pluto*, *Alecto*, and | of mingling often *Pagan* Ideas with *Christian* Mythology.[5] 'Tis strange that none of the modern Poets are free from that Fault. It seems that our Devils and our Christian Hell have something in them low and mean, and must be rais'd by the Hell of the *Pagans*, which

---

[1] 1728 Syllogismi.
[2] Rolli (*Remarks*, p. 91) found fault with this anecdote, saying: "Pray where is the Wit? Where the Comparison?" In the French version it was omitted.
[3] 1728 prophesy.
[4] Cf. Rapin, *Réflexions*, p. 79: "Et c'est en vain que le Tasse veut sauver cette faute par l'allégorie, dans un grand discours qu'il a fait. C'est justifier une chimère par une autre chimère." This sentence does not appear in the French.
[5] Cf. p. 118, note 3, *ante*.

owes its Dignity to its Antiquity. Certain it is that the Hell of the Gospel is not so fitted for Poetry as that of *Homer* and *Virgil.* The Name of *Tisiphone* sounds better than that of *Beelzebub;*[1] but with all that, it is as preposterous in a Poet to bring *Michael* and *Alecto* together, as in some *Italian* and *Flemish* Painters to have represented the Virgin *Mary* with a Chaplet[2] of Beads hanging at her Girdle, to have plac'd some *Swiss* Guards at the Door of the Apartment of *Pharao,*[3] and to have mix'd Cannons and Carabines with the ancient Arrows in the Battle of Josuah.[4]

DON ALONZO D'EREILLA Y CUNIGA.[5]

At the End of the sixteenth Century, *Spain* produc'd an *Epick* Poem, famous for some peculiar Beauties that shine in it, as well as for the Singularity of its Subject, but still more illustrious by the Character of the Author.

|*Alonzo* of *Ereilla y Cuniga,* Gentleman of the Bed Chamber 93 to the Emperor *Maximilian,* was bred up in the House of *Philip* the second, and fought under his Orders at the Battle of *St. Quentin,*[6] where the *French* were utterly defeated.

Philip after such a Success, being less desirous to augment his Glory abroad, than to settle his Affairs at home, went back to *Spain.* The young *Alonzo* of *Ereilla,* led by an insatiable Avidity of true Learning, I mean of knowing Men and of seeing the

---

[1] Voltaire was too faithful a classicist to admit the poetical possibilities of the Christian religion, which were not to be thoroughly recognized until the time of Chateaubriand. Cf. Boileau, *Art poétique,* III, ll. 193 ff.:
 "C'est donc bien vainment que nos auteurs déçus,
 Bannissant de leurs vers ces ornements reçus,
 Pensent faire agir Dieu, ses saints, et ses prophètes,
 Comme ces dieux éclos du cerveau des poëtes;

 . . . .
 De la foi d'un chrétien les mystères terribles
 D'ornements égayés ne sont point susceptibles."

[2] 1728 Chapelet.
[3] 1728 Pharaoh.
[4] 1728 Joshuah.
 This is an early evidence of Voltaire's feeling for local color, rare in the France of his time, seen later in his dramas and in his historical works and akin to his ideas regarding comparative literature. This particular sentence is omitted in the French. Cf. p. 110, note 2, *ante.*

[5] Cf. *Essai,* p. 347, Chapitre VIII, *Don Alonzo de Ercilla.* As has been said, this chapter remains practically unchanged, the French of the 1733 edition having been almost word for word that of Abbé Desfontaines' translation.

[6] 1728 Quintin. Saint Quentin in the department of Aisne, France, where the army of Philip II under the duke of Savoy defeated the French under Constable de Montmorency, Aug. 10, 1557. In the French version of the essay, Voltaire corrected the statement that Philip was present at this battle.

World, travell'd through all *France*, saw *Italy*, *Germany*, and stay'd a long while in *England*. Whilst he was in *London*, he heard some Provinces of *Peru*, and *Chily*, had taken Arms against the *Spaniards*, their Conquerors; which struggle for their Liberty is, by the by, stil'd Rebellion by the *Spanish* Authors. His Thirst of Glory, and his eager Desire of seeing, and doing new and singular Things, carry'd him without any Hesitation, or Delay, into those Countries. He went to *Chily*, at the Head of a few Troops,[1] and he stay'd in these parts all the Time of the War.

Near the Borders of *Chily*, towards the *South*, lies a small, mountainous Country, call'd *Araucana*, inhabited by a Race of Men, stronger and more fierce, than all the Nations of that new 94 World. They | fought for their Liberty, longer than the other *Americans*,[2] and were the last who were subdu'd. *Alonzo* waged against them a toilsome and dangerous War, underwent inexpressible hardships, saw and atchiev'd the most surprising Deeds, the Prize whereof was only the Honour of reducing some Rocks and barren Countries, in another Hemisphere, to the Crown of *Spain*.[3]

Alonzo, in the Course of that War, conceiv'd the Idea to immortalize his Enemies and himself, he was at once the Conqueror and the Poet. He made use of the Intervals of the War to sing it, and as he wanted Paper, he wrote the first Part of his Poem upon little Pieces of Leather, which afterwards he had much ado to set right, and to bring together. The Poem is call'd the *Araucana*, from the Name of the Country.

It begins with a geographical Account of *Chily*, and with a Description of the Manners and Customs of the People; such a Beginning, which would be quite flat and intolerable in any other Poem, is necessary, and not unpleasant in a Subject where the Scene lies under the other Tropick, and where the Heroes he writes of, are barbarous *Americans*, who must have been for-95 ever unknown, | if he had not conquer'd and celebrated them.

As the Subject was quite new, so it gave Birth to new Thoughts.[4]

---

[1] Ercilla was not in command of troops in this expedition but accompanied Captain Aldrete.

[2] Cf. pp. 35, 40, *ante*.

[3] Ercilla's subject-matter, as it is set forth by Voltaire, recalls that of J. M. de Hérédia, centuries later.

[4] Cf. p. 65, note 1, *ante*.

There is one which I present to the Readers, both as an Example of Novelty, and as a Spark of the Fire which animated sometimes the Author.

" The *Araucani*, *says he*, were surpris'd at first, to see Creatures like Men, with Fire in their Hands, and dreadful Monsters fighting under them. They thought they were the immortal Gods, descending from above, with Thunder and Destruction. They submitted, though with Reluctance; but afterwards being more acquainted with their Conquerors, they saw their Vices, and judg'd they were Men; then on a sudden, asham'd of being oppress'd by their fellow Mortals, they swore by their Shame, to wash off their Error with the Blood of the Deceivers, and to execute a Vengeance exemplary, dreadful, and irrevocable." [1]

It will be usefull[2] perhaps, to take Notice of a Passage in the second Book, which bears a near Resemblance to the Beginning of the *Iliad*, and which being handled quite differently, deserves to be presented to the little Number of impartial Readers, that they may judge between *Homer* and *Alonzo* in that particu|lar. 96 The first Action of the *Araucana*, is a Quarrel which happen'd between all the barbarous Chiefs, as in *Homer* between *Achilles* and *Agamemnon*. The Dispute was not about a Woman, but about the Right of commanding the Army.[3] Every one of those savage Warriors assumes an uncontroul'd Behaviour upon the Consciousness of his own Worth, and at last the Dispute grew so high, that they were ready to fight one against another, when one of the Casiques call'd *Colocolo*, as old as *Nestor*, and less boasting of himself than the *Grecian*, made the following speech:

"Casiques, ye illustrious Defenders of our Country, the vain Desire of Empire does not move me to speak to you. I do not complain that you all contend so eagerly for an Honour which perhaps is due to my old Age, and should adorn my Decline. 'Tis my Love to you, 'tis the Duty that I owe to my Country,

---

[1] *La Araucana* por Don Alonso de Ercilla y Zuñiga, 1569-1590 (Biblioteca de Autores Espanoles, XVII, p. 4), Canto I, stanza 64 ff. Voltaire's English, although it appears in quotation-marks, is by no means a direct translation but rather a very free summary of several stanzas of the poem.

His appreciation of this passage and of certain others of Ercilla may be considered characteristic of the attitude of the eighteenth century toward so-called savage countries and their inhabitants. Cf. Rousseau; Voltaire's *Alzire*, *Ingénu*, *Candide*, etc.

[2] 1728 useful.

[3] In the *Henriade*, also, there was no woman who played a leading part.

which forces me to intreat you to attend to my feeble Voice. Alas ! How can we be so assuming, as to pretend to any Grandeur whatever, and to claim honourable Titles, we, who have been Subjects, nay, miserable Slaves, to the *Spaniards.* Your 97 Anger, Casiques, your Fury, would be better employ'd | against our Tyrants; why do you turn against your Breasts, those Arms which might exterminate your Enemies and revenge our World ? Ah ! If Death be your Desire, seek a Death that is honourable ! Shake of[1] the shameful Yoke with one Hand, assault the *Spaniards* with the other, and shed not in an unprofitable Quarrel, those last Drops of Blood of this State, which the Gods have left in it for its Revenge. I am not displeas'd, I confess, to see the undaunted Haughtiness of your Courages. This very Fierceness which I blame, heightens the Hopes I conceive of our Designs; but let not your ill-govern'd Valour prey upon itself, and destroy with its own Force, the Country you rise to defend. If you persist in your Quarrels, let your Swords first be imbru'd in my Blood, already frozen with old Age. I have liv'd too long. Happy is he who dies before his Countrymen are unfortunate, and unfortunate by their own Fault. Attend then to what I dare propose for your Welfare. Your Valour, O Casiques, is equal, you are all equally illustrious by the Honours of the War, by your Birth, by your Power and Riches, your Souls are noble in an equal 98 Degree, all worthy | to command, and able to subdue our World. Those heavenly Gifts are the present Subject of your great Contests, you want a Chief, and every one of you is equal to that noble Charge; then since there is no Difference between your Courages, let the Strength of the Body decide what the Equality of your Virtues would keep undecided for ever, &c." [2]

---

[1] 1728 off. Cf. *Errata.*

[2] *Araucana,* Canto II, stanzas 28-36. Again Voltaire's rendering cannot by any means be called a translation. In most places the wording departs entirely from the Spanish and there are various additions and omissions. Cf. Ticknor, *Hist. of Sp. lit.,* II, pp. 467-468, note 11: " The great praise of this speech by Voltaire, in the Essay prefixed to his ' Henriade,' 1726, first made the Araucana known beyond the Pyrenees; and if Voltaire had read the poem he pretended to criticise, he might have done something in earnest for its fame . . . But his mistakes are so gross as to impair the value of his admiration."

Cf. also James Fitzmaurice Kelley, *Littérature Espagnole,* Paris, 1913, p. 253: "Voltaire loua avec raison le discours du vieux chef Colocolo; c'est précisément dans ce genre d'éloquence déclamatoire qu' Ercilla brille, et il a fait mieux encore dans les discours de Lautaro et de Caupolican."

Rather than any real desire to glorify Ercilla, there appears in Voltaire's high praise of this passage, a wish to exalt the savage at the expense of the civilized and to belittle the fame of Homer at any cost.

Then that old Man proposes a Game, fit only for a barberous Nation, and consequently very proper. It was to carry a ponderous Beam, and he who could sustain the Weight longest, was to be the Chief.

Now since the best Way of improving our Taste, is that of comparing together Things of the same Nature, let us bring in the Discourse of *Nestor*, in Opposition to this of *Colocolo*, and laying aside that Worship, which our Minds justly prejudiced pay to the great Name of *Homer*, let the Reader weigh the two Speeches in the Ballance of Equity and Reason.

As soon as *Achilles* warn'd and inspir'd by *Minerva*, the Goddess of Wisdom, has call'd *Agamemnon* Drunkard, Dog, and Stag, the wise N*estor* arose to calm the ruffled Minds of those Heroes, and among other Things which I wave, to come closely to the Point of | Comparison, thus he said, " What a Satisfaction will 99 it be to the *Trojans*, when they hear of your Dissentions ! [1] Young Men, you must respect my Years, and submit to my Wisdom, I have liv'd in my Youth with Heroes, by far superior to you, no, my Eyes will never see such Men as the undaunted *Piritous*,[2] the bold *Ceneus*, the divine *Theseus*, &c. I went to war with them, and though younger, I sway'd their Strength by my persuasive Eloquence; they list'n'd[3] to, they obey'd *Nestor*. If in my early Years they deem'd me so wise, you, young Warriors, attend to the Advice of my old Age. *Atrides*, do not seize on the Slave of *Achilles*, you Son of *Thetis*, do not treat our Prince with Pride. *Achilles* is the greatest, the most couragious[4] of the Warriors, *Agamemnon* is the greatest of Kings, &c." [5] Thus spoke the wise *Nestor*, and his Speech prov'd en-

----

[1] 1728 Dissensions.
[2] 1728 Pirithous. Cf. *Errata*.
[3] 1728 listened.
[4] 1728 courageous.
[5] Cf. *Iliad*, I, ll. 254-281. A comparison of Voltaire's rendering with the original and with Pope's translation (Pope, *Iliad*, I, ll. 339-369) shows that it is far from faithful (cf. *Oeuvres*, VIII, p. 351, note 1) and makes it evident that Voltaire had Pope before him as he wrote. Cf., for instance, Voltaire's version with the following passage from Pope, I, ll. 358-364:
" *Yet these with soft persuasive arts I sway'd;*
When Nestor spoke, *they listen'd and obey'd.*
If in *my youth, e'en these esteem'd me wise,*
Do *you, young warriors, hear my age advice.*
Atrides, *seize* not on the beauteous *slave;*
That prize the Greeks by common suffrage gave:
Nor thou, Achilles, *treat our prince with pride.*"
The borrowing is the more evident when the lines are compared with the original. A nearly literal translation of the corresponding passage in Homer

tirely ineffectual, for *Agamemnon* commended his Eloquence and neglected the Advice.

Let the Readers consider on one Part, the Endearments by which the barbarous *Colocolo* ingratiates himself into the Favour of the Casiques, the awful Majesty with which he checks their 100 Animosity, the Tenderness with which he sof|tens their Boisterousness, how the Love of his Country animates him, how the true Sense of Glory enlivens his Speech, in what a prudent Manner he praises their Valour, when he curbs their Fury, with what Art, he gives Superiority to none, and is at the same Time an inoffensive Censor, and a noble Panegyrist: So that all submit to his Reason, and comply with his Advice, confessing the Force of his Eloquence, not by empty Commendations, but by a sudden Obedience.

On the other Side, one may judge, if *Nestor* is so wise in talking so much of his Wisdom, if it is a good Way to reconcile the Attention of the *Greek* Princes, by telling them that they are by far inferior to their Fore-fathers; if to say to *Agamemnon*, that *Achilles* is the most valorous of the present Chiefs, ought to be very acceptable to *Agamamnon*;[1] and after having compar'd the haughty Talkativeness of *Nestor*, with the modest Eloquence of *Colocolo*; the Injury offered by one to all the *Greeks*, by the offensive Superiority ascrib'd to their Predecessors, with the engaging Praises bestow'd upon the Casiques then present: The odious Comparison between the Power of *Agamamnon*,[1] and the Valour of 101 *Achilles*; with that equal Share of Grandeur and | Courage artfully extoll'd in all the Casiques: Then let the Reader pronounce. And if there is a General in the World, who would hear his inferior preferr'd to him in Point of Courage, if there is any Assembly who would bear without Resentment a Speaker talking to them with Contempt, and villifying them, by extolling at their Expence their Predecessors, let then *Homer* be preferr'd to *Alonzo* in that Particular.[2]

reads: "And they laid to heart my counsels and hearkened to my voice. Even so hearken ye also, for better is it to hearken. Neither do thou, though thou art very great, seize from him his damsel, but leave her as she was given at the first by the sons of the Achaians to be a meed of honour; nor do thou, son of Peleus, think to strive with a king, might against might" (translation of Lang, Leaf and Meyers).

[1] 1728 Agamemnon.

[2] Cf. Perrault, *Paralelle*, III, pp. 48-49: "Mais je ne puis prendre plaisir à voir le sage Nestor qui dit à Agamemnon et à Achilles, qu'il a conversé avec des gens qui valoient mieux qu'eux; et qui ajoute, en parlant encore à Agamemnon, qu' Achilles est plus vaillant que luy. Cela n'est guere civil . . . "

It is true, that if *Alonzo* is above *Homer* in this Point, he is in all the rest inferior to the meanest of the Poets. It is wonderful, how he falls so low from so high a Flight. There is undoubtedly a great deal of Fire in his Battles, but no Design, no Invention, no Variety in the Descriptions, no Unity in the whole Frame; the Poem is more wild, then[1] the Nations who are the Subject of it. In the latter End of the Work, *Alonzo*, who is one of the chief Actors in the Poem, makes a long and tedious March with some Soldiers by Night; and to divert the Time, he raises a Dispute between them about *Virgil*, and chiefly on the Episode of *Dido; Alonzo* takes his Opportunity, in the Conversation of relating the History of *Dido*, as it is reported by some antient Authors, and in order to give the Lie[2] to *Virgil*, and to restore *Dido* to her for|mer Glory, he spends two long Canto's in descanting upon her. 102

One of the greatest Exceptions besides, which may be taken against it, is that the Book consists of thirty-six long Cantos. The Reader will think it probable, that a Man who does not know how to stop, is not qualified to run such a Carrier.[3]

So many Defects have not deterred the celebrated *Michel*[4] *Cervantes* from writing, that the *Araucana* may cope with the best Authors of *Italy*.[5]

The Judgement of *Cervantes* was misled in that Point by an overweaning Inclination towards his Countrymen. The true Love of our Country is to do good to it, to contribute to its Liberty, as far as it lies in our Power; but to contend only for the Superiority of our Authors, to boast of having among us better Poets than our Neighbors, is rather Self-love than Patriotism.

MILTON.[6]

Milton is the last in *Europe* who wrote an *Epick* Poem, for I wave all those whose Attempts have been unsuccessful, my

---

[1] 1728 than.
[2] 1728 Lye.
[3] 1728 Career.
[4] 1728 *Michael.*
[5] *Don Quijote de la Mancha*, ed. Marín, I, Capitulo VI, pp. 170-171: " Y aquí vienen tres, todos juntos: *La Araucana* de don Alonso de Ercilla, *La Austríada* de Juan Rufo, jurado de Córboda, y *El Monserrate* de Cristóbal de Virués, poeta valenciano.—Todos esos tres libros—dijo el Cura—son los mejores que, en verso heroico, en lengua castellana están escritos, y pueden competir con los más famosos de Italia: guárdense como las más ricas prendas de poesía que tiene España."
[6] John Milton (1608-1674) had died about fifty years before the time of Voltaire's visit to England. *Paradise Lost* appeared in 1667 but was not duly appreciated until much later.

Intention being not to descant on the many who have contended
for the Prize, but to speak only of the | very few who have gain'd
it in their respective Countries.[1]

Milton, as he was travelling through *Italy* in his Youth, saw
at *Florence* a Comedy call'd *Adamo*, writ by one *Andreino* a
Player, and dedicated to *Mary de Medicis* Queen of *France*.[2]
The Subject of the Play was the *Fall of Man*; the Actors, God,
the Devils, the Angels, *Adam, Eve*, the Serpent, Death, and the
Seven Mortal Sins. That Topick so improper for a Drama, but
so suitable to the absurd Genius of the *Italian* Stage, (as it was
at that Time) was handled in a Manner intirely conformable to
the Extravagance of the Design.[3] The Scene opens with a

Cf. *Essai*, p. 352, Chapter IX, *Milton*. The French chapter is shorter
than the English by about one third. We have already commented in some
detail upon the marked difference in tone between the French and the English
and upon the probable reasons for the change. Cf. pp. 68 ff., *ante*. Our notes
will show various omissions and alterations which helped to produce that change
and tended in some cases to make the French chapter less liberal and of less
value as a contribution to comparative literature. In the French much un-
trustworthy biographical information was added.

[1] The opening sentence of the French chapter reads: " On trouvera ici, touch-
ant Milton, quelques particularitiés omises dans l'abrégé de sa *Vie* qui est au-
devant de la traduction française de son *Paradis perdu*. Il n'est pas étonnant
qu'ayant recherché avec soin en Angleterre tout ce qui regarde ce grand homme,
j'aie découvert des circonstances de sa vie que le public ignore." Some of the
added information is far from accurate. Cf. Lounsbury, *Shakespeare and Voltaire*, p. 49. Enumerating certain of these inaccuracies Lounsbury gives the
impression that they were to be found in the English essay whereas they appeared only in the French version.

[2] Giovanni Battista Andreini (1578—cir. 1650) was born in Florence and
died in Paris. He was the author of *Adamo*, a mystery play. Cf. *Grande
Encyclopédie*, II, p. 1042: "Adamo, sorte de mystère d'où quelques Italiens
ont prétendu que Milton, voyageant à cette époque en Italie, avait pris l'idée
du *Paradis perdu*. Ce n'est pas impossible. Cette hypothèse, accréditée par
Rolli, le traducteur italien du *Paradis perdu*, a eu quelque cours en Angleterre
et il paraît que si le volume est devenu si rare en Italie c'est que les Anglais
en ont acheté peu à peu presque tous les exemplaires connus."
Cf. Rolli, *Remarks*, 103: " It was at Milan, they wouldn't have borne with
it in Florence." In his French essay Voltaire, no doubt in accordance with
Rolli's comment, has replaced Florence by Milan: " Milton . . . vit représenter
à Milan une comédie intitulée *Adam*." P. 353.
In the French, too, it is added that Milton originally intended to write a
tragedy based on Andreino's and even went so far as to compose an act and a
half. Voltaire explains the source of his information: "Ce fait m'a été assuré
par des gens de lettres, qui le tenaient de sa fille, laquelle est morte lorsque
j'étais à Londres" (p. 353).

[3] Cf. *Essai*, p. 353: " Ce sujet, digne du génie absurde du théâtre de ce temps-
là . . . " and "J'avertis seulement les Français qui en iront que notre théâtre
ne valait guère mieux alors; que la *Mort de Saint Jean-Baptiste*, et cent autres
pièces, sont écrites dans ce style; mais que nous n'avions ni *Pastor fido* ni *Aminte*."
In this same connection occurs the sentence: " Il y a surtout dans ce sujet
je ne sais quelle horreur ténébreuse, un sublime sombre et triste qui ne convient
pas mal à l'imagination anglaise." Cf. p. 70, *ante*.

Chorus of Angels, and a Cherubim thus speaks for the Rest: " Let the Rainbow be the Fiddlestick of the Fiddle of the Heavens, let the Planets be the Notes of our Musick, let Time beat carefully the Measure, and the Winds make the Sharps, &c." Thus the Play begins, and every Scene rises above the last[1] in Profusion of Impertinence.

Milton pierc'd through the Absurdity of that Performance to the hidden Majesty of the Subject, which being altogether unfit for the Stage, yet might be (for the Genius of *Milton*, and for his only) the Foundation of an *Epick* Poem.

|He took from that ridiculous Trifle the first Hint of the noblest 104 Work, which human Imagination hath ever attempted, and which he executed more than twenty Years after.[2]

In the like Manner, *Pythagoras* ow'd the Invention of Musick to the Noise of the Hammer of a Blacksmith. And thus in our Days Sir *Isaak*[3] *Newton* walking in his Gardens had the first Thought of his System of Gravitation, upon seeing an Apple falling from a Tree.[4]

If the Difference of Genius between Nation and Nation, ever appear'd in its full Light, 'tis in *Milton's* Paradise lost.[5]

---

[1] 1728 first. Cf. *Errata.*

[2] This enthusiastic judgment of the poem is not found in the French. The sentence there which may be said to correspond to it shows at the outset the difference in spirit between the two chapters: "Il imagina un poème épique, espèce d'ouvrage dans lequel les hommes sont convenus d'approuver souvent le bizarre sous le nom de merveilleux." P. 354.

[3] 1728 Isaac.

[4] The story of Newton and the apple does not appear in the French version. Voltaire says elsewhere that it was told him by Mrs. Conduit, Milton's niece. *Oeuvres,* XXII, pp. 434, 520. Cf. Lanson, *Lettres phil.,* II, pp. 19-20, Letter 15, *Sur le Système de l'attraction:* " S'étant retiré en 1666 à la campagne près de Cambridge, un jour qu'il se promenoit dans son jardin, & qu'il voïoit des fruits tomber d'un arbre, il se laissa aller à une méditation profonde sur cette pesanteur, dont tous les Philosophes ont cherché si long-tems la cause en vain." *Ibid.,* II, p. 31, Lanson shows that the source of this part of the letter is *A view of Isaac Newton's philosophy* by Dr. Pemberton, London, 1728, but he continues (p. 33): " On voit que Pemberton ne fait pas allusion à l'anecdote fameuse de la pomme. Voltaire la rappelle . . . Fontenelle n'en parle pas; et le mémoire que Conduit avait envoyé à Fontenelle pour faire son *Éloge,* n'en dit rien non plus."

Cf. Churton Collins, *V. M. R,* p. 33: " It is perhaps worth mentioning that we owe to Voltaire the famous story of the falling apple. . . . It is not, so far as I can discover, to be found in any publication antecedent to the *Lettres sur les Anglais.*" Churton Collins leaves out of account this passage of the English *Essay on Epic Poetry* which precedes by several years the telling of the story in the *Lettres philosophiques.*

[5] This idea is not expressed in the French. The short sentence in which Voltaire boasts of having made Milton known in France (p. 357): "Je fus le premier qui fis connaître aux Français quelques morceaux de Milton et de Shake-

The *French* answer with a scornful Smile, when they are told there is in *England* an *Epick* Poem, the Subject whereof is the Devil fighting against God, and *Adam* and *Eve* eating an Apple at the Persuasion of a Snake. As that Topick hath afforded nothing among them, but some lively Lampoons, for which that Nation is so famous; they cannot imagine it possible to build an *Epick* Poem upon the subject of their Ballads. And indeed such an Error ought to be excused; for if we consider with what Freedom the politest Part of Mankind throughout all *Europe*, both Catholicks and Protestants, are wont to ridicule in Conversation 105 those consecrated | Histories; nay, if those who have the highest Respect for the Mysteries of the Christian Religion, and who are struck with Awe at some Parts of it, yet cannot forbear now and then making free with the *Devil*, the *Serpent*, the Frailty of our first Parents, the Rib which *Adam* was robb'd of, and the like; it seems a very hard Task for a profane Poet to endeavour to remove those Shadows of Ridicule, to reconcile together what is Divine and what looks absurd, and to command a Respect that the sacred Writers could hardly obtain from our frivolous Minds.[1]

What *Milton* so boldly undertook, he perform'd with a superior Strength of Judgement, and with an Imagination productive of Beauties not dream'd of before him. The Meaness[2] (if there is any) of some Parts of the Subject is lost in the Immensity of the Poetical Invention. There is something above the reach of human Forces to have attempted the Creation without Bombast, to have describ'd the Gluttony and Curiosity of a Woman without Flatness, to have brought Probability and Reason amidst the Hurry of imaginary Things belonging to another World, and as 106 far remote from the Limits of our Notions as they | are from our Earth; in short to force the Reader to say, " If God, if the Angels, if Satan would speak, I believe they would speak as they do in *Milton*."

I have often admir'd how barren the Subject appears, and how fruitful it grows under his Hands.

The *Paradise Lost* is the only Poem wherein are to be found in a perfect Degree that Uniformity which satisfies the Mind and

---

speare," is not found in the 1733 edition of the *Essay*, having been added some years later, between 1756 and 1768, as was the passage defending Milton against the charge of plagiarism. Cf. pp. 159-160, *post*.

[1] This whole passage was omitted in the French.

[2] 1728 Meanness.

that Variety which pleases the Imagination. All its Episodes being necessary Lines which aim at the Centre of a perfect Circle.[1] Where is the Nation who would not be pleas'd with the Interview of *Adam* and the *Angel ?* With the Mountain of Vision, with the bold Strokes which make up the Relentless, undaunted, and sly Character of Satan? But above all with that sublime Wisdom which *Milton* exerts, whenever he dares to describe God, and to make him speak? He seems indeed to draw the Picture of the Almighty, as like as human Nature can reach to, through the mortal Dust in which we are clouded.

The *Heathens* always, the *Jews* often, and our Christian Priests sometimes, represent God as a Tyrant infinitely powerful. But the God of *Milton* is always a Creator, a Father, and a Judge, nor is his Vengeance jarring with his Mercy, | nor his Predetermi- 107 nations repugnant to the Liberty of Man. These are the Pictures which lift up indeed the Soul of the Reader. *Milton* in that Point as well as in many others is as far above the ancient Poets as the Christian Religion is above the *Heathen* Fables.[2]

But he hath especially an indisputable Claim to the unanimous Admiration of Mankind, when he descends from those high Flights to the natural Description of human Things. It is observable that in all other Poems Love is represented as a Vice, in *Milton* only 'tis a Virtue. The Pictures he draws of it, are naked as the Persons he speaks of, and as venerable. He removes with a chaste Hand the Veil which covers everywhere else the enjoyments of that Passion. There is Softness, Tenderness and Warmth without Lasciviousness; the Poet transports himself and us, into that State of innocent Happiness in which *Adam* and *Eve* continued for a short Time: He soars not above human, but above corrupt Nature, and as there is no Instance of such Love, there is none of such Poetry.[3]

---

[1] None of the very favorable comment contained in this and in the preceding sentences is found in the French chapter.

[2] Cf. Addison in *Spectator*, II, p. 386: " [Milton's] survey of the whole Creation . . . is . . . as much above that, in which *Virgil* has drawn his *Jupiter*, as the Christian Idea of the Supreme Being is more Rational and Sublime than that of the Heathens." All the praise of Milton's treatment of God is reduced in the French to the sentence: "On admira les traits majesteux avec lesquels il ose peindre Dieu."

[3] Cf. Addison in *Spectator*, II, p. 504: " The Love which is described in it is every way suitable to a State of Innocence . . . The Sentiments are chaste, but not cold; and convey to the Mind Ideas of the most transporting Passion, and of the greatest Purity." The last sentence "He soars . . . poetry" is translated exactly in the French essay.

How then it came to pass that the *Paradise Lost* had been so long neglected, (nay almost unknown) in *England*, (till the Lord 108 *Sommers*[1] in some Measure *taught | Mankind to admire it*,) is a Thing which I cannot reconcile, *neither* with the Temper, *nor* with the Genius of the *English* Nation.

The Duke of *Buckingham*[2] in his Art of Poetry gives the Preference to *Spencer*. It is reported in the Life of the Lord *Rochester*,[3] that he had no Notion of a better Poet than *Cowley*. Mr. *Dryden's* Judgement on *Milton* is still more unaccountable. He hath bestow'd some Verses upon him, in which he puts him upon a Level with, nay above *Virgil* and *Homer;*

> The Force of Nature could not further go,
> To make a third she join'd the former two.[4]

The same Mr. *Dryden* in his Preface upon his Translation of the *Æneid*, ranks *Milton* with *Chapellain* and *Lemoine* the most impertinent Poets who ever scribbled.[5]   How he could extol him so much in his Verses, and debase him so low in his Prose, is a Riddle which, being a Foreigner, I cannot understand.[6]

In short one would be apt to think that *Milton* has[7] not obtained his true Reputation till Mr. *Adisson*,[8] the best Critick as well as the best Writer of his Age, pointed out the most hidden Beauties of the *Paradise Lost*, and settled forever its Reputation.[9]

109 |It is an easy and a pleasant Task to take Notice of the many Beauties of *Milton* which I call universal: But 'tis a ticklish

---

[1] Lord John Somers, 1651-1716, a politician and writer of poems, pamphlets, etc.   He encouraged the publisher Tonson to re-edit the *Paradise Lost*.

[2] John Sheffield, Duke of Buckingham, 1648-1721, author of a rhymed *Essay on Poetry* first published in 1682 and highly praised by Pope and Addison.   Cf. Spingarn, *Critical Essays of the Seventeenth Century*, II, pp. 286-296.

[3] John Wilmot, Earl of Rochester, 1647-1680. Cf. Spingarn, II, pp. 282–285.

[4] These lines were published under Milton's portrait in Tonson's folio edition of the *Paradise Lost*, 1688, issued under the patronage of Lord Somers. Cf. Dryden, *Works*, XI, p. 162.

[5] *Ibid.*, XIV, p. 144.

[6] Cf. *Essai*, p. 359: " C'est ce grand nombre de fautes grossières qui fit sans doute dire à Dryden, dans sa préface sur *l'Enéide*, que Milton ne vaut guère mieux que notre Chapelain et notre Lemoyne; mais aussi ce sont les beautés admirables de Milton qui ont fait dire à ce même Dryden que la nature l'avait formé de l'âme d'Homère et de celle de Virgile." Cf. p. 68, *ante*.

[7] 1728 had.

[8] 1728 Addison.

[9] The letters on Milton appeared in the *Spectator* on Saturdays, between January 5 and May 3, 1721.
    Cf. *Essai*, p. 356: " Depuis, le célèbre M. Addison écrivit en forme, pour prouver que ce poëme égalait ceux de Virgile et d'Homère.   Les Anglais commencèrent à se le persuader, et la réputation de Milton fut fixée."

Undertaking to point out what would be reputed a Fault in any other Country.

I am very far from thinking that one Nation ought to judge of its Productions by the Standard of another, nor do I presume that the *French* (for Example) who have no *Epick* Poets, have any Right to give Laws on *Epick* Poetry.[1]

But I fancy many *English* Readers, who are acquainted with the *French* language, will not be displeas'd to have some Notion of the Taste of that Country: And I hope they are too just either to submit to it, or despise it barely upon the Score of its being foreign to them.[2]

Would each Nation attend a little more than they do, to the Taste and the Manners of their respective Neighbours, perhaps a general good Taste might diffuse itself through all *Europe* from such an intercourse of Learning, and from that useful Exchange of Observations.[3] The *English* Stage, for Example, might be clear'd of mangled Carcasses, and the Style of their tragick Authors, come down from their forced Metaphorical Bombast to a nearer Imitation of Nature. The *French* would learn from the *English* to animate their Tragedies with more | Action, and would con- 110 tract now and then their long Speeches into shorter and warmer Sentiments.[4]

The *Spaniards* would introduce in their Plays more Pictures of human Life, more Characters and Manners, and not puzzle

---

[1] Omitted in the French.

[2] A direct plea for the *Henriade*. This sentence naturally did not appear in the French.

[3] This sentence is found in the French essay at the end of the introduction where it seems logically to belong.

[4] The comparison of the French and English stage has been transferred to the introductory chapter of the French essay. Cf. *Discours sur la Tragédie*, *Oeuvres*, II, p. 314, 318: " Il a manqué jusqu'à présent à presque tous les auteurs tragiques de votre nation [England] cette pureté, cette conduite régulière, ces bienséances de l'action et du style, cette élégance, et toutes ces finesses de l'art qui ont établi la réputation du théâtre français depuis le grand Corneille; mais vos pièces les plus irrégulières ont un grand mérite, c'est celui de l'action . . . Nous avons en France des tragédies estimées, qui sont plutôt des conversations qu'elles ne sont la représentation d'un événement . . . Je suis bien loin de pro- poser que la scène devienne un lieu de carnage, comme elle l'est dans Shakes- peare et dans ses successeurs." Cf. *Essai*, p. 307: " Chez les Français, c'est pour l'ordinaire une suite de conversations en cinq actes, avec une intrigue amour- euse.   En Angleterre, la tragédie est véritablement une action."   Cf. Lanson, *Lettres phil.*, II, p. 139: " Les Anglais ont beaucoup profité des ouvrages de notre langue, nous devrions à notre tour emprunter d'eux après leur avoir prêté: nous ne sommes venus, les Anglais & nous, qu'après les Italiens qui en tout ont été nos maîtres, & que nous avons surpassés en quelque chose.   Je ne sçai à laquelle des trois nations il faudra donner la préférence; mais heureux celui qui sait sentir leurs différens mérites."

themselves always in the Entanglements of confus'd Adventures, more romantick than natural. The *Italian* in Point of Tragedy would catch the Flame from the *English*, and all the Rest from the *French*. In Point of Comedy, they would learn from Mr. *Congreve*[1] and some other Authors, to prefer Wit and Humour to Buffoonery.

To proceed in that View, I'll venture to say that none of the *French* Criticks could like the Excursions which *Milton* makes sometimes beyond the strict Limits of his Subject.[2] They lay down for a Rule that an Author himself ought never to appear in his Poem; and his own Thoughts, his own Sentiments must be spoken by the Actors he introduces. Many judicious Men in *England* comply with that Opinion, and Mr. *Adisson*[3] favours it.[4] I beg Leave in this place to hazard a Reflection of my own, which I submit to the Reader's Judgement.

Milton breaks the Thread of his Narration in two Manners. 111 The first consists of two or three kinds of Prologues, | which he premises at the Beginning of some Books. In one Place he expatiates upon his own Blindness; in another he compares his Subject and prefers it to that of the *Iliad*, and to the common Topicks of War, which were thought before him the only Subject fit for *Epick* Poetry; and he adds that he hopes to soar as high as all his Predecessors, unless the cold Climate of *England damps his Wings*.

His other Way of interrupting his Narration, is by some Observations which he intersperses now and then upon some great

---

[1] William Congreve, English dramatist, 1670-1729. Cf. Lanson, *Lettres phil.*, II, p. 108; p. 104, note 7, *ante*.

[2] In the French essay Voltaire enumerates, as having displeased French critics, most of the parts of *Paradise Lost* which he had mentioned in the English, as likely to displease them. Cf.: " Mais tous les critiques judicieux, dont la France est pleine, se réunirent à trouver que le diable parle trop souvent" (p. 357) and the closing sentence: " Lorsque j'étais à Londres, j'osai composer en anglais un petit *Essai sur la poésie épique*, dans lequel je pris la liberté de dire que nos bons juges français ne manqueraient pas de relever toutes les fautes dont je viens de parler. Ce que j'avais prévu est arrivé . . . " P. 360.

[3] 1728 Addison.

[4] Cf. Addison in *Spectator*, II, pp. 318, 319: " In the Structure of his Poem he has likewise admitted of too many Digressions. It is finely observed by *Aristotle*, that the Author of an Heroic Poem should seldom speak himself . . . *Milton's* Complaint [for] his Blindness, his Panegyrick on Marriage, his Reflections on *Adam* and *Eve's* going naked, of the Angels eating, and several other Passages in his Poem, are liable to the same Exception, tho' I must confess there is so great a Beauty in these very Digressions, that I would not wish them out of his Poem."

Incident, or some interesting Circumstance. Of that Kind is his
Digression on Love in the fourth Book;

> *Whatever* Hippocrites[1] *austerely talk*
> *Defaming as impure, what God declares*
> *Pure, and commands to some, leaves free to all.*
> *Our Maker bids increase, who bids abstain*
> *But our Destroyer foe to God and Men* ?
> *Hail wedded Love, &c.*[2]

As to the first of these two Heads, I cannot but own that an
Author is generally guilty of an impardonable Self-love, when he
lays aside his Subject to descant on his own Person; but that
human Frailty is to be forgiven in *Milton;* nay, I am pleas'd with
it. He gratifies the Curiosity, it raises in me about his Person,
when I admire the Author, I dessre[3] | to know something of 112
the Man, and he whom all Readers would be glad to know, is
allow'd to speak of himself. But this however is a very dangerous
Example for a Genius of an inferior Order, and is only to be justified by Success.

As to the second Point I am so far from looking on that Liberty
as a Fault, that I think it to be a great Beauty.[4] For if Morality
is the aim of Poetry, I do not apprehend why the Poet should be
forbidden to intersperse his Descriptions with moral Sentences
and useful Reflexions,[5] provided he scatters them with a sparing
Hand, and in proper Places either when he wants Personages to
utter those Thoughts, or when their Character does not permit
them to speak in the Behalf of Virtue.

'Tis strange that *Homer* is commended by the Cricticks for his
comparing *Ajax* to an Ass[6] pelted away with Stones by some

---

[1] 1728 Hypocrites.

[2] Milton, *Paradise Lost*, IV, ll. 744-750. Line 745 ("Of purity and place, and innocence,") is omitted by Voltaire.

[3] 1728 desire.

[4] The discussion of Milton's digressions did not find a place in the French.

[5] 1728 Reflections.

[6] Cf. Le Bossu, I, p. 210: " On raille fort la comparaison d'Ajax avec un asne, qu'Homère a emploiée dans l'Iliade. Elle seroit maintenant indécente & ridicule parcequ'il seroit ridicule & indécent à un Seigneur de se servir de cette monture. Mais cet animal étoit plus noble autrefois, les Rois & les Princes ne les dédaignoient pas comme font les Bourgeois aujourd'hui." *Ibid.*, p. 211: " [La comparison] d'Ulysses à de la Graisse. Le Saint-Esprit même qui ne peut avoir de mauvais goût, commence l'éloge du Roi David par cette idée: David est comme de la graisse toute pure. En ces premiers temps où l'on sacrifioit des animaux dans la Religion véritable aussi bien que dans la fausse, le sang et la graisse étoient les choses les plus nobles, les plus augustes et les plus saintes."

Children, *Ulysses* to a Pudding, the Council-board of *Priam* to Grashoppers. 'Tis strange, I say, that they defend so clamorously those Similes tho' never so foreign to the Purpose, and will not allow the natural Reflexions,[1] the noble Digressions of *Milton* tho' never so closely link'd to the Subject.[2]

I will not dwell upon some small Errors of *Milton*, which are
113 obvious to eve|ry Reader, I mean some few Contradictions and those frequent Glances at the *Heathen* Mythology,[3] which Fault by the by is so much the more unexcusable[4] in him, by his having premis'd in his first Book that those Divinities were but Devils worshipp'd under different Names, which ought to have been a sufficient Caution to him not to speak of the Rape of *Proserpine*, of the Wedding of *Juno* and *Jupiter*, &c. as Matters of Fact.

I lay aside likewise his preposterous and aukward Jests, his Puns, his too familiar Expressions so inconsistent with the Elevation of his Genius, and of his Subject.

To come to more essential Points and more *liable* to be debated. I dare affirm that the Contrivance of the *Pandaemonium* would have been entirely disapprov'd of by Criticks like *Boyleau*,[5] *Racine*, &c.

That Seat built for the Parliament of the Devils, seems very preposterous: Since Satan hath summon'd them altogether, and harangu'd them just before in an ample Field. The Council was necessary; but where it was to be held, 'twas very indifferent. The Poet seems to delight in building his *Pandaemonium* in *Doric* Order with Freeze and Cornice, and a Roof of Gold.[6] Such a Contrivance savours more of the wild Fancy of our Father
114 *le Moine*, then[7] of the seri|ous spirit of *Milton*. But when

---

[1] 1728 Reflections.
[2] This unfavorable allusion to Homer seems very forced. There is little connection between his comparisons and Milton's digressions. It is interesting to compare with this passage, which does not appear in the French, another which does: "On a reproché à Homère de longues et inutiles harangues, et surtout les plaisanteries de ses héros; comment souffrir dans Milton les harangues et les railleries des anges et des diables pendant la bataille qui se donne dans le ciel ?" *Essai*, p. 359.
[3] Cf. Addison in *Spectator*, II, p. 319: "Another Blemish [that] appears in some of his Thoughts, is his frequent Allusion to Heathen Fables, which are not certainly of a Piece with the Divine Subject, of which he treats." Cf. p. 110, note 2, *ante*.
[4] 1728 inexcusable.
[5] 1728 Boileau.
[6] Cf. Addison in *Spectator*, II, p. 321: "When he is upon Building he mentions *Doric Pillars, Pilasters, Cornice, Freeze, Architrave.*"
[7] 1728 than.

afterwards the Devils turn dwarfs to fill their Places in the House, as if it was impracticable to build a Room large enough to contain them in their natural Size; it is an idle Story which would match the most extravagant Tales. And to crown all, Satan and the chief Lords preserving their own monstrous Forms, while the rabble of the Devils shrink into Pigmees,[1] heightens the Ridicule of the whole Contrivance to an unexpressible Degree. Methinks the true Criterion for discerning what is really ridiculous in an *Epick* Poem, is to examine if the same Thing would not fit exactly the Mock heroick. Then I dare say that no-thing is so adapted to that ludicrous way of Writing as the Metamorphosis of the Devils into Dwarfs.

The Fiction of *Death* and *Sin* seems to have in it some great Beauties and many gross Defects.[2] In order to canvass this Matter with Order. We must first lay down that such shadowy Beings, as *Death, Sin, Chaos*, are intolerable when they are not allegorical.[3] For Fiction is nothing but Truth in Disguise. It must be granted too, that an Allegory must be short, decent and noble. For an Allegory carried too far or too low, is like a beautiful Woman who wears always a | Mask. An Allegory is a long 115 Metaphor; and to speak too long in metaphor's must be tiresom,[4] because unnatural. This being premis'd, I must say that in general those Fictions, those imaginary beings, are more agreeable to the Nature of *Milton's* Poem, than to any other; because he hath but two natural Persons for his Actors, I mean *Adam* and *Eve*. A great Part of the Action lies in imaginary Worlds, and must *of course* admit of imaginary Beings.

---

[1] 1728 Pigmies.

[2] It is related that while Voltaire was at Eastbury, the guest of Doddington, probably in 1727, an argument arose concerning *Paradise Lost*. Voltaire criticized severely the episode of Death and Sin and the poet Young who was defending Milton was inspired to make an epigram:
    " You are so witty, profligate and thin,
        At once we think thee Milton, Death and Sin."
Some years later Young referred to this incident in a poem called *Sea Piece* which he dedicated to Voltaire:
    " On Dorset's downs, when Milton's page,
        With sin and Death provoked thy rage,
        Thy rage provoked, who soothed with gentle rhymes?"
Cf. Churton Collins, *V. M. R.*, p. 31; Ballantyne, pp. 96 ff; Foulet, *Corr.*, p. 37, note 3.

[3] Cf. Addison in *Spectator*, II, p. 235: " He has brought into it two Actors of a Shadowy and Ficticious Nature, in the Persons of *Sin* and *Death* . . . I cannot think that Persons of such a Chymerical Existence are proper Actors in an Epic Poem."

[4] 1728 tiresome.

Then *Sin* springing out of the Head of Satan, seems a beautiful Allegory of Pride, which is look'd upon as the first Offence committed against God. But I question if *Satan*, getting his Daughter with Child, is an Invention to be approv'd off.[1] I am afraid that Fiction is but a meer Quibble; for if Sin was of a masculine Gender in *English, as it is in all the other Languages,*[2] that whole Affair Drops, and the Fiction vanishes away. But suppose we are not so nice, and we allow Satan to be in Love with *Sin, because this Word is made feminine in* English (as Death passes also for masculine) what a horrid and loathsome Idea does *Milton* present to the Mind, in this Fiction? *Sin* brings forth Death, this Monster inflam'd with Lust and Rage, lies with his Mother, as she 116 had done with her Father. From | that new Commerce, springs a Swarm of Serpents, which creep in and out of their Mother's Womb, and gnaw and tear the Bowels they are born from.

Let such a Picture be never so beautifully drawn, let the Allegory be never so obvious, and so clear, still it will be intolerable, on the Account of its Foulness. That Complication of Horrors, that Mixture of Incest, that Heap of Monsters, that Loathsomeness so far fetch'd, cannot but shock a Reader of delicate Taste.

But what is more intolerable, there are Parts in that Fiction, which bearing no Allegory at all, have no Manner of Excuse. There is no Meaning in the Communication between Death and Sin, 'tis distasteful without any Purpose; or if any Allegory lies under it, the filthy Abomination of the Thing is certainly more obvious than the Allegory.

I see with Admiration, *Sin*, the *Portress* of Hell, opening the Gates of the Abiss,[3] but unable to shut them again; that is really beautiful, because 'tis true.[4] But what signifies Satan and Death quarrelling together, grinning at one another, and ready to fight?

The Fiction of *Chaos, Night,* and *Discord,* is rather a Picture, 117 than an Allegory; and for ought I know, deserves | to be approv'd, because it strikes the Reader with Awe, not with Horror.

I know the Bridge built by Death and Sin, would be dislik'd

[1] 1728 of.
[2] Cf. die Sünde.
[3] 1728 Abyss.
[4] Cf. Addison in *Spectator*, II, p. 367: "And how properly *Sin* is made the Portress of Hell, and the only Being that can open the Gates to that World of Tortures."

in *France*. The nice Criticks of that Country would urge against that Fiction, that it seems too common, and that it is useless; for Men's Souls want no paved Way, to be thrown into Hell, after their Separation from the Body.

They would laugh justly at the Paradise of Fools, at the Hermits, Fryars, Cowles,[1] Beads, Indulgences,[2] Bulls, Reliques, toss'd by the Winds, at St. *Peter's* waiting with his Keys at the Wicket of Heaven. And surely the most passionate Admirers of *Milton*, could not vindicate those low comical Imaginations, which belong by Right to *Ariosto*.[3]

Now the sublimest of all the Fictions calls me to examine it. I mean the War in Heaven. The Earl of *Roscommon*,[4] and Mr. *Addison* (whose Judgement seems either to guide, or to justify the Opinion of his Countrymen) admire chiefly that Part of the Poem. They bestow all the Skill of their Criticism and the Strength of their Eloquence, to set off that favourite Part.[5] I may affirm, that the very Things they admire, would not be tolerated by the *French* Criticks. The Reader will perhaps see with Pleasure, *in* | *what consists so strange a Difference*, and what 118 may be the Ground of it.

First, they would assert, that a War in Heaven being an imaginary Thing, which lies out of the Reach of our Nature, should be contracted in two or three Pages, rather than lengthen'd out into two Books; because we are naturally impatient of removing from us the Objects which are not adapted to our Senses.

According to that Rule, they would maintain that 'tis[6] an idle Task to give the Reader the full Character of the Leaders of that War, and to describe *Raphael, Michael, Abdiel, Moloch*, and *Nisroth*, as *Homer* paints *Ajax, Diomede*, and *Hector*.

For what avails it to draw at length the Picture of these Beings, so utterly Strangers to the Reader, that he cannot be affected any Way towards them; by the same Reason, the long Speeches of

---

[1] 1728 Cowls.

[2] 1728 Indulgencies.

[3] Cf. *Essai*, p. 358: "Voilà des imaginations dont tout lecteur sensé a été révolté; et il faut que le poëme soit bien beau d'ailleurs pour qu'on ait pu le lire, malgré l'ennui que doit causer cet amas de folies désagréables."

[4] Wentworth, Dillon, Earl of Roscommon, 1633?-1685, *Essay on Translated Verse*, 1684. Cf. Spingarn, *Critical Essays of the Seventeenth Century*, II, pp. 297-309. Roscommon's essay was praised by Addison, *Spectator*, II, p. 166.

[5] Cf. Earl of Roscommon, *Essay on Translated Verse*, ed. Spingarn, pp. 308, 309; Addison in *Spectator*, II, pp. 436, 500; *ibid.*, III, p. 4.

[6] 1728 it is.

these imaginary Warriors, either before the Battle or in the Middle of the Action, their mutual Insults, seem an injudicious Imitation of *Homer.*

The aforesaid Criticks would not bear with the Angels plucking up the Mountains, with their Woods, their Waters, and their Rocks, and flinging them on the Heads of their Enemies. Such 119 a Contrivance (they would say) is the | more puerile, the more it aims at Greatness. Angels arm'd with Mountains in Heaven, resemble too much the Dipsodes in *Rabelais,* who wore an Armour of *Portland* Stone six Foot thick.[1]

The Artillery seems of the same Kind, yet more trifling, because more useless.

To what Purpose are these Engines brought in? Since they cannot wound the Enemies, but only remove them from their Places, and make them tumble down: Indeed (if the Expression may be forgiven) 'tis to play at Nine-Pins. And the very Thing which is so dreadfully great on Earth, becomes very low and ridiculous in Heaven.

I cannot omit here, the visible Contradiction which reigns in that Episode. God sends his faithful Angels to fight, to conquer and to punish the Rebels. *Go (says He, to* Michael *and* Gabriel)

> ....*And to the Brow of Heaven*
> *Pursuing, drive them out from God and Bliss,*
> *Into their Place of Punishment, the Gulph*
> *Of* Tartarus, *which ready opens wide*
> *His fiery Chaos to receive their Fall.*[2]

How does it come to pass, after such a positive Order, that the Battle hangs doubtful? And why did God the Father com- 120 mand *Gabriel* and *Raphael,* to | do what He executes afterwards by his Son only.

I leave it to the Readers, to pronounce, if these Observations are right, or ill-grounded, and if they are carried to[3] far. But in case these Exceptions are just, the severest Critick must how-

---

[1] Cf. Rabelais, *Pantagruel,* Book I, Chap. XXVIII: " Comment Pantagruel eut victoire bien estrangement des Dipsodes et des Géans." Chap. XXIX: "Comment Pantagruel deffit les troys cens Géans armez de pierre de taille."
  Portland stone, from quarries on the Isle of Portland, a peninsula off Dorsetshire, was used in the construction of many English buildings, notably St. Paul's Cathedral, begun in 1675.
[2] *Paradise Lost,* VI, ll. 51-55.
[3] 1728 too.

ever confess there are Perfections enough in *Milton,* to attone for
all his Defects.

I must beg leave to conclude this Article on Milton with two
Observations.

His Hero (I mean *Adam,* his first Personage) is unhappy. That
demonstrates against all the Criticks, that a very good Poem
may end unfortunately, in Spight of all their pretended Rules.[1]
Secondly, the *Paradise Lost* ends compleatly. The Thread of
the Fable is spun out to the last. *Milton* and *Tasso* have been
careful of not stopping short and abruptly. The one does not
abandon *Adam* and *Eve,* till they are driven out of *Eden.* The
other does not conclude, before *Jerusalem* is taken. *Homer* and
Virgil took a contrary Way, the *Iliad* ends with the Death of
Hector, the *Æneid,* with that of *Turnus:* The Tribe of Commentators have upon that enacted a Law, that a House ought
never to be finish'd, because *Homer* and *Virgil* did not compleat
their own;[2] but if *Homer* had taken *Troy,* and *Virgil* married
Lavinia to *Æneas,* | the Criticks would have laid down a Rule 121
just the contrary.[3]

Was I sway'd by the common Affectation of commending our
native Country abroad, I would endeavour in this Place, to set
off to the best Advantage, some of our *Epick* Poems; but I must
frankly own, among more than fifty which I have read, there
is not one tolerable.[4] Then instead of throwing away an un-
available Criticism upon some wretched *French* Poem, I am reduced to inquire, why we have not a good one;[5] for it seems a

---

[1] Cf. Addison in *Spectator,* II, p. 316: " The first Imperfection which I shall
observe in the Fable is that the Event of it is unhappy." Cf. Le Bossu, p. 263:
" Mais s'il faut s'arrêter à l'autorité je ne sais s'il se trouvera quelque exemple
d'un Poète qui finisse son ouvrage par le malheur de son Héros."

[2] Rapin, *Réflexions,* p. 23: " Il n'y a presque qu'Homère et Virgile qui sçachent
finir les choses, où il faut les finir."

[3] This paragraph is omitted in the French.

[4] Cf. *Essai,* p. 360: *Conclusion.* The French conclusion is only about half
as long as the English. Although in each case the discussion resolves itself
into an attempt to determine why the French have no epic poem and thereby
to pave the way for the *Henriade,* only a few of the ideas brought out in the
English are touched upon in the French and then rather lightly. As we have
seen, all the passages dealing with lack of liberty in France and in French literature, as contrasted with England, have been omitted.

[5] Cf. Addison in *Spectator,* I, p. 471: " I have only considered our Language
as it shows the Genius and national Temper of the *English* . . . We might
perhaps carry the same Thought into other Languages, and deduce a greater
Part of what is peculiar to them from the Genius of the People who speak them."

little strange, that a Nation who boasts of having succeeded so well in all the other Parts of Poetry, falls so short of herself in that Particular.

I have heard the *French* tongue arraigned in *England* of Insufficiency, as being neither strong nor lofty enough to reach the Sublimity of *Epick* Poetry.

I am apt to think, that every Language has its own particular Genius, flowing chiefly from the Genius of the Nation, and partly from its own Nature.[1]

On the one Side, more or less Liberty in the Government,[2] and in Religion, a more or less free Conversation between the two Sexes, the Influence of the first Authors, who have written 122 with Suc|cess, and whose Stile is become the general Standard, all these Means have a great Share in determining the Nature of a Language, in making it extensive or stinted, strong or weak, sublime or low.

On the other Side, the Roughness of too many Consonants, the Softness of predominant Vowels, the Length, or the Shortness or the Words, more or less Articles, and the like, give a strong Bias to an Idiom, and render it more or less susceptible of some particular Ways of Writing.

Thus if we consider the Softness and Effeminacy into which the Luxuriancy of Vowels emasculates the *Italian* Tongue, and the Idleness in which the *Italians* spend all their Life,[3] busy only in the pursuit of those Arts which soften the Mind; we must not wonder if that Language passes (as it were) for the Language of Love.

The Freedom of Society in *France*, and the Turn of the Phrases, which, as they admit of no Transposition, are the more perspicuous, qualify exceedingly the *French* Tongue for Conversation. The former Roughness of the *English* language, now improv'd into Strength and Energy, its Copiousness, its admitting of many Inversions, fit it for more sublime Performances. Besides, the 123 Force | of that Idiom is wonderfully heighten'd, by the Nature of the Government, which allows the *English* to speak in Pub-

---

[1] Voltaire's attitude has changed somewhat in the French: " Nous n'avions point de poëme épique en France, et je ne sais même si nous en avons aujourd'hui. *La Henriade*, à la vérité, a été imprimée souvent." *Essai*, p. 360.

[2] Cf. p. 145, note 1, *post*.

[3] This passage was omitted in the French conclusion.

lick,[1] and by the Liberty of Conscience, which makes them more
conversant in the Scripture, and hath rendered the Language of
the Prophets so familiar to them, that their Poetry savours very
much of that *Eastern* out of the way Sublimity; nay, sixty or
eighty Years ago, all the Speeches in Parliament were cramm'd[2]
with Expressions taken from the *Jewish* Writings.[3] But such predominant Qualifications of a Language, do not imply an Exclu-
sion of any other Aptitude in it. Lofty Performances have been
made in *Italian*. Some *English* Poets have written gracefully
upon Love, and it is not impossible for the *French* to have an
Epick Poem.

The *French* Tongue has Strength and Majesty enough in *Cor-
neilles* Tragedies. Nay, now and then it soars up in his Plays,
beyond the true Measure of the Sublime. Far from wanting
Force or Grandeur, I dare affirm it labours under a contrary
Defect. And this is a Secret which I unfold willingly. We can
hardly express common Things with Felicity in our Heroic[4] Poetry.
The Genius of the Nation, and consequently the Turn of the
Language, does not allow us to | come down to the Description 124
of the Trappings of a Horse, of the Wheels of a Chariot, &c. We
can commend rural Life in General, but not specify, with Dignity,
the little Particularities belonging to it. This Task, is avoided
by all our skilful Writers, who are conscious of the Defectiveness
of the Language in that respect. In short, such is our Disad-
vantage, that there are infinite Things,[5] which we dare neither
call by their Names, nor express by a Paraphrase.[6] Mr. *Pope,*

---

[1] Cf. Lanson, *Lettres phil.*, II, pp. 119-120: " En Angleterre communément
on pense, & les lettres y sont plus en honneur qu'en France. Cet avantage
est une suite nécessaire de la forme de leur gouvernement. Il y a à Londres
environ huit cent personnes qui ont le droit de parler en public, & de soutenir
les intérêts de la Nation; . . . ainsi toute la Nation est dans la nécessité de
s'instruire."

[2] 1728 crammed.

[3] Cf. Addison in *Spectator*, II, p. 697: "And it happens very luckily, that
the *Hebrew* Idioms run into the *English* tongue with a peculiar Grace and Beauty.
Our Language has received innumerable Elegancies and Improvements, from
the Infusion of *Hebraisms*, which are derived to it out of the Poetical Passages
in Holy Writ. They give a Force and Energy to our Expressions, warm and
animate our Language and convey our Thoughts in more ardent and intense
Phrases, than any that are to be met with in our own Tongue." *Ibid.*, p. 479:
"*Milton* has shewn his Judgment very remarkably . . . in duly qualifying
those high Strains of *Eastern* Poetry." Cf. Texte, pp. 86-87: " Le premier
sans doute des critiques français, Voltaire a signalé cette parenté du génie bri-
tannique et du génie de la Bible, qui est le premier des livres anglais."

[4] 1728 Heroick.

[5] 1728 There is an infinite Number of Things. Cf. *Errata.*

[6] 1728 Periphrase. Cf. *Errata.*

in his Translation of *Homer*, may without any Risque, wound a Hero, *where the Bone and the Bladder meet*, or pierce him through the *right Shoulder*. He may say after his Original:

>........*the Dart*.........*pierced a vital Part,*
>*Full in his Face it entered, and betwixt*
>*The Nose and the Eye-Ball, the proud* Lician *fixt,*
>*Crash'd all his Jaws, and cleft the Tongue within,*
>*Till the bright Point look'd out beneath the Skin.*[1]

The like Attempt in *French* would be thought Burlesque. The Fields of Nature lie wide and open for the *English* to range through 125 at Pleasure, whilst we | are stinted and oblig'd to walk with too much Circumspection.

To this happy Freedom, that the *British* Nation enjoys in every Thing,[2] are owing many excellent poetical Versions of the ancient Poets; whereas the *French* are reduced to translate *Virgil Homer, Lucretius,* and *Ovid* in Prose.

[1] 1728 Chin. Cf. *Errata*. Pope, *Iliad*, V, ll. 351-356. In Pope ll. 351-352 read:
" He spoke, and, rising, hurl'd his forceful dart,
Which, driven by Pallas, pierc'd a vital part."

[2] It is interesting to compare with the allusions to English liberty in our text extracts from those letters of Voltaire written in England in which the same idea found expression.

Cf. Foulet, *Corr.*, p. 45 (to Thieriot, August 12, 1726): "C'est un pays où l'on pense librement et noblement, sans être retenu par aucune crainte servile." *Ibid.*, p. 61 (to Thieriot, October 26, 1726): " I am weary of courts, my dear Thiriot; all that is king, or belongs to a king, frights my republican philosophy, I won't drink the least draught of slavery in the land of liberty." Foulet, p. xii, says in regard to this letter: " Elle renferme le plus chaleureux éloge de l'Angleterre qui soit jamais tombé de la plume d'un Français." *Ibid.*, pp. 138-139 (à M. . . . March 31, 1728): " I think and write like a free Englishman," . . . "A country [England] where one obeys to the laws only and to one's whims. Reason is free here and walks her own way. . . . No manner of living appears strange."

Cf. Lanson, *Lettres phil.*, I, p. 89: " Le fruit des guerres civiles à Rome a été l'esclavage, & celui des troubles d'Angleterre la liberté. La Nation Anglaise est la seule de la terre, qui soit parvenue à régler le pouvoir des Rois en leur résistant, et qui d'efforts en efforts ait enfin établi ce Gouvernement sage, où le Prince tout puissant pour faire du bien, a les mains liées pour faire le mal, où les Seigneurs sont Grands sans insolence & sans Vassaux, & où le peuple partage le gouvernement sans confusion." *Ibid.*, II, p. 5: " Son grand bonheur [Newton's] a été non-seulement d'être né dans un païs libre . . ." In a letter to Towne dated July 27, 1728, there is a sentence in which Voltaire speaks definitely, as he had in the Essay, of the influence upon the English language of the freedom enjoyed by the nation. Foulet, *Corr.*, pp. 169-170: "A language [the English] which gives life and strength to all the subjects it touches. The *Henriade* has at least in itself a spirit of liberty which is not very common in France; the language of a free nation as yours is the only one that can vigourously express what I have but faintly drawn in my native tongue: the work will grow under your hands, worthy of the British nation, and that tree transplanted in your soil and grafted by you will bear a new and a better sort of fruit." Cf. p. 149, *post*.

Mr. *de la Motte*, a Member of the *French* Academy, is the only Man of some Reputation, who attempted the *Iliad* in Verse; but he was forced to contract the four and twenty Books of *Homer* into twelve, yet those twelve do not contain so many Verses, as four Books of *Homer* do. His *Iliad* is a short Abridgment of the *Greek*, and yet is judg'd to be exceedingly too long.[1]

After all, if that Slavery, if that Coyness of the *French* Language, makes it unfit for translating *Homer*, and *Virgil*, yet I do not perceive how that should hinder the Nation from having an *Epick* Poem of her own Growth?

A Poem, methinks, might subsist very well, without the Help of mechanick, or anatomical Descriptions. We rather require of an Author, to excite our Passions, to unfold the most intricate Recesses of the Soul, to describe the Customs of the Nations, to mark the Differences[2] which arise in the Characters of | Men, 126 from the different Governments they are born under, in short to speak the Language of the polite World; than to play the Surgeon, the Carpenter or the Joiner, though never so elegantly.

Cardinal of[3] *Rets*, and the Earl of *Clarendon*,[4] in their Memoirs, unravel all the Springs of the Civil Wars, and draw at full Length, the Pictures of those whose Ambition shook the Foundation of their respective Countries. But neither of these two great Writers, makes it his particular Care to describe with Accuracy, how such a Colonel was wounded through the Bladder, and such a Captain in the Kidneys. Nor do they throw away their Time in describing elegantly of what Wood the Benches of the House of Parliament were made. Why then should an *Epick* Poet, lie under the Necessity of elaborating those little Descriptions, which every noble Historian avoids with Care?

Some impute our Want of an *Epick* Poem, to the Shackles of Rhime. They say that the gingling[5] Return of the same Sounds,

---

[1] Cf. *Essai*, p. 317 (Chapter on Homer): " Peu d'ouvrages sont écrits avec autant d'art, de discrétion, et de finesse, que ses dissertations [Lamotte's] sur Homère." But (p. 319): " Lamotte a ôté beaucoup de défauts à Homère [in his translation], mais il n'a conservé aucune de ses beautés; il a fait un petit squelette d'un corps démesuré et trop plein d'embonpoint. En vain tous les journaux ont prodigué des louanges à Lamotte; en vain avec tout l'art possible, soutenu de beaucoup de mérite, s'était-il fait un parti considérable; son parti, ses éloges, sa traduction, tout a disparu, et Homère est resté." This passage first appeared in the French essay between 1742 amd 1746. Cf. p. 153, *post*.
[2] 1728 Differences.
[3] 1728 de.
[4] Edward Hyde, Earl of Clarendon, 1608-1674.
[5] 1728 jingling.

which are chiming on, in the same Stops, Measures, Pauses, without any Variety, or any Relief to the Ear, must needs Occasion an insupportable Uniformity throughout all the Work. They 127 urge, that Slavery cramps the no|blest Genius, and a Poet, instead of using Rhime, as an Ornament, serviceable to his Sense, makes his own Thoughts subservient to Rhime.[1]

They add, Rhime is a barbarous *Gothick* Invention, owing to the dull Sprightliness of the Monks, and contend that nothing Good can be built with so bad a Material.

First, I must confess we are Slaves to Rhime in *France*, and our Slavery is altogether irretrievable.[2] Nay, all our Tragedies ought to be rhimed.[3] For our Poetry being fetter'd by too strict Rules, admitting of no Inversions, nor of Verses incroaching upon one another, would have nothing but Loftiness of Stile, to distinguish it from Prose, if it were not for Rhime.[4] We have no Manner of Pretence to blank Verse, we must keep to Rhime necessarily, and whosoever would attempt to throw off a Burthen which Mr. *Boyleau*,[5] *Racine* and *Corneille*, have so gloriously sustained, would be thought rather weak than bold, and certainly would meet with a very unkind Reception.[6]

As to that pretended Uniformity, and Tediousness objected against Verses in Rhime, it is not to be found in Authors truly good, of whatsoever Country. *Tasso* is read with Pleasure, though 128 all his | Verses, nay, almost all his Syllables, end in *a, e, i, o*. And those who say Rhime is an Invention of the Monks of the seventh Century, are utterly in the Wrong. All the Nations whose Lan-

---

[1] *Discours sur la tragédie, Oeuvres*, II, pp. 313-314: "Je sais combien de disputes j'ai essuyées sur notre versification en Angleterre, et quels reproches me fait souvent le savant évêque de Rochester sur cette contrainte puérile, qu'il prétend que nous nous imposons de gaieté de coeur."

[2] *Ibid.*, p. 312: "Malgré toutes ces réflexions et toutes ces plaintes, nous ne pourrons jamais secouer le joug de la rime; elle est essentielle a la poésie française." Cf. Voltaire's discussion of rhyme in the Preface of *Oedipe*.

[3] *Ibid.*, p. 313: "Il y a grande apparence qu'il faudra toujours des vers sur tous les théâtres tragiques, et, de plus, toujours des rimes sur les nôtres."

[4] *Ibid.*, p. 312: "Notre langue ne comporte que peu d'inversions; nos vers ne souffrent point d'enjambement, du moins cette liberté est très rare; . . . nos césures et un certain nombre de pieds ne suffiraient pas pour distinguer la prose d'avec la versification."

[5] 1728 Boiloau.

[6] *Discours sur la tragédie, Oeuvres*, II, p. 312: "De plus, tant de grands maîtres qui ont fait des vers rimés, tels que les Corneille, les Racine, les Despréaux, ont tellement accoutumé nos oreilles à cette harmonie que nous n'en pourrions pas supporter d'autres; et, je le répète encore, quiconque voudrait se délivrer d'un fardeau qu'a porté le grand Corneille serait regardé avec raison, non pas comme un génie hardi qui s'ouvre une route nouvelle, mais comme un homme très-faible qui ne peut marcher dans l'ancienne carrière."

guages are known to us, have Verses in Rhime, except the *Greeks* and the *Romans*.

The return of the same Sounds, is a Kind of natural Musick, more obvious to the Ear, and more easily reduc'd into an Art, than the *Quantity* of Syllables.   It is true, that Distinction between long and short Syllables afforded to the *Romans* and *Greeks* an harmonious Variety of Sounds, which by their Quickness, or Gravity, were wonderfully expressive of the impetuous, or slow Motions of the Soul.   But we ought not (because we want so great an Advantage) to neglect the only one we are in Possession of, and in Room of which, we have nothing to set up.   Shou'd we not manure our own Soil, because some others are more fruitful ?

After these little Hints upon our Language, and our Versification, I will own, that an *Epick* Poem is a harder Task in *France*, than in any other Country whatever;[1] not purely because we *Rhime*, but because our *Rhimes*, as well as the other Parts of our Versification, are ty'd down | to most insupportable and insig- 129 nificant Rules;[2] not because our Language wants Loftiness, but because it wants Freedom.   For it is with our Heroick Poetry, as with our Trade, we come up to the *English* in neither, for want of being a free Nation.[3]

Slavery is generally an Obstacle to Abundance.   Our coy Language is not as copious as it should be.   We have discarded a Multitude of old energetic Expressions, the Loss of which has weakened the Stock of the *French* Tongue, as the compelling our Protestants away hath thinned the Nation.   The *English* have naturalized many of our antiquated Words, as they have done

---

[1] *Discours sur la tragédie, Oeuvres,* II, p. 313: " Voilà pourquoi il est plus aisé de faire cent vers en toute autre langue que quatre vers en français."

[2] *Ibid.,* p. 312: " Ce qui m'effraya le plus en rentrant dans cette carrière, [i.e., after his return from England] ce fut la sévérité de notre poésie, et l'esclavage de la rime . . . Un poëte, disais-je, est un homme libre qui asservit sa langue à son génie; le Français est un esclave de la rime. . . . L'Anglais dit tout ce qu'il veut, le Français ne dit que ce qu'il peut."

These remarks concerning French versification did not appear in the French version of the essay which was published two years later than the *Discours sur la tragédie.*

Cf. Pope, *Essay on Criticism,* III, ll. 712-714:
        " But critic-learning flourished most in France;
          The rules a nation, born to serve, obeys;
          And Boileau still in right of Horace sways."

[3] Cf. Lanson, *Lettres phil.,* I, p. 120: " Le Commerce qui a enrichi les Citoïens en Angleterre a contribué à les rendre libres, & cette liberté a étendu le Commerce à son tour; de là s'est formée la grandeur de l'Etat."

our Countrymen, and so they have increased their Language, as well as their People, at our Expence.[1]

But the greatest Enemy to *Epick* Poetry in *France*, is the Turn of the Genius of our Nation. It is almost impossible for us to venture on any Machinery. The antient Gods are exploded out of the World. The present Religion cannot succeed them among us.[2] The Cherub, and the Seraph, which act so noble a Part in *Milton*, would find it very hard to work their Way into a *French* Poem. The very words of *Gabriel, Michael, Raphael,* 130 would run a great Hazard of being made a Jest of. Our | Saints who make so good a Figure in our Churches, make a very sorry one in our *Epick* Poems. St. *Denis,*[3] St. *Christopher*, St. *Rock*, and St. *Genevieve*, ought to appear in Print no where, but in our Prayer-Books, and in the History of the Saints; a noble Volume, which contains more Wonders than any Machinery could afford.

To conclude, the best Reason I can offer for our ill Success in *Epick* Poetry is the Insufficiency of all who have attempted it. I can add nothing further, after this ingenuous Confession.[4]

---

[1] Religious intolerance was one of the subjects on which Voltaire felt most keenly. Here he draws an interesting parallel between the Revocation of the Edict of Nantes, which had occurred only nine years before his birth, and the intolerant rejection, on the part of the Academy and of classic writers, of a vast number of energetic words and expressions. Voltaire had had an opportunity to see how England in both cases had profited by France's intolerance of the French.

[2] Cf. p. 123, note 1, *ante*.

[3] 1728 *Dennis*.

[4] The essay closes with personal and characteristic touches, an ironical allusion to religious superstition and a final indirect but crystal-clear appeal for the *Henriade*.

F I N I S .

APPENDIX

The more important variants of the Essai sur la poésie épique—
Voltaire's further treatment of the poets discussed in the essays.

The marked differences existing between the *Essay upon Epic Poetry* and the *Essai sur la poésie épique* lead one to wonder to what extent the latter was altered during the forty-five years which the author lived after its first publication.

A comparison of the text found in the standard modern edition of Voltaire's works[1] and that of 1733,[2] with the text as it appeared in seven other representative editions published during the author's lifetime[3] and in the Kehl edition of 1784,[4] gives interesting results. It is clear that this brief piece of writing in its French form was considerably worked over, because, no doubt, of the importance its connection with the *Henriade* continued to give it in the poet's eyes. The collation of the ten editions in question reveals more than one hundred and fifty variants involving changes in wording, omissions and additions, exclusive of corrections in spelling and punctuation. The alterations are often unimportant. In some cases, however, they are of real significance either as corrections of inaccurate statements occurring in previous editions or as the result of a change of opinion, slight, complete or gradual on the part of the author.

---

[1] *Oeuvres*, Garnier frères, 1877-1885, VIII, p. 306.
[2] Cf. p. 29, note 5, *ante.*
[3] *Oeuvres de M. Voltaire*, Amsterdam, ed. Ledet et Cie., 1738-39, t. I. (Cf. Bengesco, IV, p. 5.)
    Oeuvres mêlées de M. de Voltaire, Genève, Bousquet, 1742, t. I. (Cf. Bengesco, IV, p. 20.)
    Oeuvres diverses de M. de Voltaire, Londres, Trévoux, Nourse, 1746. (Cf. Bengesco, IV, p. 24.)
    Oeuvres de M. de Voltaire, Paris, Lambert, 1751, t. II. (Cf. Bengesco, IV, p. 42.)
    Oeuvres (Collection Complète) de M. de Voltaire, Genève, Cramer, 1756. (Cf. Bengesco, IV, p. 50.)
    Collection complète des Oeuvres de M. de Voltaire, Genève, Cramer, et Paris, Bastien, 1768, t. I. (Cf. Bengesco, IV, p. 73.)
    La Henriade, Divers autres poèmes et toutes les pièces relatives à l'épopée, Genève, Cramer et Bardin, 1775. (Cf. Bengesco, IV, p. 94.)
[4] *Oeuvres Complètes de Voltaire*, De l'imprimerie de la société littéraire topographique, Kehl, 1784 et 1785-89, t. X. (Cf. Bengesco, IV, p. 105.)

Practically all these changes belong to the period of Voltaire's lifetime. Most of them are of such a kind and are so definitely accepted in succeeding editions that it is well nigh certain that they are the work of the author. Examination of the texts in question shows that the greater number of the alterations, nearly sixty, were made between 1751 and 1756. In 1751 Voltaire was in Germany. He returned in 1753 and in 1756, at the age of sixty-one or sixty-two, he was established in Switzerland. About half as many variants date from the period between 1742 and 1746 when the writer was about fifty years of age and was living at Cirey or had just returned to Paris. A smaller, but still considerable, number of changes were made between 1746 and 1751, the years immediately preceding Voltaire's departure for Germany; about twenty between 1738 and 1742 and only ten or so between 1733 and 1738. Those made later than 1756 are few and scattering. A table of the more interesting variants follows.

Chapitre I.   Des différents goûts des peuples.
  Oeuvres (Garnier ed.), VIII.
  p. 309.[1]   Pourvu que vous confessiez que c'est un ouvrage [le Paradis perdu] aussi admirable en son genre que *l'Iliade*. 1784, '75, '68, '56, '51.

---

  que *l'Enéide*,[2] 1746, '42, '38, '33.
  p. 313.   Il faut peindre avec des couleurs vraies comme les anciens, mais il ne faut pas peindre les mêmes choses. 1784, '75, '68, '56.

---

  en sorte qu'un Poëte épique entouré de tant de nouveautés, doit avoir un génie bien stérile, ou bien timide, s'il n'ose pas être neuf lui-même.[3] 1751, '46, '42, '38, '33.

Chapitre 11.   Homère.
  p. 314.   deux générations après la guerre de Troie, 1784, '75, '68, '56, '51.

---

[1] All page references are made to the Garnier edition.
[2] It is suggestive that the substitution of the *Iliad* for the *Aeneid* was made at a period when Voltaire was becoming less favorable to both Homer and Milton.
[3] This earlier and more forceful form was an almost exact translation of the English. Cf p. 87, note 4, *ante*.

trois générations, 1746, '42, '38, '33.

p. 316. maître de la moitié de l'univers, 1784, '75, '68, '56, '51, '46.

---

maître de l'univers,[1] 1742, '38, '33.

p. 316. les nations du nord ont conquis notre hémisphère, 1784, '75, '68, '56, '51, '46.

---

ont conquis toute la terre,[1] 1742, '38, '33.

p. 319. C'est ici sans doute qu'on ne peut surtout s'empêcher d'être un peu révolté contre feu Lamotte Houdar de l'Académie française, qui, dans sa traduction d'Homère, étrangle tout ce beau passage . . . Son parti, ses éloges, sa traduction, tout a disparu, et Homère est resté. 1784, '75, '68, '56, '51, '46.

---

not found,[2] 1742, '38, '33.

p. 320. Malheur à qui l'imiterait dans l'économie de son poëme! heureux qui peindrait les détails comme lui! et c'est précisément par ces détails que la poésie charme les hommes.[3] 1784, '75, '68, '56.

---

not found, 1751, '46, '42, '38, '33.

Chapitre III. Virgile.

p. 321. Cependant il nous reste de très-beaux vers de Cicéron. Pourquoi Virgile n'aurait-il pu descendre à la prose, puisque Cicéron s'éleva quelquefois à la poésie ? 1784, '75, '68, '56.

---

[1] These two changes show the same trend.

[2] The fact that this passage was added over ten years after the first publication of the *Essai* explains the difference in tone between it and the other allusion to La Motte contained in the French version, the very favorable judgment of his dissertation on Homer.

[3] Cf. *Essai*, p. 336 (*Camoëns*): "Les aventures se succèdent les unes aux autres, et le poète n'a d'autre art que celui de bien conter les détails; mais cet art seul, par le plaisir qu'il donne, tient quelquefois lieu de tous les autres." Voltaire's ideas concerning detailed description in poetry seem to have varied somewhat. Cf. pp. 145 ff., *ante*.

Si cela est, le Poète a eu un mérite que l'orateur n'avait point: c'était de connaître sa portée. Du moins Virgile n'a-t-il point laissé après lui de mauvaise prose: au lieu que nous avons des vers de Cicéron qui font honte à sa mémoire.[1] 1751, '46, '42, '38, '33.

Chapitre V. Le Trissin.

p. 330. Il cueille les fleurs du poëte grec, mais elles se flétrissent dans les mains de l'imitateur. 1784, '75, '68, '56, '51, '46.

Il faut bien de l'adresse pour cueillir et pour assembler les fleurs des anciens; elles se fânent entre les mains ordinaires, 1742, '38.

Les vrais génies n'imitent que rarement, et cependant il n'y a qu'eux qui puissent imiter avec succès. Il faut . . . ordinaires (as above),[2] 1733.

Chapitre VI. Le Camoëns.

p. 332. dans les dernières années du règne célèbre de Ferdinand et d'Isabelle,[3] 1784, '75, '68, '56, '51, '46, '42.

-----

[1] This diametric change of opinion occurring between 1751 and 1756, is of particular interest in the light of the fact that in 1749 Voltaire became much interested in Cicero (cf. *Oeuvres*, V, pp. 199 ff.) writing a play, *Rome Sauvée ou Cataline*, in which Cicero was a leading character. In a private performance Voltaire himself played that part with signal success. In a preface to *Rome Sauvée* printed in 1753 the author writes (*ibid.*, p. 206): " Ce que peu de personnes savent, c'est que Cicéron était encore un des premiers poëtes d'un siècle où la belle poésie commençait à naître." Voltaire then translated a few verses from Cicero, apologizing for the inadequacy of his translation.

[2] The gradual changing of this passage from the strong general statement to an unimportant comment upon the individual poet gives it a place in the history of Voltaire's attitude toward the ancients and the moderns.

[3] In this later form the passage reads: " Camoëns . . . naquit en Espagne dans les dernières années du règne célèbre de Ferdinand et d'Isabelle, tandis que Jean II régnait en Portugal. Après la mort de Jean, il vint à la cour de Lisbonne, la première année du règne d'Emmanuel le Grand." This passage gives incorrect information concerning the date and place of Camoens' birth (he was born in some Portuguese city, probably Lisbon, in 1524, according to modern opinion, 1517 being the date previously accepted) but "dans les dernières années du règne", although still thirty years out of the way, more nearly approaches the truth than " sous le règne."

A translation of Camoens' poems was published in France in 1735 by du Perron de Castera. In the *Essai* as it appeared in the edition of his works of 1738-39, in the publication of which he himself had a part (cf. Bengesco, IV, p. 5), Voltaire made no reference to this translation. The fact that, as

sous le règne, 1738, '33.

pp. 332–333. Camoëns n'accompagna point Vasco de Gama dans son expédition, comme je l'avais dit dans mes éditions précédentes . . . Tant d'exemples doivent apprendre aux hommes de génie que ce n'est point par le génie qu'on fait sa fortune, et qu'on vit heureux. 1784, '75, '68, '56, '51, '46, '42.

Camoëns qui était intime ami de Velasco de Gama, s'embarqua avec lui . . . , introducing an account of the poet's life much like that found in the English essay. 1738, '33.

p. 335. J'apprends qu'un traducteur du Camoëns prétend que dans ce poëme Vénus signifie la sainte Viërge. . . . Baccus et la viërge Marie se trouveront tout naturellement ensemble.[1] 1784, '75, '68, '56, '51, '46, '42.

---

not found, 1738, '33.

p. 335. et qu'il ait toujours péché contre le costume, 1784, '75, '68, '56.

---

not found, 1751, '46, '42.

---

contre la coutume, 1738.

---

contre le costume,[2] 1733.

p. 336. Mais de tous les défauts de ce poème . . . qui doit en connaître les fautes, 1784, '75, '68, '56, '51, '46, '42.

Ces bévues reviennent assez souvent, & cela seul prouve que l'Ouvrage est plein de très grandes beautés puis-

the author of the Lettres Philosophiques, he had found himself forced to leave Paris in 1734 and had taken up his abode in Cirey in 1736 may account for his apparent ignorance of the publication of a work in which he would have felt a great interest. It would appear that he became acquainted with the French Lusiads between 1738 and 1742, for in the 1742 edition of the essay, he writes: "J'apprends qu' un traducteur du Camoëns prétend . . .," and evidently consulting this translation, he makes various corrections and additions in his biographical account of the Portuguese poet, which remains, however, far from accurate.

[1] Cf. p. 110, note 2, ante.

[2] Cf. Oeuvres, VIII, p. 336, note of Beuchot: " L'édition de 1738 porte: contre la coutume; et c'est probablement cette faute d'impression qui aura décidé quelque éditeur, qui n'avait pas le texte, à supprimer le membre de phrase."

qu'il fait depuis plus de cent ans les délices d'une
nation spirituelle qui certainement en connoît les
fautes. 1738, '33.

Chapitre VII. Le Tasse.
  pp. 336, 337. Il y aura même quelques lecteurs qui s'étonneront
que l'on ne place point ici l'Arioste parmi les poëtes
épiques. . . .et d'outrer la nature que de la suivre.[1]
1784, '75, '68, '56.

———————

parmi les poëtes épiques, mais il faut qu'ils songent
qu'en fait de Tragédie, il serait hors de propos de citer
l'*Avare* et le *Grondeur;* et, quoique plusieurs Italiens
en disent, l'Europe ne mettra l'Arioste avec le Tasse
que lorsqu 'on placera l'*Enéide* avec *Don Quichotte*, et
Callot à côté du Corrége. Le Tasse naquit . . .
1751.

———————

parmi les poëtes épiques, mais en fait de tragédie il
faudrait citer l'*Avare* ou le *Grondeur;* quoique plusieurs
Italiens en disent, on ne mettra Arioste avec le Tasse
que lorsqu'on placera l'*Enéide* avec *Don Quichotte* et
le Callot avec le Corrége. L'Arioste est un poëte charmant mais non pas un poëte épique. Le Tasse naquit
. . . 1746.

———————

mais en fait de tragédie, faudrait-il citer l'*Avare* ou
le *Grondeur ?* Quoique plusieurs Italiens en disent, l'Europe ne mettra l'Arioste avec le Tasse que lorsqu'on
placera l'*Eneide* avec *Don Quichotte* et Callot avec le
Corrége. L'Arioste est un poëte charmant, mais non
pas un poëte épique. Je suis bien loin de rétrécir la
carrière des arts et de donner des exclusions; mais
enfin, pour être poëte épique il faut, au moins, avoir
un but; et l'Arioste semble n'avoir que celui d'entasser
fable sur fable; c'est un recueil de choses extravagantes
écrit d'un style enchanteur. Je n'ai pas osé placer
Ovide parmi les poëtes épiques, parceque ses *Méta-*

———————

[1] Most of the variants of this passage are quoted in the Garnier edition
(*Oeuvres*, VIII, p. 337, note).   They reveal Voltaire's increasing admiration for
Ariosto and show that the position of the Italian poet was a question to which
he gave much thought.

morphoses, toutes consacrées qu'elles sont par la religion des anciens, ne font pas un tout, ne sont pas un ouvrage régulier; comment donc y placerais-je l'Arioste, dont les fables sont si fort au-dessous des *Métamorphoses ?* Le Tasse naquit . . . , 1742.

---

mais en fait de tragédie il ne quadrerait pas de citer *l'Avare* et quoique plusieurs Italiens en disent, l'Europe ne mettra l'Arioste avec le Tasse que lorsqu'on placera *l'Enéide* avec *Don Quichotte* et Callot à côté du Corrége. Le Tasse naquit . . . , 1738.

---

parmi les poètes épiques. Mais il faut qu'ils songent qu'en fait de tragédie il serait hors de propos de citer *l'Avare* et *le Grondeur*; et quoique plusieurs Italiens en disent, l'Europe ne mettra l'Arioste avec le Tasse que lorsqu'on placera *l'Enéide* avec *le Roman comique*, et Callot à côté du Corrége. Le Tasse naquit . . . , 1733.

---

p. 342. mais dont les Italiens sont entièrement désabusés, 1784, '75, '68, '56, '51, '46.

---

not found, 1742, '38, '33.

p. 343. Encore ces imaginations, dignes des contes de fées, n'appartiennent-elles pas au Tasse; elles sont copiées de l'Arioste . . . au dessus du Tasse, 1784, '75, '68, '56.

---

not found, 1751, '46, '42, '38, '33.

Chapitre VIII. Ercilla.[1]
p. 348. Philippe, qui n'était point à cette bataille, moins jaloux d'acquérir de la gloire[2] . . . , 1784, '75, '68, '56.

---

[1] It is evident that Voltaire took the chapter on Ercilla bodily from Desfontaines' translation. Cf. p. 46, note 1, *ante*. The variants occurring in this chapter show that in practically every case where the modern editions of the *Essai* give different readings from Desfontaines' version, Voltaire's early editions followed Desfontaines' word for word. Of the fourteen variants involved, five represent changes between 1751 and 1756; three between 1746 and 1751; five between 1742 and 1746; one between 1733 and 1738.

[2] As a matter of fact Philip was not present at the battle of St. Quentin as Voltaire had implied in the English essay.

Après un tel succès Philippe, moins jaloux d'acquérir de la gloire . . . , 1751, '46, '42, '38, '33; also Desf. (Desfontaines' translation), 1728 and 1732.

p. 348.   contre les Espagnols leurs conquérants, 1784, '75, '68, '56.

_____

leurs conquérants et leurs tirans, 1751, '46, '38, '33; Desf. '28 and '32.

p. 348.   cette tentative des Américains, 1784, '75, '68, '56, '42.

_____

des Africains,[1] 1751, '46, '38, '33; Desf. '28 and '32.

p. 348.   pour recouvrer leur liberté, 1784, '75, '68, '56, '51.

_____

pour leur liberté, 1746, '42, '38; '33; Desf. '28 and '32.

p. 348.   l'entraînèrent dans ces pays, 1784, '75, '68, '56, '51.

_____

l'entraînèrent sans hésiter dans ce pays, 1746, '42, '38, '33; Desf. '28 and '32.

p. 349.   il s'agit du commandement, 1784, '75, '68, '56, '51.

_____

mais par rapport au commandement, 1746, '42, '38, '33; Desf. '28 and '32.

p. 349.   demander attention, 1784, '75, '68, '56, '51, '46.

_____

demander quelque attention, 1742, '38, '33; Desf. '28 and '32.

p. 350.   de porter une grosse poutre, et de déférer à qui en soutiendrait le poids plus longtemps l'honneur du commandement, 1784, '75, '68, '56.

_____

de porter une grosse poutre, afin que celui qui en soutiendrait le poids le plus longtemps fût revêtu du commandement, 1751, '46, '42, '38, '33; Desf. '28 and '32.

p. 351.   non par de vaines louanges, 1784, '75, '68, '56, '51, '46.

_____

non par des louanges, 1742, '38.

_____

[1] The fact that this curious error, corrected in the edition of 1742, recurred in 1746 and 1751 would be illuminating in a critical study of the relationship of the different texts.

non par de fades louanges, 1733; Desf. '28 and '32.

p. 351. l'odieuse différence qu'il met entre, 1784, '75, '68, '56, '51, '46. _____

l'odieuse comparaison entre, 1742, '38, '33; Desf. '28 and '32.

p. 351. un harangueur, 1784, '75, '68, '56, '51, '46, '42, '38. _____

un harangueur pédant, 1733; Desf. '28 and '32.

p. 351. leur parlant, 1784, '75, '68, '56. _____

qui leur parle, 1751, '46, '42, '38, '33; Desf. '28 and '32.

p. 351. un seul endroit, 1784, '75, '68, '56, '51, '46 (misprint, endroit omitted). _____

un endroit, 1742, '38, '33; Desf. '28 and '32.

p. 352. Le véritable et solide amour, 1784, '75, '68, '56, '46. _____

cependant le véritable et solide amour,[1] 1751, '42, '38, '33; Desf. '28 and '32.

Chapitre IX. Milton.

p. 356. édition que Milton n'eut jamais la consolation de voir. 1784, '75, '68, '56. _____

n'eut jamais la consolation d'avoir dans ses mains, 1751, '46. _____

not found,[2] 1742, '38, '33.

pp. 356-357. Il peut avoir imité . . . la seconde est la beauté des détails. 1784, '75, '68, '56 (y avoir in certain cases). _____

not found, 1751, '46, '38, '33.

p. 357. Je fus le premier qui fis connoître aux Français quelques

_____

[1] Here again we find a reading, once changed, reappearing in later editions before its final rejection.

[2] Cf. Lounsbury, p. 49: "A special contribution of his own Voltaire also made to the swelling mass of misstatement about the favor or rather disfavor with which the great epic had been received at the time of its appearance. He assures us that Milton never lived to see a second edition of his principal work."

morceaux de Milton et de Shakespeare, 1784, '75, '68. *not found,*[1] 1756, '51, '46, '42, '38, '33.

Conclusion.

p. 360.   Les artistes ne sont bien jugés que quand ils ne sont plus. 1784, '75, '68, '56.

Un écrivain qui pendant sa vie ne sera point protégé par son Prince, qui ne sera dans aucun poste, qui ne tiendra à aucun parti, qui ne se fera valoir par aucune cabale, n'aura probablement de réputation qu'après sa mort.[2]   1751, '46, '42, '38, '33.

p. 363.   Les cornes et les queues des diables ne sont tout au plus que des sujets de raillerie; on ne daigne pas même en plaisanter. 1784, '75, '68, '56.

-----

not found, 1751, '46, '38, '33.

p. 363.   et au temps seul à désarmer l'envie, 1784, '75, '68, '56.

-----

[1] The variants of the chapter on Milton show that three additions of some importance were made at three different times; the first between 1742 and 1746, the second between 1751 and 1756 and the third between 1756 and 1768. The second is noticeably more favorable in tone than the greater part of the chapter in which it is contained. The third shows the author, as in the case of Shakespeare, anxious to be recognized as having made known to his countrymen an English writer who had gained renown in France but whom he himself had come to dislike for one reason or another.

It is interesting in this connection to quote a passage concerning *Paradise Lost* found in the *Dictionnaire Philosophique* (*Oeuvres,* XVIII, p. 588): "Nous n'avions jamais entendu parler de ce poëme en France, avant que l'auteur de la *Henriade* nous en eût donné une idée dans le neuvième chapitre de son *Essai sur la Poésie épique.* Il fut même le premier (si je ne me trompe) qui nous fît connaître les poëtes anglais, comme il fut le premier qui expliqua les découvertes de Newton et les sentiments de Locke . . . On songea alors à traduire ce poëme épique anglais dont M. de Voltaire avait parlé avec beaucoup d'éloges à certains égards."

There is a certain amount of vagueness in this passage. From the words "neuvième chapitre" and the form of the title it would seem that Voltaire had reference to his own French version of the essay, yet that version was not published until over three years after the French translation of *Paradise Lost* had appeared and in the opening sentence of his chapter on Milton Voltaire referred to that translation. It is of course possible that he had in mind here Dœfontaines' translation of his essay which appeared in France a year before the translation of Milton's poem and where, as a matter of fact, *Paradise Lost* was spoken of "avec beaucoup d'éloges à certains égards." His allusion is at any rate not clear.

[2] This passage, bitter and personal in tone, dates from the period when Voltaire had definitely left the capital.

le temps seul peut désarmer l'envie, 1751, '46.

---

not found, 1742, '38, '33.

The variants of the *Essai sur la Poésie Epique* indicate no real change of opinion on the part of the author in regard to the eight poets whose names head the chapters. Yet from Voltaire's correspondence and his other works it is evident that his estimate of these poets did not in every case remain the same throughout his life.

The history of his attitude toward Homer is rather a complicated one, two phases of which we have seen in our study of the French and English essays.[1] Wholly unappreciative of the Greek poet in 1727, he was soon to attain a degree of real sympathy with him, only to return in after years to his early position and to take it still more strongly. Voltaire's *Stances sur les poètes épiques* of which the first five date from 1731 at the latest[2] gives us an extremely informal judgment of four of the poets treated in the essay. The first stanza deals with Homer and in tone as well as in date stands half-way between the two versions of the essay:

" Plein de beautés et de défauts,
   Le vieil Homère a mom estime.
   Il est, comme tous ses héros,
   Babillard, outré, mais sublime."

A few extracts from letters and other writings of Voltaire will serve to show how true are Rigault's words: " Mais, en vieillissant, Voltaire devient moins homérique." [3] In the *Siècle de Louis XIV* (1751) the author returns to the idea expressed in the English essay: " Que de gens encore en Italie qui, ne pouvant lire Homère qu'avec dégoût et lisant tous les jours l'Arioste et le Tasse avec transport, appellent encore Homère incomparable ! " [4] In *Candide* (1759) the judgment of Homer is put in the mouth of Pococurante but has been considered Voltaire's own and is of particular interest here, reproducing as it does several ideas found in the English essay written some thirty years before. " ' Il [Homère] ne fait pas les miennes [mes délices];' dit froidement

---

[1] Cf. pp. 66, 67, *ante*.
[2] *Oeuvres*, VIII, p. 505 and note.
[3] Rigault, p. 474.
[4] *Oeuvres*, XIV, p. 115.

Pococurante; ' on me fit accroire autrefois que j'avais du plaisir en le lisant;[1] mais cette répétition continuelle de combats qui se ressemblent tous . . . cette Hélène qui est le sujet de la guerre et qui à peine est une actrice dans la pièce . . . tout cela me causait le plus mortel ennui. J'ai demandé quelque fois à des savants s'ils s'ennuyaient autant que moi à cette lecture; tous les gens sincères m'ont avoué que le livre leur tombait des mains, mais qu'il fallait toujours l'avoir dans sa bibliothèque, comme un monument de l'antiquité, et comme les médailles rouillées qui ne peuvent être de commerce.' " [2] In *l'ABC* (1762-69) Voltaire speaks of the " roman monotone de *l'Iliade* " [3] and in the *Dictionnaire Philosophique* (1764) we read: " Son poème qui n'est point du tout intéressant pour nous, était donc très précieux pour tous les Grecs. Ses dieux sont ridicules aux yeux de la raison, mais ils ne l'étaient pas à ceux du préjugé; et c'était pour le préjugé qu'il écrivait." [4]

Voltaire's opinion of Virgil seems never to have undergone any radical change, as is quite natural in view of the facts already cited in connection with the two essays, his thorough familiarity with Latin, his lasting preference for the polished rather than the rugged in literature and the *Henriade's* resemblance to the *Æneid*. The second of the *Stances sur la poèsie épique* contains, as one might expect, a comparison between Homer and Virgil, favorable to Virgil. It also suggests the judgment upon the latter part of the *Aeneid* already expressed in the essay:

" Virgile orne mieux la raison
    A plus d'art, autant d'harmonie,
    Mais il s'épuise avec Didon
    Et rate à la fin Lavinie."

In a letter written to Mme. du Deffand in 1754, it is evident that Voltaire still defends Virgil as " the Pattern of all Poets," [5] as unflinchingly as twenty-five years earlier. " Ne mettons rien," he says, " à côté de Virgile . . . Je vous plains, madame, avec le goût et la sensibilité éclairée que vous avez, de ne pouvoir lire

[1] Here Voltaire may well be thinking of his personal experience.
[2] *Oeuvres*, XXI, p. 202.
[3] *Oeuvres*, XXVII, p. 377.
[4] *Oeuvres*, XVIII, p. 567.
[5] Cf. p. 97, *ante* .

Virgile." [1] Moreover the frequency with which Voltaire quoted Virgil throughout his life shows that the *Æneid* remained one of his favorite works.

In Voltaire's later writings there seems nothing to indicate any change of opinion concerning Lucan.

Trissino is mentioned several times but as the author of *Sophonisba* rather than of an epic. There is no reason to suppose that the Frenchman had any thorough acquaintance with *L'Italia liberata dai Goti* or any particular interest in the poem, either at the time of writing the English essay or later. He seems, likewise, to have concerned himself very little with the *Lusiads* after commenting in the *Essai* upon certain phases of the French translation of 1735. Toward the last of his life, however, he still had the Portuguese poet in mind for in September, 1773, he wrote La Harpe concerning the latter's *Ode sur la navigation:* "J'ai vu avec grand plaisir le fantôme du cap de Bonne Espérance, plus majestueux et plus terrible dans vous que dans Camoëns." [2] Three years later he wrote in regard to La Harpe's translation of Camoens,—" quoique je ne le croie pas tout à fait digne d'être traduit pas M. de la Harpe." [3]

The third of the *Stances* deals with Tasso. Here Voltaire mentions the defects of the *Gerusalemme liberata* which he had discussed at length in the English essay and places Tasso somewhat below Virgil:

> " De faux brillants, trop de magie,
> Mettent le Tasse un cran plus bas,
> Mais que ne tolère-t-on pas
> Pour Armide et pour Herminie ? "

In after years Voltaire spoke of Tasso frequently and remained consistent in his praises. As in the case of Virgil, his evident familiarity with the poem and the likeness of the *Henriade* to it combined to preserve this consistency. A brief sentence found in the *Dictionnaire Philosophique*, 1764, (*Oeuvres*, XVIII, p. 573) is of interest in this connection: "On renvoie le lecteur à ce qu'on a dit du Tasse dans *l'Essai sur la Poésie épique.*" Voltaire referred more than once to Boileau's very severe criticism of the

---

[1] *Oeuvres*, XXXVIII, p. 219.
[2] *Oeuvres*, XLVIII, p. 449.
[3] *Oeuvres*, L, p. 94.

Gerusalemme liberata. In the *Epître à Boileau* (1769), he expressed at the same time his idea of Tasso's place among epic poets:

> " Et si ton goût sévère a pu désapprouver
> Du brillant Torquato le séduisant ouvrage,
> Entre Homère et Virgile, il aura mon hommage." [1]

In the *Essai sur les moeurs* this superiority of Tasso to Homer is emphasized: " Encore quelques siècles," we read, " et on n'en fera peut-être pas de comparaison." [2]

Voltaire's interest in Ercilla seems to have died down with the writing of his essays, indeed with that of the English, for it will be remembered how little he concerned himself thereafter with the chapter on the Araucana. [3]

The stanza of the half mocking poem already quoted, which deals with Milton, although echoing at first a bit of the praise of 1727, has even more in common with the unfavorable chapter of 1733:

> " Milton plus sublime qu'eux tous
> A des beautés moins agréables.
> Il semble chanter pour les fous
> Pour les anges et pour les diables."

Voltaire's judgment of Milton grew more severe, in part because of changing circumstances, but chiefly, no doubt, because of the French poet's inherent dislike of the very qualities which made Milton great. In 1749, for instance, (*Mélanges*) he speaks of the " poëme bizarre du *Paradis perdu*, de Milton " and of " l'extra-ordinaire et le sauvage du fond." [4] In the *Siècle de Louis XIV*, there is an interesting passage in which the writer groups together Milton, Homer and Dante, three poets whose work came to be, as we have seen, thoroughly displeasing to him. " Milton reste la gloire et l'admiration de l'Angleterre: on le compare à Homère, dont les défauts sont aussi grands; et on le met audessus du Dante, dont les imaginations sont encore plus bizarres." [5] *Candide* (1759) contains a savage attack upon the author of *Paradise Lost*, who is

---

[1] *Oeuvres*, X, p. 402.
[2] *Oeuvres*, XII, p. 247.
[3] Cf. p. 46, note 1, *ante.*
[4] *Oeuvres*, XXIII, p. 420.
[5] *Oeuvres*, XIV, p. 560.

spoken of at the outset as " ce grossier imitateur des Grecs qui défigure la création." The passage ends with the following sentence: "Ce poème obscur, bizarre et dégoûtant, fut méprisé à sa naissance; je le traite aujourd'hui comme il fut traité dans sa patrie par les contemporains." [1] Shortly after, Mme. du Deffand wrote to Voltaire, "Je ne saurais vous dire le plaisir que j'ai eu de trouver dans *Candide* tout le mal que vous dites de Milton." [2] In 1770 in a letter to George Gray concerning the latter's parody of *Paradise Lost*, Voltaire speaks of the original as the work of a " fanatique éloquent." [3]

BIBLIOGRAPHY

Athenaeum, January 11, 1913.
Baldensperger, F., La chronologie du séjour de Voltaire en Angleterre et les Lettres philosophiques. Archiv für das Studium der Neueren Sprachen und Literaturen, 1913.
Ballantyne, A., Voltaire's Visit to England. London, 1893.
Baretti, G., A Dissertation upon the Italian Poetry, in which are interspersed some Remarks on Mr. Voltaire's Essay on the Epic Poets. London, 1753.
Baretti, G., Discours sur Shakespeare et sur M. de Voltaire (1777). Lanciano, 1911.
Bengesco, G., Voltaire, Bibliographie de ses Oeuvres. 1882-1890.
Bibliothèque française, 1728.
Boileau-Despréaux, N., Oeuvres, ed. Amar. Paris, 1824.
Boulting, W., Tasso and his Times. New York and London, 1907.
Bouvy, E., Voltaire et l'Italie. Paris, 1898.
British Journal, 1727.
Brunetière, F., L'Evolution des genres dans l'histoire de la littérature française. Paris, 1890.
Camões, Don Luiz de, Lusiadas. Reprint of edition of 1626, De Vinne Press, 1903.
Cervantes, Don Quijote, ed. Marín. Madrid, 1911-1913.
Chénier, André, Oeuvres poétiques, ed. Chénier. Paris, 1874.
Chetwood, W. R., A General History of the Stage. London, 1749.
Chinard, G., L'Amérique et le rêve exotique dans la littérature française au XVIIe et au XVIIIe siècles. Paris, 1913.
Claretie, L., Le Sage, romancier. Paris, 1890.
Collins, J. Churton, Bolingbroke, a Historical Study, and Voltaire in England. New York, 1886.
Collins, J. Churton, Voltaire, Montesquieu and Rousseau in England. London, 1908.
Collman, O., Gil Blas und die Novela picaresca. Archiv für das Studium der Neueren Sprachen und Literaturen, 1870.
Denham, Sir John, Poems, The Work of the English Poets from Chaucer to Cowper, ed. Chalmers. London, 1810, VII, pp. 221 ff.
Desfontaines, Abbé G., Voyage de Gulliver . . . [translation], Tome I. Paris, 1727.
Desfontaines, Abbé G., La Voltairomanie (avec le Préservatif). Londres, 1739.

---

[1] *Oeuvres*, XXI, p. 204.
[2] *Oeuvres*, XL, p. 205.
[3] *Oeuvres*, XLVII, p. 138. Again in the *Dictionnaire Philosophique* there appeared an article on Milton (*Oeuvres*, XVIII, pp. 580-592) full of inaccurate statements and surprising critical opinion. Cf. Lounsbury, p. 48.

Desnoiresterres, G., Voltaire et la société française au XVIIIe siècle. 1871-1876.
Dryden, J., Works, ed. Scott-Saintsbury. Edinburgh and London, 1882-1893
Duvernet, T., Vie de M. de Voltaire. Genève, 1787.
English Review, February, 1914.
Ercilla y Zuñiga, Alonso de, La Araucana. Biblioteca de Autores Españoles, XVII.
Faguet, Emile, Voltaire. Paris, 1895.
Fanshawe, R., Camoens, the Lusiad [translation]. London, 1655.
Farinelli, A., Dante e la Francia. Milano, 1908.
Fitzmaurice–Kelly, J., Littérature espagnole. Paris, 1913.
Fontenelle, B. de, Oeuvres. Paris, 1825.
Foulet, L., Le Voyage de Voltaire en Angleterre. Rev. d'Hist. Litt. de la France. 1906.
Foulet, L., Voltaire en Angleterre. Rev. d'Hist. Litt. de la France. 1908.
Foulet, L., Correspondance de Voltaire (1726-1729). Paris, 1913. [Foulet, Corr.]
Genlis, Mme. la Comtesse de, Mémoires sur le XVIIIe siècle. Paris, 1825.
Goldsmith, O., Works, ed. Gibbs. London, 1884-1886.
Harwood, E., Biographia Classica. London, 1778.
Hoole, J., Jerusalem Delivered (translation from Tasso). London, 1783. The Works of the English Poets, from Chaucer to Cowper, ed. Chalmers. London, 1810, XXI, pp. 385 ff.
Journal des Sçavans, 1728, 1731.
Jusserand, J., Shakespeare in France, under the Ancien Régime. New York, 1899.
La Motte-Houdar, A. de, L'Iliade, poëme, avec un discours sur Homère. Paris, 1714.
Lanson, G., Voltaire. Paris, 1906.
Lanson, G., Lettres philosophiques [de Voltaire], édition critique. Société des Textes français modernes. Paris, 1909. [Lanson, Lettres phil.]
Le Bossu, R., Traité du poëme épique. Paris, 1675.
Lounsbury, T. R., Shakespeare and Voltaire. New York, 1902.
Lowndes, W. T., The Bibliographer's Manual. London, 1857-64; London, 1881-85.
Magasin encyclopédique, 1807.
Martino, P., L'Orient dans la littérature française au XVIIe et au XVIIIe siècle. Paris, 1906.
Mercure de France, 1728.
Mickle, William J., The Lusiad of Luis de Camoëns [translation]. The Works of the English Poets from Chaucer to Cowper, ed. Chalmers. London, 1810, XXI, pp. 517 ff.
Milton, J., Poetical Works, ed. D. Masson. London, 1903.
Montagu, Mrs. Elizabeth, An Essay on the Writings and Genius of Shakespear. Dublin, 1769.
Montesquieu, Oeuvres. Paris, 1796.
Morel-Fatio, Etudes sur l'Espagne. Paris, 1890-95.
Oxford Dictionary.
Parton, J., Life of Voltaire. Boston, 1881.
Perrault, Charles, Paralelle des Anciens et des Modernes. Paris, 1692.
Pierron, A., Voltaire et ses Maîtres. Paris, 1866.
Pope, A., Iliad, The Works of the English Poets, from Chaucer to Cowper, ed. Chalmers. London, 1810, XIX.
Pope, A., Works, ed. Elwin and Courthope. London, 1871-89.
Rapin, R., Réflexions sur la Poétique de ce temps et sur les Ouvrages des Poètes anciens et modernes. Paris, 1675.
Rigault, H., Histoire de la Querelle des Anciens et des Modernes. Paris, 1856.
Rolli, P., Remarks upon M. Voltaire's Essay on the Epick Poetry of the European Nations. London, 1728.
Rolli, P., Examen de l'essai de M. de Voltaire sur la Poésie Epique traduit de l'anglais par M.L.A. . . . à Paris, 1728.
Rowe, Nicholas, Lucan's Pharsalia, translated into English verse. London, 1722.

Saintsbury, G., A History of Criticism. London, 1900-1904.
Spectator, ed. Morley. London, 1891.
Spence, J., Anecdotes, Observations and Character of Books and Men, ed. Singer. London, 1820.
Spingarn, J., Critical Essays of the Seventeenth Century. Oxford, 1908-1909.
Spingarn, J., A History of Literary Criticism in the Renaissance. New York, 1908.
Tasso, T., La Gerusalemme liberata. Firenze, 1823.
Texte, J., Jean Jacques Rousseau et les orignes du Cosmopolitisme littéraire. Paris, 1895.
Ticknor, George, History of Spanish Literature. Boston, 1864.
Trissino, G. G., L'Italia liberata da' Goti. Parigi, 1729.
Voltaire, An Essay upon the Civil Wars of France extracted from Curious Manuscripts, and also upon the Epic Poetry of the European Nations From Homer down to Milton, By Mr. de Voltaire, London, Printed by Samuel Jallason, in Prujean's Court, Old Baily, 1727.
Voltaire, Ibid. By Mr. de Voltaire, Author of the Henriade, The second Edition, Corrected by Himself, London; Printed for N. Prevost and Comp. at the Ship, over against Southampton street, in the Strand, 1728.
Voltaire, Ibid. By Mr. de Voltaire, Author of the Henriade. The fourth Edition corrected, to which is now prefixed A Discourse on Tragedy. With Reflections on the English and French Drama by the Same Author, London, Printed for N. Prevost and Company over against Southampton Street in the Strand, 1731.
Voltaire, Ibid. By Mr. de Voltaire, To which is prefixed a short account of the Author by J.S.D.D.D.S.P.D., printed for William Ross, Bookseller in Grafton Street, Dublin, 1760.
Voltaire, Essai sur la poésie épique, traduit de l'anglais de M. de Voltaire, par M. A Paris chez Chaubert à l'Entrée du Quai des Augustins près le Point Saint Michel à la Renomée et à la Prudence, 1728.
Voltaire, Essai sur la poésie epique, traduit de l'anglais de M. de Voltaire, par M. A la Haye chez G. M. de Merville, 1728.
Voltaire, La Henriade, Nouvelle édition, à Londres chez Hierome Bold-Truth à la Vérité, 1730.
Voltaire, La Henriade et l'Essai sur la Poésie Epique par M. de Voltaire, Nouvelle édition à Londres, 1734, (reprint of edition of 1733, La Henriade à Londres). Cf. Bengesco, I, p. 105.
Voltaire, La Henriade, Divers autres Poèmes et toutes les Pièces relatives à l'Epopée, Genève, Cramer et Bardin, 1775.
Voltaire, Oeuvres de M. Voltaire, Nouvelle édition, Revue, augmentée et corrigée par l'Auteur, Amsterdam, chez Etienne Ledet, 1732.
Voltaire, Oeuvres de M. Voltaire, Amsterdam, ed. Ledet et Cie, 1738-39.
Voltaire, Oeuvres mêlées de M. de Voltaire, Genève, Bousquet, 1742.
Voltaire, Oeuvres diverses de M. de Voltaire, Londres, Trévoux, Nourse, 1746.
Voltaire, Oeuvres de M. de Voltaire, Paris, Lambert, 1751.
Voltaire, Oeuvres (Collection Complète) de M. de Voltaire, Genève, Cramer, 1756.
Voltaire, Oeuvres (Collection Complète) de M. de Voltaire, Genève, Cramer, et Paris, Bastien, 1768.
Voltaire, Oeuvres Complètes de Voltaire, De l'imprimerie de la société littéraire typographigue, Kehl, 1784, et 1785-89.
Voltaire, Oeuvres de Voltaire, ed. Moland, Garnier frères, Paris, 1877-1885.
Voltaire, Préservatif le (La Voltairomanie avec), François Jores, Londres, 1739.
Waller, Edmund, Works, published by Mr. Fenton, London, 1729.

For further bibliography of the period in question the reader is referred to G. Lanson, Manuel bibliographique de la littérature française moderne, III, Dix-huitième siècle, Paris, 1911; and for that of Voltaire's works to G. Bengesco, Voltaire, Bibliographie de ses Oeuvres, 1882-1890.